Pure Emotion

Susan H Lawrence

WestBow
PRESS
A DIVISION OF THOMAS NELSON

Scripture taken from the New Century Version. Copyright © 2005 by Thomas Nelson, Inc. Used by permission. All rights reserved.
Scripture taken from the HOLY BIBLE, NEW INTERNATIONAL VERSION®. Copyright © 1973, 1978, 1984 Biblica. Used by permission of Zondervan. All rights reserved.
Scripture quotations taken from the New American Standard Bible®, Copyright © 1960, 1962, 1963, 1968, 1971, 1972, 1973, 1975, 1977, 1995 by The Lockman Foundation. Used by permission.
Holman Christian Standard Bible ® Copyright © 2003, 2002, 2000, 1999 by Holman Bible Publishers. Used by permission. All rights reserved.
Scripture quotations taken from the Amplified® Bible, Copyright © 1954, 1958, 1962, 1964, 1965, 1987 by The Lockman Foundation. Used by permission.

WestBow Press books may be ordered through booksellers or by contacting:

WestBow Press
A Division of Thomas Nelson
1663 Liberty Drive
Bloomington, IN 47403
www.westbowpress.com
1-(866) 928-1240

Because of the dynamic nature of the Internet, any web addresses or links contained in this book may have changed since publication and may no longer be valid. The views expressed in this work are solely those of the author and do not necessarily reflect the views of the publisher, and the publisher hereby disclaims any responsibility for them.

Any people depicted in stock imagery provided by Thinkstock are models, and such images are being used for illustrative purposes only.

Certain stock imagery © Thinkstock.

ISBN: 978-1-4497-1769-8 (sc)
ISBN: 978-1-4497-1770-4 (e)

Library of Congress Control Number: 2011928960

Printed in the United States of America

WestBow Press rev. date: 5/13/2011

"Women were created with a wide array of emotions. It's what we do with those emotions that affects every single aspect of our Christian walk. *Pure Emotion* dives deeply into the heart of our emotions, biblically addressing emotions like fear, jealousy, anger, anxiety, frustration, joy and guilt. This is a study for ALL women, in ALL circumstances, at ANY stage of life. It encourages women to honestly look at the effects of emotions in their lives so they can live an emotionally pure life in Christ!"

Lori Macmath, Owner, Internet Cafe Devotions

"Studying *Pure Emotion* was much like an in-depth conversation with a good friend whose godly counsel spurs me toward spiritual growth. *Pure Emotion* helped me examine personal beliefs, identify ungodly thought patterns and habits, and move toward emotional health. The study both encouraged and equipped me to further commit to Christ and reassured me from the beginning to end that my God is committed to me. It is a must have for any women!"

Tracie Johnson, Author and Founder, Response to Grace Ministries

"I was blessed and encouraged after working through *Pure Emotion*. It is a wonderful study for women who want to dig deep into the Word to discover who they are in Christ. Over the years, I can't tell you how many times I have heard these words: 'a woman is just too emotional to make a good decision.' This statement frustrates me for good reason! I can make good decisions and so can you. As you work through the *Pure Emotion*, you'll find that our God is an emotional God. As we can cling to him and seek his guidance, we can work through any issue facing us. *Pure Emotion* will encourage and strengthen you."

Major Mariam Rudd, The Salvation Army

"I have done many Bible studies, and God has taught me so much through each one. For that I'm grateful, but this study was altogether different for me. It was like for the first time, so much made sense to me. *Pure Emotion* engaged me from the first page. You see, as a little girl, I was a sexually abused by my father. By the time I was 12, he was in prison and later moved back into our house. I remember begging God to make it all go away. By the time I was sixteen, I was pregnant, getting married, and had the title wife and mother. My emotions were all over the place. Anger, jealousy, envy – I had them all!

"It was through *Pure Emotion* that I realized how much of an impact my emotions had on my life. I felt the emotions, but when my life was distant from God, these emotions were so unproductive, nothing good came from them. Just self-pity. Even now, 20 years later, I can easily forget that regardless of what I may be going through, God has something amazing to teach me if I go through it alongside him.

"I often get asked 'why are you so happy?' My problems aren't any less now, but I don't respond to them with unproductive emotions. I more readily crawl onto Jesus' lap. I've done this study with him and often found myself quietly smiling and thinking, 'Wow! God, you are something else.' My focus isn't on my emotions; God is my focus.

"Week Nine was the turning point for me: 'The thing is....whether or not life is fair is irrelevant. God doesn't want us to get stuck in this life. He wants to correct our eyesight so we see into eternity.' Praise God! I found myself in tears as I worked through the week's studies. I thanked Jesus for this study as he once again helped me to see into eternity. As I surrender to him, my emotions become Godly emotions, and it doesn't get any better than that.

Speak it.

Personalize it.

Live it.

These words now hold such meaning for me."

Kimberly

Table of Contents

Introduction

Do not be shaped by this world; instead be changed within by a new way of thinking. Then you will be able to decide what God wants for you; you will know what is good and pleasing to him and what is perfect. Romans 12:2

While leading a *Pure Purpose* women's group, I was captivated by the emotions women experience. Emotions are certainly not always positive, but the passion behind them convicted me to explore the emotions of God. After all, we're created in his image. Yet so many of the emotions we experience entangle us. We feel like puppets responding to and making decisions based on our emotions. We excuse erratic behavior because of our emotions. We also enjoy life because of emotions. We passionately serve out of emotions.

As I consult with women in ministry around the world, I hear the emotions pouring through their words. I see emotions dancing and weeping in their eyes as I speak at conferences. I sit across the table in a coffee shop and listen to pain, joy, fear, and anxiety.

Women feel, and we feel with passion.

Pure Emotion is a journey. In the pages that follow, I trust you will meet God wherever you are. He'll encourage you, and he'll challenge you to question some assumptions you make about your own and his emotions. He'll reveal himself to you so you can declare the truth of his character, his emotions, and his purpose for you.

I'm thrilled to take these next steps by your side. Each week, we'll begin with a Starter Session. If you're meeting with other women for this study, you'll experience the Starter Session together. If you're studying on your own, you'll find it to be an enriching personal experience. For study groups, questions and experiences marked with an asterisk (*) can be discussed in small groups. Additional tips are included in *Tips for Group Facilitators*.

Following each Starter Session are five Make It Personal sessions for you to work through on your own. While each week is not identical, all weeks have at least three personal study sessions and two additional sessions, including Planting Seeds of Truth and, beginning Week Three, Emotional Check-Up. We'll dig into, reflect upon, and live out God's Word.

All Scriptures are included within the study guide so everyone can easily explore. Verses are from the New Century Version unless otherwise noted. I encourage you to dig into additional translations to enrich your study experience.

Pure Emotion has been a roller-coaster journey for me. As God will so often do, he's blessed me with firsthand experiences as I've studied and written. It hasn't been a comfortable journey, but it's been beyond worthwhile. I'm closing the last page closer to him. I'm more familiar and vulnerable with God, and my life is richer and faith is deeper because of the journey.

I may not know your name or your specific life circumstance, but I've prayed for you every step of the way, and I continue to trust God will bless you as you open up your heart, soul and mind to him along the journey of *Pure Emotion*.

Seeking Pure Emotion,
Susan
purepurposebook.wordpress.com
facebook.com/PurePurpose

Tips for Group Facilitators

Whether you're facilitating a group for the first time, or you've had decades of experience, I want to encourage you as you begin *Pure Emotion*. Facilitating a group can be overwhelming, but I hope the tips I've provided will support you…like a personal assistant!

There are two main lessons I've learned when facilitating small group studies through the years. First, you'll learn and grow through the process. As you spend time in preparation, God will challenge you and reveal himself to you in ways that spur you to trust him and grow closer to him. He'll prepare you beyond the time you're spending on this particular study. As you're sensitive to God's leading, you'll hear him speak to you through other teachers, books, relationships, and situations, which will nourish you as a facilitator.

Second, it's not about you as the "teacher." God is entrusting a group of women to you for a season, but they are God's, not yours. As you're obedient to him, you'll receive exactly what you need. When we're consumed about "messing up" as leaders, we're distorting our trust in God's guidance. When it becomes about *our* abilities, issues, concerns, and shortcomings, the study becomes about us. The study is about God and helping individual women grow in their relationships with him. It's not about teaching. It's about learning. Facilitate women's learning. God will do the rest.

I may not know your name or location, but I know God does, and I trust him to guide and care for you. I hope you'll connect with me through my website (purepurposebook.wordpress. com) or Facebook (facebook.com/PurePurpose). I'd love to hear your story of *Pure Emotion*!

Before your first session…

Pray. Ask a group of women to commit to regularly pray for the *Pure Emotion* study group. Let them know specific prayers as your group proceeds. Start with praying for guidance as you're making decisions about the study…when to meet, where to meet, how to promote, etc. Pray for women who will be in your study group, even if you don't know their names. God does! As the study continues, let your prayer supporters know what topics you're studying each week. If someone is struggling or shares personal concerns, keep specifics confidential, but you can ask your prayer supporters to continue to pray for all the people and situations brought up during sessions. Again, God knows the details, and that's enough.

Promote. Use your typical promotional avenues such as bulletins, church newsletters, website, and fliers. Then consider other creative ways to promote your study. Not every woman will respond to the same style of invitation. The most effective way to invite women is personal. Create a buzz. Encourage women currently in studies to reach out to others. Consider where women gather in your community, and create invitations that target specific groups of women. Provide small invitation cards or postcards, making it easy for women in your church to pick up a stack to invite their family, friends, neighbors and coworkers. (Deliver with a piece of good chocolate!)

Anticipate and answer women's questions on promotional materials. Time, day, starting date, cost (if applicable). Will childcare be provided? If so, is there a cost? Are reservations necessary?

Always let women know they can invite their friends. Women are usually more comfortable when they can grab a friend to tag along.

Prepare. Personal preparation is essential. What's your personal spiritual condition? Do you feel insecure and inadequate? God will provide! You're not chosen to facilitate a study because you're perfect. At the same time, if you're in a time of personal crisis, assuming a leadership role might not be the best choice for this season of your life – yet God will meet you right where you are and use anything you're going through. Trust God's guidance. If he's prompting you to lead, and you're hesitant and find yourself making excuses, you need to listen, be obedient, and trust. If you're assuming leadership because "no one else will" or because you've "always led this study," take a step back and confirm God is prompting to lead. Your obedience is essential. If you say "yes" when God intends someone else to say "yes," you're not allowing someone else to choose obedience.

Spend time in prayer. Ask others to pray. Be prepared. I recommend working ahead of the group's pace. When discussing with the group, focus on what they've experienced that particular week instead of sharing everything you've experienced but they haven't. However, it's important you know what's coming. When someone brings up a question or concern, and you know it's later addressed, you can inform women they'll study that topic soon and stay on task for the particular session.

During your first session...

Get to know each other. Spend a few minutes at the beginning of the first session getting to know each other. Check out resources for icebreakers or ask women to introduce themselves with their names and an answer to a question such as

- If money was no object, where would you vacation and why?
- What is your favorite room in your house and why?
- If you had a magic wand to organize something in your life, what would you choose and why?

Avoid questions or information that might divide women or cause them to feel uncomfortable because they would have nothing to share or have answers that don't match everyone else. When you ask something that is opinion or dream-based instead of information-based, even women who feel self-conscious will be put at ease.

During the first session and throughout all sessions, avoid statements such as "We're so glad you could join us." "We have a visitor today." "Let's have our guests introduce themselves." Concentrate on helping everyone feel welcome. Terms such as "we" and "us" can feel divisive when you're not part of the "we" and "us." Structure the first session as if no one knows each other. You'll be surprised what you'll learn about each other even if you've been meeting for years.

If someone joins your group after the first week and is the only new person in attendance, spend the first few minutes going around the room answering a basic, fun question like the ones above. Let your guests know that it's just as important that she gets to know everyone in the room than it is for you to get to know her. As a guest leaves, instead of saying, "We hope you'll come back and see us next week," speak for yourself: "I'm so glad I got to meet you, and I hope I'll see you again next week. Let me know if you have any questions as you study this week." And then connect by phone, email, or a handwritten note within a couple days.

Gather contact information. Pass out index cards and ask everyone to share her name, mailing address, email address, and phone number, so you can keep in touch. Assure everyone you won't sell contact information to a marketing agency; you simply want to help everyone stay connected. As the facilitator, you'll try to connect with everyone occasionally, but it is important women are able to connect with each other as well. Women will often make a comment that resonates or concerns someone else. Instead of having to contact you and explain the concern, she can follow up directly. Help women connect and build relationships. You're the facilitator, not the gatekeeper. Create a contact list to share with everyone the following week. Be sure to leave room to add women who start the group the following weeks.

Talk about accountability. Let women know they can talk as little or as much as they want (although you might make a joke about leaving the option of gently curbing extremely lengthy discourses to conserve time!). As women share, we're to hold one another accountable...in love. That means someone who says she feels she should confront someone or verbally forgive them, let her know you'll be checking in with her. Then do it. If someone is trying to break a habit, encourage her.

As women connect and develop relationships, they'll want to help one another. They'll invest in each other's lives. Ask women to let someone know if they can't attend a session, so you'll know why women are missing. As the facilitator, you need to be held accountable, too. Respect your women's time by starting and ending each session on time.

Agree to confidentiality. Confidentiality is critical to individual and group health. Women can easily mask gossip as prayer requests. We want to support each other and our loved ones in prayer. In order for all women to feel safe within the group, it's essential to create a community in which "what's said in the group stays in the group." Encourage women to be careful when and where they check in with group members outside the group. Asking someone, "Did your test results come back okay this week?" in a crowded store or worship center is likely going to generate hearsay and gossip among others.

Determine your default setting in small group to keeping what's shared in the group confidential unless (1) it involves a serious threat to someone's safety, or (2) the person sharing requests others to share (applicable specifically with prayer requests). Apply the same principle when sharing outside prayer requests. If you have a person's permission to share the prayer request, it's fine. If not, simply say, "I have an unspoken prayer request." We don't need names and details. God knows, and that's good enough.

During each session...

Start and end on time. Each Starter Session is designed for an hour and a half, but time can vary based on the length and depth of discussions. Keep on track. If you want to extend the time, two hours will work with *Pure Emotion*, but be sure to set the length of time before the study begins. Two hours might be too long for young moms or for women in an evening study who like to be home by a certain time. It's not about appeasing everyone, but you need to weigh the pros and cons of your dates and times before beginning with your small group. Set and communicate the guidelines and expectations – in a welcoming way.

Share needs with each other.

Model the responses, habits, and attitudes you know God expects.

Allow time for women to share. As noted in the Introduction, experiences and questions marked with an asterisk (*) can be shared in small groups of 3-4 women. It's tempting for some facilitators to plow through these experiences, sharing their own answers or allowing only a small number of women to respond. However, everyone will not have time to respond in a large group, nor will everyone be comfortable sharing in a large group. Plus, learning is significantly more impactful if women experience and debrief together. You might feel like you're giving up control. You are. You're giving control to God.

You'll also want to allow time for women to share their at-home study with each other. You won't have time to completely go through each day's study, and you won't want to, because many of the questions are too personal or sensitive to share with a group. However, many women will want to ask questions to clarify something or share an "a-ha" moment experienced through the week. Let women's needs guide the discussion as you place enough structure to provide stability and time constraints.

For example, during the first session, you can encourage women to mark their at-home study pages in a way that makes it easy to discuss when you gather together. They can create their own marking systems, but here are a few simple approaches I use:

- Exclamation marks in the margins indicate an "a-ha" thought, moment, or experience.
- Question marks in the margins indicate a question I need to ask (or dig into on my own later).
- Underlining text helps me mark the main points God is highlighting to me.

When you get together for group sessions, before beginning the next Starter Session, you can casually lead women through their at-home study pages by asking simple questions, such as,

- "Does anyone have anything in Day One's study that they want to discuss?"
- "What jumped out at you as you studied Day Two?"
- "Are there any questions or comments you'd like to share from Day Three?"

Keeping the questions general gently invites women to be involved. Have a general idea of the time you want to set aside for discussing the at-home study. If it's 20 minutes, and discussion of Day One's pages approaches five minutes, gently transition into Day Two's pages. Pace the discussion to allow women to share questions and reflections from all five days.

You may have women who do not complete the at-home study. While you want to encourage everyone to complete it as you begin *Pure Emotion*, be careful not to put women on the spot during sessions. Let women know that if they don't get their at-home study done, you don't want them to miss group sessions. Of course, women will get the most out of completing all of the study, but if someone only attends the group sessions and doesn't study at all outside of the group sessions, she's still hearing God's Word and building relationships with other women. You might want more for each woman, but trust God to guide and provide. Each woman must decide how deeply to commit.

Optional Ending Session

While *Pure Emotion* is a ten-week study, you can host an optional eleventh session. Because women will have completed at-home work following your tenth Starter Session, you can get together to discuss the at-home work as usual. I encourage you to keep the discussion structure consistent with the other weeks of your group gatherings. If you usually allow twenty minutes for discussion of at-home study, keep the eleventh week's discussion to around twenty minutes.

Because you won't have another Starter Session to consume the remainder of your time, consider hosting a celebration to commemorate the journey you've taken together! Ask women to bring basic finger foods. You can simply hang out and connect, or you can place fun questions on the tables to generate discussions in small groups. Here are a few ideas:

- What's one way you "wasted time" in the past week?
- How often do you clip and use coupons?
- Which do you dislike the most: stubbing your toe, hitting your funny bone, or biting your tongue?
- When was the last time you were locked out of something or somewhere?
- What's the worst tasting thing you've ever eaten?
- What's your strongest sense?
- What's one fashion trend you hope never comes back?
- Where are you most ticklish?
- What kitchen utensil do you use most often?
- What's one part of your morning routine you can't live without?

Commit to praying for and encouraging each other. You might commit to a small group of 2-4 women, checking in with each other in the coming weeks and months to ask how the journey of growing in pure emotions is going and help each other through the rough experiences. It's fantastic when God entwines our lives with others to equip and encourage each other!

Let us think about each other and help each other to show love and do good deeds. You should not stay away from the church meetings, as some are doing, but you should meet together and encourage each other. Do this even more as you see the day coming. Hebrews 10:24-25

Pure Emotion Follow Up...

Week Ten is just the beginning of your *Pure Emotion* journey. Women connect and build relationships with each other and with God. Be intentional about following up with women, showing women pathways to continue their journeys. Share upcoming studies, women's events, retreats, and conferences. Keep an email list to continue to keep in touch even with the women who don't jump into another study right away. Encourage women to stay in touch with each other and to continue to invite other women, fostering relationships with each other and others as they encourage each other in their daily lives, discovering the pure purpose God intends for them.

Week One: *The Emotional Experience*

Starter Session

*What emotion(s) do you struggle with the most?

*What emotion(s) would you never want to live without?

These are two of the questions I presented to women in a survey on emotions. You'll have an opportunity to answer more of the questions in a few minutes, and I'll share some of the survey results throughout *Pure Emotion*.

You'll likely not agree with all the responses. We're all different, and we experience the world differently. But the truth is – whether you want to admit it or not, whether you're comfortable with it or not – we're all emotional people. We have emotions, and we experience the world through emotions.

*Consider a situation you experienced or responded to with negative emotions. How did those emotions enhance the experience and your memory of it?

*Consider a situation you experienced or responded to with positive emotions. How did those emotions enhance the experience and your memory of it?

I wish I could sit with you right now – with warm drinks in our hands, of course – and listen to your story. This journey called life is rough…and thrilling. Like roller coasters. I've ridden many roller coasters, and my experiences have widely varied. Frightening. Lame. Rickety. Jerky. Exhilarating. Kind of like the experiences of my life. The season I'm in right now is a roller coaster. Whether your knuckles are white from gripping in fear or your voice is weak from loud squeals of joy, I'd like to hear about it. My experiences wouldn't be exactly the same, but I'm confident we'd have a lot in common. Even when the details of life are different, the emotions we experience are similar. We can connect because we've felt fear, jealousy, anger, anxiety, peace, frustration, guilt, shame, and joy. Different situations, different intensities, same emotions.

*What questions do you have about emotions?

*What perplexes, frustrates, or encourages you about emotions?

Here are a few questions I've considered.
Are emotions inherently good or bad?
Can we mature our emotions?
How do we use one emotion to hide another?

I've been exploring these questions – and many more – in preparation for *Pure Emotion*, and we'll be digging in over the next ten weeks. I'm confident we'll have many more questions along the way. We'll explore those, too!

When I was in high school, someone gave me a pin-on button that said "Moody, but cute." I liked the cute part. But moody? I was a happy-go-lucky person. Or so I thought. When I started thinking about it, I had to admit…yep, I'm moody, too. In fact, I was more certain of my moodiness than my cuteness! I guess I didn't notice my moodiness much because it was just the way I experienced life – different emotions for different moments. My emotions made sense to me. In fact, they helped me make sense of the world. Taking a step back, I decided I had a lot to learn because, to be quite honest, my emotions weren't always appropriate. They often poked out all over the place, spearing the people around me.

I learned early that being emotional was "normal." I don't know if it was because I was raised in a family of girls (and I was the youngest), but emotions were expected and accepted. Well, perhaps not *always* accepted, but the variety of emotions didn't seem to take anyone by surprise. If the emotion was negative, the offender was often ignored. I remember many pity parties the family refused to join in. Oh, not necessarily my own (although I had my fair share!).

And then there have been my aha emotional moments, particularly when my emotions haven't matched someone else's in a situation – whether the intensity or the emotion itself differed. One person was angry while I was joyful. I was frustrated when someone else was peaceful. The differences in and of themselves caused tension at times. Like when my family was on vacation in Florida…

I was around five years old and heard my parents talking about a toll bridge. Except I didn't hear "toll bridge." I heard "troll bridge" – and I was scared.

Being scared quickly escalated to petrified when my sisters – on either side of me in the backseat – began sharing troll stories. I was scared enough just thinking of the trolls in *Three Billy Goats Gruff*, and those were drawings. When my sisters started describing the menacing, vengeful trolls of their twisted imaginations, I couldn't take it any longer. We had to cross the toll bridge, but I didn't have to look. I crouched on the floorboard and tried to slide as far under the seat as possible.

The trolls didn't get me, and my now apparent fear got my mom's attention. She reprimanded my sisters, but it didn't do much good. They'd seen the fear in my eyes, and they were going to carry this as far as they could.

Each night in the hotel, two of us would share a bed, Mom and Dad would get a bed, and the other girl slept on a rollaway bed. I loved the rollaway bed, so I looked forward to my nights. As we approached the hotel later in the toll bridge day, whichever sister had the rollaway assignment for the night asked if I wanted to trade nights. Of course, I did! At least *something* was going right in my day.

I should have known. My sister didn't offer to exchange nights out of the goodness of her heart. It was a conspiracy to torment me. You see, the rollaway would be placed in the open space by the balcony overlooking the ocean. A beautiful view – until my sisters started sharing stories of how the trolls trudged out of the ocean every evening looking for little girls to eat and how trolls ate the first girl they saw, which would obviously be the one closest to the ocean. I think they also told me something twisted like the only way the troll wouldn't get me is if I was really still and didn't say anything about being scared. A slick way to get me *not* to tell Mom and Dad I was terrified!

· I remember what that room looked like in the light and in the dark, what the crashing waves sounded like, and what my sisters' occasional muffled giggles sounded like. I didn't know if I would survive the night, but of course, I did. I don't know if Mom or Dad put a stop to the torment or not, but I don't remember any more nights of terror. The next day wasn't as scary in the daylight, and I enjoyed beach time.

A half dozen years later, I opened a gift from my sisters. It was an ugly troll. Very funny. What did I learn about emotions? First, they can be stirred up even when imagination doesn't match reality. Second, my emotions don't always match someone else's in the same situation. Third, our emotional responses can make us vulnerable.

*What about you? What's one experience you recall that taught you something about emotions?

Now let's dig into your emotions. I encourage you to be completely honest with your responses. You're not going to be asked to share these responses with anyone, but you'll refer to these responses over the next ten weeks. Some areas might not change much, but you might be surprised that as you learn more about the biblical truths of emotions and common misconceptions and assumptions, you'll begin to respond in fresh ways – not to a simple survey but to situations.

1. What do you believe about the following emotions?

	Mainly positive.	Could be positive or negative.	Mainly negative.
Discouragement	❑	❑	❑
Pain/Suffering	❑	❑	❑
Anger	❑	❑	❑
Love	❑	❑	❑
Desire	❑	❑	❑
Jealousy	❑	❑	❑

Peace	❏	❏	❏
Happiness	❏	❏	❏
Joy	❏	❏	❏
Grief	❏	❏	❏
Fear	❏	❏	❏
Anxiety	❏	❏	❏
Frustration	❏	❏	❏
Confusion	❏	❏	❏
Loneliness	❏	❏	❏
Rejection	❏	❏	❏

2. What's your personal experience with each of the following emotions?

	Mainly positive.	Could be positive or negative.	Mainly negative.
Discouragement	❏	❏	❏
Pain/Suffering	❏	❏	❏
Anger	❏	❏	❏
Love	❏	❏	❏
Desire	❏	❏	❏
Jealousy	❏	❏	❏
Peace	❏	❏	❏
Happiness	❏	❏	❏
Joy	❏	❏	❏
Grief	❏	❏	❏
Fear	❏	❏	❏
Anxiety	❏	❏	❏
Frustration	❏	❏	❏
Confusion	❏	❏	❏
Loneliness	❏	❏	❏
Rejection	❏	❏	❏

3. Which best describes your belief about emotions?
    ❏ Emotions are indicators and enhancements of experiences.
    ❏ Emotions are the result of a situation or circumstance.
    ❏ Emotions are the driving force of behavior.
    ❏ Emotions are symptoms of something deeper.
    ❏ Other:_____

4. What is the source of emotions?
   ❑ God-given.
   ❑ Situational.
   ❑ Biological.
   ❑ Hormonal.
   ❑ Other:_____

5. To what extent do each of the following affect your emotions (either positively or negatively)?

Relationships	Not affected at all.	Minimally affected.	Somewhat affected.	Definitely affected.
Finances	Not affected at all.	Minimally affected.	Somewhat affected.	Definitely affected.
Specific Situations	Not affected at all.	Minimally affected.	Somewhat affected.	Definitely affected.
Others' Emotions	Not affected at all.	Minimally affected.	Somewhat affected.	Definitely affected.
Music	Not affected at all.	Minimally affected.	Somewhat affected.	Definitely affected.
Isolation	Not affected at all.	Minimally affected.	Somewhat affected.	Definitely affected.
Crowds of People	Not affected at all.	Minimally affected.	Somewhat affected.	Definitely affected.
Others' Expectations	Not affected at all.	Minimally affected.	Somewhat affected.	Definitely affected.
Faith	Not affected at all.	Minimally affected.	Somewhat affected.	Definitely affected.
Crisis	Not affected at all.	Minimally affected.	Somewhat affected.	Definitely affected.
Uncertainty	Not affected at all.	Minimally affected.	Somewhat affected.	Definitely affected.
Weather	Not affected at all.	Minimally affected.	Somewhat affected.	Definitely affected.

6. What thrills you most about emotions?
   ❑ Emotions serve as indicators in my life.
   ❑ Any emotion enhances my experiences.
   ❑ Subdued emotions help me maintain control.
   ❑ Intense emotions add to life.

7. How much did you learn about emotions (positive or negative) from the following?

	I learned nothing.	I learned a little.	I learned nothing.	n/a
Mother	❑	❑	❑	❑
Father	❑	❑	❑	❑
Pastor/ Preacher	❑	❑	❑	❑
Bible	❑	❑	❑	❑
Childhood Friends	❑	❑	❑	❑
Formal Education	❑	❑	❑	❑
Personal Experiences	❑	❑	❑	❑
Adult Friends	❑	❑	❑	❑
Siblings	❑	❑	❑	❑
Grandparents	❑	❑	❑	❑

8. How comfortable are you with expressing your emotions?
   - ❑ I don't mind getting emotional any time.
   - ❑ I don't mind expressing emotion but I also hold back sometimes.
   - ❑ I'm comfortable sharing with a small group of people.
   - ❑ I don't want anyone to see my emotions.
   - ❑ Emotions confuse me, and I'm rarely emotional.

9. What emotion(s) do you struggle with the most?

10. What emotion(s) would you never want to live without?

11. What are your best methods for dealing with emotions? (Rank with 1 being the one you successfully use most often.)
    _____Self-help books
    _____Support groups
    _____Medication
    _____Journaling

_____Friendships

_____Prayer

_____Other:_____

12. Share a time of being overwhelmed.

This week we'll start exploring how our emotions impact everyday life. We'll also take a look at several specific emotions and what our assumptions of those emotions are. We'll begin planting seeds of truth from God's Word. Be patient. It's going to take some time to pull up the weeds of our misconceptions – responses and assumptions we've repeatedly practiced – and replant, water and grow the truth of emotions. But you can do it. I'm certain. Because I know God, and he wants no less for you than freedom from strongholds, freedom in him.

Make It Personal #1: *Everyday Emotions*

Which of the following have you experienced? Write notes beside any phrase that conjures up specific memories.

Mad enough to spit nails.

Leap for joy.

Sadder but wiser.

Bundle of joy.

Mad as a hornet.

Hold your peace.

Out of my mind with worry.

Love-hate relationship.

Guilt trip.

Labor of love.

We use all sorts of phrases when describing our response to something, and we often use emotions, because we frequently respond with emotion! Consider a world void of emotion. Oh, how we'd experience the world differently! Imagine…

A wedding…

A job interview…

A doctor's appointment…

The birth of a baby…

Watching a teenager pick on a small child…

Sledding down a snow-covered hill…

Holding the hand of a loved one as she dies…

Looking at a report card…

Worshiping God…

When asked what affects emotions, either positively or negatively, no item in the survey was listed as having no effect at all on emotions. Crowds of people and weather were most often ranked as minimally affecting. Somewhat affecting were others' emotions, isolation, others' expectations and uncertainty, and receiving the highest, "definitely" affecting response was relationships, finances, specific situations, music, faith, and crises.

Keep in mind the question included both negative and positive emotional responses, so while we might be drawn to some situations because of the emotional experience, we'll likely avoid others. Like most everything else, we'd prefer to keep the positive and get rid of the negative. It's like cleaning your closet. Keep what you like and what feels good and get rid of the things you're tired of or don't fit well.

Let's explore those emotions we'd like to toss out. Jot a few of your "toss aways." Keep in mind some of the emotions might be situational toss-aways. For example, you might want to toss out anger, because in most cases, you experience anger as negative, but when someone is being mistreated, you experience an anger of injustice, and you don't want to toss it away. If an emotion is sometimes in the toss away pile, write "sometimes" beside it.

There are several reasons we experience emotions negatively.

1. The messages we've paired with some emotions are devastating to us. With each of the following emotions, consider the messages you've received about that emotion – from parents or other relatives, teachers, pastors, friends, or others.

Fear –

Jealousy –

Anger –

Anxiety –

Peace –

Frustration –

Guilt –

Shame –

Joy –

Ask yourself if each message is actually true. If it's not, draw a line through it.

These messages come back to us in the middle of our emotions whether we've thought through and accepted them as truthful or not.

What voice interrupts you in the midst of your emotions?

When you're rejected by a close family member, do you feel worthless?

When you're anxious about a test result, do you feel incapable of proceeding?

When you're peaceful, do you feel self-sufficient or proud?

When you're fearful, do you feel victimized?

Voices of learned messages interrupt us in the middle of our emotional responses and cover the original emotion with broad sweeping strokes until our initial emotional response is painted over with a mess of random colors and design.

Not all messages that accompany our emotions are inaccurate. God can speak to us in all times, including moments of emotion. We'll dig into God's character and biblical emotions next week, but let's start by acknowledging that God is an emotional God.

Don't worship any other god, because I, the Lord, the Jealous One, am a jealous God. Exodus 34:14

Still God was merciful. He forgave their sins and did not destroy them. Many times he held back his anger and did not stir up all his anger. Psalm 78:38

The Lord your God is with you; the mighty One will save you. He will rejoice over you. You will rest in his love; he will sing and be joyful about you. Zephaniah 3:17

God is not a God of confusion but a God of peace. 1 Corinthians 14:33

There is much expression of emotion in Scripture, and we'll be studying specific emotions beginning with Week 3, but go ahead and take a look at Psalm 139: *You know when I sit down and when I get up. You know my thoughts before I think them. Where can I go to get away from your Spirit? Where can I run from you? If I rise with the sun in the east and settle in the west beyond the sea, even there you would guide me. With your right hand you would hold me. I could say, "The darkness will hide me. Let the light around me turn into night." But even the darkness is not dark to you. The night is as light as the day; darkness and light are the same to you.* (verses 2,7,9-12).

What do these verses tell you about God and emotions?

God is definitely aware of emotions. Emotions saturate Scripture. God is an emotional God – not in the same way we talk about an emotional woman or emotional person. But God is certainly aware of the runaway emotions we're referring to when we put a negative spin on emotions. We can't escape God's presence. That means he sees and hears alongside us, including our (often messy) emotions. And if we let him, God will replace those untruthful messages we've learned about emotions along the journey of life with the truthful messages reflecting his character, will, and commands.

2. Another reason we experience emotions negatively is we can feel victimized by our emotions. Emotions can make us feel as if we're on a board game. Perhaps you know some of the rules.

a. Your move is dependent on others' moves. (Your emotions are responses to others.)

b. Only one person can occupy a space at one time. (Your emotions prohibit you from some experiences.)

c. You'll incur penalties for landing on certain spaces. (Some of your emotions will only end in trouble.)

d. Where you land is determined by the roll of a die. (You don't have control over your emotions.)

e. You might need to go back several spaces. (Your emotions can get you stuck.)

When have you felt victimized by your emotions?

Read the previous question again. It strikes me as funny that we think of our emotions making us feel something. In other words, because we feel, we feel. If (insert emotion), then (insert emotion). It's no wonder we feel victimized by our emotions…we attribute more emotions to them! Which leads us to another reason we experience emotions negatively.

3. We use emotions to mask other emotions. Consider the following emotions and how they can become tied together. Draw lines from one emotion to another if you see a connection, where one might mask another. Lines can be drawn from one column to another or within the same column.

Anger	Jealousy
Hurt	Grief
Confusion	Fear
Sadness	Anxiety
Shame	Peace
Pride	Frustration
Joy	Guilt

Negative emotions can be energizing. We might not like them. We might complain about them. But we'd rather feel something than nothing, and negative emotions at least help us feel something. Because we often experience negative emotions as more intense than positive emotions, we're more energized and consumed by them…and therefore often less willing to give them up.

We want something to be changed, but we're not willing to *be* changed.

How have you experienced this in your own life?

In others' lives?

We struggle – and our struggle is often internal. But our internal battles show on the outside. Our thoughts and emotions are intricately intertwined, and they impact our behaviors. When our emotions escalate unchecked, we'll end up behaving how we feel. Behavior changes as emotions and thoughts change.

Do not be shaped by this world; instead be changed within by a new way of thinking. Then you will be able to decide what God wants for you; you will know what is good and pleasing to him and what is perfect. Romans 12:2

We'll declare Romans 12:2 many times over the next 10 weeks. Right now, let God speak it to and over you. Fill each blank with your name. Then read the entire verse, including your name, aloud. Write it on an index card and use it as a bookmark for this study book or your Bible.

_____, *do not be shaped by this world; instead,* _____, *be changed within by a new way of thinking. Then you,* _____, *will be able to decide what God wants for you; you will know what is good and pleasing to him and what is perfect,* _____.

I'm going to assume we have something in common. Do you, like me, want God to work through you? I so often cry out with that desire. But I have to constantly remind myself that in order for God to work through me, I have to be willing to allow him to work *in* me. He's changing me from the inside out. And it's not easy for me to allow him to change me.

Which do you typically choose – the hard or the easy? I want to assure you that *right* doesn't always mean *easy*. I'm not suggesting you choose the hard way just to take the hard way. You need to seek and choose God's way, but if you assume God's way is going to be easy, you're in for a surprise. I have good news for you, though. God can ordain the *hard* of life, too. I encourage you not to assume that you can discern based on your personal experiences of difficulty, struggle, peace or ease.

What, in general, do you do when you experience emotions? You might decide not to choose one option. Write notes beside each option if specific situations come to mind.

- ❑ I push them aside and forge forward.
- ❑ I feel helpless and am often stopped in my tracks.
- ❑ I sense the opportunity to look at what God's exposing about me.
- ❑ I'm motivated to change and grow.

Emotions expose us. We can feel unmasked. Emotions enhance our experiences – as if a highlighter has illuminated what's going on in our lives. What do you think of when you think about being exposed?

I think about being on an island. My first thought is of being on the beach. Not the relaxing resort beach where refreshing drinks and snacks are readily available. A deserted beach. The sun is beating down, and there's little escape if some odd creature or person wants to attack. I'm visible to everyone who is in the area as well as to the elements. I don't feel safe. Exposure feels unsafe. It's unsettling.

I can also feel exposed in the very depths of the island jungle, where the vines and bushes are overgrown and hide the path. It's a different kind of exposure. It's exposure to the unknown and uncertainty. I can easily get lost, and I consider what could be lurking in the overgrowth.

Emotions *can* lead us to depend on God. The small word "can" is critical, because emotions will not automatically lead us to depend on God.

Consider a time your emotions have led you to depend on God.

What about a time your emotions didn't lead you to depend on God?

Consider if there are specific emotions that spur you to shy away from God or run to God most times you experience them. What patterns do you see as you glance over your life and experiences with emotions – both positive and negative?

Do you respond differently to negative and positive emotions?

Both positive and negative can lead us to depend on God. We sometimes want to replace our negative emotions with positive ones. We'll explore this through *Pure Emotion*, but for now, consider what emotions you experience as negative you most often want to replace with positive emotions (and are there specific positive emotions?).

As we study more about God's emotions, we'll begin to discern what's positive and negative about the way we experience various emotions. Each week, you'll be answering several questions, so you can apply what you're learning into everyday life by quick assessments that will hopefully begin to extend from your time studying *Pure Emotion* into the small crevices of your day when you're faced with a decision of how to respond emotionally to a situation.

We often ask ourselves and others "What do I feel?"

What benefits are involved with asking this question of ourselves? Others?

What drawbacks are involved with asking this question of ourselves? Others?

I've asked this question many times, and while I don't think the question in and of itself is bad – I've learned a lot about myself and others by answering it. We can get caught up in the emotion itself without moving beyond the emotion. The emotion becomes the end result instead of a hint of what's going on or what should happen next. So, we're going to go one step forward and regularly ask ourselves:

"Where am I and where am I headed? Is it where God wants me to go?"

As we continue our study, we'll assume the "What do I feel?" as we incorporate it into "Where am I and where am I headed? Is it where God wants me to go?" For practice, start with "What do I feel?" Right now. About anything going on in your life. Take some time and write the emotion. It might also help to jot a few notes about the situation surrounding the emotion. You don't need to get specific if you prefer, but be honest. There's no reason to deceive yourself about it. You're not going to share this with anyone, and God already knows!

Now take it the next step. "Where am I and where am I headed? Is it where God wants me to go?"

If you feel paralyzed, as if you have no idea where you're headed or if it's where God wants you to go, revisit the emotion and measure it against who you know God to be. Rest on the truth of his words and his character. Let that determine if the direction that emotion usually leads you (or perhaps the place it causes you to camp) is a direction or place God would want you to go.

We get bogged down with our emotions. We're experiencing negative emotions and we want to turn them into positive emotions. We experience positive emotions and we want them to last forever. We want things our way, and we usually want them to be easy. But we don't experience easy emotions because life isn't easy. We get uncomfortable, and we want to change. No. Let me rephrase that. We often *don't* want to change. We want *something* to change more than we want to *be* changed.

Let's take a look at some changes in Scripture.

God said to Abraham, "I will change the name of Sarai, your wife, to Sarah." Genesis 17:15

When Saul turned to leave Samuel, God changed Saul's heart. All these signs came true that day. 1 Samuel 10:9

You changed my sorrow into dancing. You took away my clothes of sadness, and clothed me in happiness. Psalm 30:11

Do not be shaped by this world; instead be changed within by a new way of thinking. Then you will be able to decide what God wants for you; you will know what is good and pleasing to him and what is perfect. Romans 12:2

Our faces, then, are not covered. We all show the Lord's glory, and we are being changed to be like him. This change in us brings ever greater glory, which comes from the Lord, who is the Spirit. 2 Corinthians 3:18

By his power to rule all things, he will change our humble bodies and make them like his own glorious body. Philippians 3:21

Compare the verses about change with the following.

So God created human beings in his image. In the image of God he created them. He created them male and female. Genesis 1:27

You made my whole being; you formed me in my mother's body. I praise you because you made me in an amazing and wonderful way. What you have done is wonderful. I know this very well. Psalm 119:13-14

"I say this because I know what I am planning for you," says the Lord. "I have good plans for you, not plans to hurt you. I will give you hope and a good future. Then you will call my name. You will come to me and pray to me, and I will listen to you." Jeremiah 29:11-12

That was not because of anything we did ourselves but because of God's purpose and grace. That grace was given to us through Christ Jesus before time began, but it is now shown to us by the coming of our Savior Christ Jesus. 2 Timothy 1:9-10

Write any truths declared over your life through these verses.

I hope you recognized this one: **God didn't mess up his design of you.**

He's not capable of messing up. He created you in his image. He has a plan for your life. He even knew what mistakes you'd make throughout your life, and he still loves you and wants nothing more than to be in an ever-deepening relationship with you. He will pursue you – whether you're not following him and need to make that decision or you're following him marginally or you're passionate about him. He designed you for more, and he will pursue you, tapping you on the shoulder, whispering in your ear, and knocking on the door of your heart so that your daily life – including your decisions, attitudes, and yes, emotions – is impacted in the purity of who he created you to be and the everyday messiness of living on earth as you move ever closer to eternity – with God or without him. Rest assured, God did not mess up his design for you.

As we explore our emotions – and the emotions of God expressed in Scripture – let's continually remind ourselves that God created us in his image and he didn't mess up his design for us…so if our emotions aren't reflecting the character of God…well, we're probably distorting something and need to get back on track.

That's what this journey is about. Growing closer to God, getting to know him better, and committing to reflecting him more and more on a daily basis.

One thing is certain. Our emotions influence our daily lives. God experiences emotions, too. He responds out of love, anger, jealousy, and more. God's emotions are pure. We can reflect those pure emotions, because (1) we're created in God's image, and (2) we have God's Word and Spirit to guide us, discerning whether our emotions are a pure reflection of God or not. We can't rely on our emotions. They're influential but not very reliable. God's emotions are reliable, so the more we know and trust his emotions, the more we can grow toward healthy emotions. That's what *Pure Emotion* is all about: getting to know God and growing toward healthy emotions. With his help, we can grow in our emotions and responses to them.

Week One

Make It Personal #2: *Emotional Assumptions*

It's important to benchmark where you are to measure your growth (or lack of it) along your journey. Spend time reflecting on and completing the following to identify your assumptions and experiences of particular emotions. Jot immediate thoughts you have, but also allow God to continue to bring memories and reminders to you in the coming days and commit to observing the reality of your emotional assumptions as the week continues. We'll revisit a similar experience toward the end of *Pure Emotion*.

Fear
Positive Assumptions and Experiences…

Negative Assumptions and Experiences…

How I typically respond to others' expressing this emotion…

Jealousy
Positive Assumptions and Experiences…

Negative Assumptions and Experiences…

How I typically respond to others' expressing this emotion…

Anger
Positive Assumptions and Experiences…

Negative Assumptions and Experiences…

How I typically respond to others' expressing this emotion…

Anxiety   Positive Assumptions and
Experiences...

Negative Assumptions and
Experiences...

How I typically respond to others'
expressing this emotion...

Peace   Positive Assumptions and
Experiences...

Negative Assumptions and
Experiences...

How I typically respond to others'
expressing this emotion...

Frustration   Positive Assumptions and
Experiences...

Negative Assumptions and
Experiences...

How I typically respond to others'
expressing this emotion...

Guilt   Positive Assumptions and
Experiences...

Negative Assumptions and
Experiences...

How I typically respond to others'
expressing this emotion...

Shame   Positive Assumptions and
Experiences...

Negative Assumptions and
Experiences…

How I typically respond to others'
expressing this emotion…

Joy   Positive Assumptions and
Experiences…

Negative Assumptions and
Experiences…

How I typically respond to others'
expressing this emotion…

Other: _____ Positive Assumptions and
Experiences…

Negative Assumptions and
Experiences…

How I typically respond to others'
expressing this emotion…

Other: _____ Positive Assumptions and
Experiences…

Negative Assumptions and
Experiences…

How I typically respond to others'
expressing this emotion…

WEEK ONE

Make It Personal #3: *Raw Emotions*

Raw. *(1)* being in or nearly in the natural state : not processed or purified *(2)* not diluted or blended *b* : unprepared or imperfectly prepared for use *c* : not being in polished, finished, or processed form.[1]

List as many emotions as you can. (No Googling necessary. It's not a competition – just include what comes to mind!)

Now read the definitions for *raw* again. Circle all the emotions you've experienced as raw at some point in your life or another.

Before we continue, let's clarify something about the first definition of raw - *being in or nearly in the natural state: not processed or purified.* This study is all about looking at God's pure emotions so we can hold ours up to the same standards. It's going to take some retraining, but we can determine to let God define our emotions instead of letting our emotions define us! With that said, let's clarify the use of the word natural. Does it refer to how God created us and intends us to be or the messy (wo)manhood in us? *Natural* typically refers to our carnality, our humanness, and differs from our spiritual being. Our spiritual selves are who God created us to be, but while we're here on earth, our spiritual selves are residing in our natural selves. As we grow spiritually, our natural selves slowly die to sacrificially reveal our maturing spiritual selves. It's not worth getting stuck on for now, but I want to mention the raw emotions we're going to be referring to are not God-intended, God-reflected emotions. For today's study, the second part of the definition most accurately applies: *unprepared or imperfectly prepared for use; not being in polished, finished, or processed form.*

What negatives of reacting with raw emotions can you identify?

What positives of reacting with raw emotions can you identify?

I venture to guess most people can come up with more negatives than positives. There are definitely some positives. Raw emotions enhance an experience, and if that experience is joyful, responding in the purity of joy can be thrilling. A marriage proposal, a surprise visit from a dear friend, an unexpected promotion, the long-awaited arrival of a child. (I recognize not everyone

---

1   www.merriamwebster.com

experiences these particular situations as joyful. If not, it's okay. Choose your own joyful memory.) Go ahead and share a moment of raw, positive emotion.

These are often the highlights of our lives.

But we also remember the flip side of enhanced experiences because of raw emotions. Unbridled anger. Paralyzing fear. Unfathomable grief. Crushing shame.

Do any of these resonate with you? Something else might come to mind. Go ahead and share it. Perhaps you've never admitted the intensity of the moment. Take your time. God knows and is ready to catch you in his compassion.

My Grammy and I were close since I was little. I loved spending time with her. She spoiled me in little ways, mainly with the sweet treats I got to eat when I visited her. I loved spending the night with her. We'd sit side-by-side at her kitchen counter and play Solitaire, each with our own deck. I remember when she patiently taught me, and to this day, I don't play Solitaire without thinking of her. She also taught me to cook some of her famous dishes like lasagna and custard.

As she got older, I went on several day trips with her. We often went to the grocery store together. Actually, we went to several stores, so she could save a couple cents on bananas or some other item she "needed." Then our relationship changed. Our relationship became as equally distant as it had been close. She accused me of hurtful things. I tried to understand, attributing it to her health going downhill and not being comfortable with the process of goodbye. While my mom and she hadn't been super close as mother-daughter, their relationship improved as mine deteriorated. I tried to take comfort in that, but it was a struggle to say the least. My mom and I decided it was best if I didn't visit her in the hospital.

When I got the call that Grammy had died, my emotions were raw. I hung up the phone and yelled, "How dare she die before resolving things with me!" I was angry. Perhaps more hurt than angry. I had been grieving my relationship with Grammy for months. I hadn't hoped much for a resolution over those months, but my emotional response wasn't pretty. It was raw and ugly. But very real.

Only my husband was around that night. My raw response didn't hurt anyone or a relationship. It was authentic. While I didn't rationalize it at the time, I know God can handle my intense emotions of doubt, fear, and anger when I respond to a situation. The problem comes when (1) the intense emotion becomes the norm instead of a temporary reaction, or (2) the displaced emotion harms relationships I have with others or God.

Check any of the following you've experienced either on the giving or the receiving side.

❑ I've responded to someone in misguided anger.

❑ I've felt insecure and wrongly made assumptions or accusations about someone else.

❑ My frustration has boiled over from one situation or person onto another unrelated situation or person.

❑ My jealousy has prompted me to do things uncharacteristically.

❑ I've withdrawn because of intense hurt.

❏ I've been paralyzed by fear.

❏ My guilt has been a heavy burden to bear.

❏ I have felt so ashamed, I wasn't sure if or how I could take it to God.

Next, let's dig a bit deeper into the ones you checked. It's okay if you checked them all. Well, not okay in the sense that you can stay where you are and the responses you checked are acceptable, but okay in the sense that…you're human. Hopefully, one of the reasons you're working through this study is to seek insight into what pure emotions – given by God – are and what they should look like in our daily lives. This is a journey. You're being honest with where you've been and where you are now. Let's not sugar-coat how we're living daily life. After all, it's only through authenticity that we're going to grow, and besides, God already knows, so you might as well stop playing charades with yourself and others.

Revisiting the list, place a #1 or #2 behind each statement you checked.

1 = This intense emotion has (or had) become a pattern in my life, not just a temporary reaction.

2 = This displaced emotion has harmed (or is harming) relationships I have with others or God.

Let's take one step deeper in honesty. This time, it's God's honesty. He's not going to sugar-coat for you. These are words you can rely on as absolute truth and firmly stand on them as you declare them as promises in God's Word. What do you learn from each of these verses?

Wisdom will make your life pleasant and will bring you peace. Proverbs 3:17

When you lie down, you won't be afraid; when you lie down, you will sleep in peace. Proverbs 3:24

I am the Lord. There is no other God; I am the only God. I will make you strong, even though you don't know me, so that everyone will know there is no other God. From the east to the west they will know I alone am the Lord. I made the light and the darkness. I bring peace, and I cause troubles. I, the Lord, do all these things. Isaiah 45:5-7

I also made a promise to you and entered into an agreement with you so that you became mine, says the Lord God. Ezekiel 16:8

Love each other like brothers and sisters. Give each other more honor than you want for yourselves. Romans 12:10

Now that your obedience to the truth has purified your souls, you can have true love for your Christian brothers and sisters. So love each other deeply with all your heart. 1 Peter 1:22

We respond to others and to situations. Sometimes we assess the situation well and respond appropriately, and sometimes we don't. Whether our emotions are raw or processed and thought through, consider several ways we respond to people and situations.

1. ***When we sense someone is against us, we feel attacked.***

What emotional responses do you think of when you consider being attacked? Perhaps a specific situation comes to mind.

We often get defensive and have a knee-jerk reaction. Yet we don't respond to attacks only with raw emotions. Sometimes our emotions are well-thought through over a period of time... but still not healthy. We hold grudges, and out of those grudges come anger, jealousy, and fear. Retaliation is often the driving motivation – whether we're active in our retaliation or we're mulling it over in our thoughts.

2. ***When we sense someone is moving away from us, leaving us, we feel abandoned.***

What emotional responses do you think of when you consider being abandoned? Perhaps a specific situation comes to mind.

We respond in a variety of ways. Some people retreat; some retaliate. Some experience loneliness, anger, fear, and anxiety. Nearly all experience rejection. Even when we're abandoned through nothing we personally did, we take it personally. It's difficult not to. We feel like a doormat. We feel unworthy. We feel isolated or ostracized. Keep in mind feelings of abandonment don't have to involve someone completely leaving our lives. It could be an emotional retreat or disconnectedness that stirs the feelings of abandonment inside us.

3. ***When we sense someone is moving toward us, connecting with us, we often feel loved.***

What emotional responses do you think of when you consider being loved? Perhaps a specific situation comes to mind.

Because we *feel* love doesn't mean our responses will be appropriate and healthy. We can respond out of neediness or fear or anxiety. We can try to please others. We can run from one relationship to another. We can stay in a rut of abuse or disrespect. *Feeling* love isn't *being* loved. We can say that about any of the emotions we experience.

Feeling lonely doesn't mean we're alone.

Feeling rejected doesn't mean we're being rejected.

Feeling jealous doesn't mean there's reason for jealousy.

Feeling a myriad of tumultuous emotions doesn't mean you're life is a torrent.

Before you send me angry messages of "How dare you tell me my feelings are unjustified!," let me assure you that's not my intent. I'm not saying your feelings aren't what you're experiencing. I'm not invalidating your feelings. You feel what you feel. What I'm suggesting is this: Consider that feelings might not reflect the reality of a situation. That's why we're studying emotions in the context of who God is and who he created us to be. Emotions are intended to enhance life. Sometimes they're positive and sometimes they're negative. We're not going to get rid of all negative emotions, because life isn't always going to go smoothly. But our emotions can be godly, which means our emotions will accurately reflect the reality of the situation and help us respond in healthy ways.

Think about the dashboard gauges in your vehicle. What happens when something goes wrong in the mechanics of the gauges, and the indicators are off? What if your emotional indicators are off?

Let's let God lift the hood and make the adjustments he has to make to help our gauges reflect reality. It's not going to be easy. He's willing to do the adjusting, but you have to be willing to (1) be adjusted, and (2) trust the adjusted gauges even though they might seem odd and uncomfortable for a while.

How will (or do) you struggle with God's adjustments?

You can trust God. You might struggle with trust. You might struggle with God. But I pray you invite him to adjust and transform your life. You will not overcome something until it becomes unacceptable to you.

Every good action and every perfect gift is from God. These good gifts come down from the Creator of the sun, moon, and stars, who does not change like their shifting shadows. James 1:17

These two things cannot change: God cannot lie when he makes a promise, and he cannot lie when he makes an oath. These things encourage us who came to God for safety. They give us strength to hold on to the hope we have been given. Hebrews 6:18

The Lord is not slow in doing what he promised—the way some people understand slowness. But God is being patient with you. He does not want anyone to be lost, but he wants all people to change their hearts and lives. 2 Peter 3:9

Do not be shaped by this world; instead be changed within by a new way of thinking. Then you will be able to decide what God wants for you; you will know what is good and pleasing to him and what is perfect. Romans 12:2

WEEK ONE

Make It Personal #4: *Planting Seeds of Truth*

God wants you to know his Word.

In the beginning there was the Word. The Word was with God, and the Word was God. He was with God in the beginning. All things were made by him, and nothing was made without him. John 1:1-3

God's Word is who he is, so being familiar with the Word is being familiar with God. The more intimate you are with what's in Scripture, the more intimate you'll be with God himself. We need to spend time in God's Word on a regular basis!

Let's go beyond simply reading the Bible and actually interact, experience and live out the words included in the Word. Each week, we'll dedicate one or two days to specifically interact with God's Word. Of course, verses are also firmly planted on every other day as well, so you can apply the same principles on a daily basis, but these are days to specifically focus your attention on what God is saying and interact with him to listen to what he's specifically saying to you and what it means in your daily life.

Following each verse, you'll find some basic instructions. I caution you not to become legalistic in your approach. You don't need to fill all the blanks on a page, but it's critical for you to fill all the spaces of your heart! Let God guide you to interact with his Word. One caution: if you find yourself employing only one approach week after week, verse after verse, consider stretching yourself. God is a creative God, and he'll direct you to search him completely through a variety of lenses. When we get used to the same old routine, we can become hearing and sight impaired in our faith journey.

Here's an overview:

Speak It. Say it out loud – several times if you prefer! God's spoken Word has power. Plus, you'll be using several senses to experience God's Word. You're taking it in with your eyes, forming the words with your mouth, and hearing the words. It's like a double exclamation point!

Personalize It. What's God specifically saying to you in this season of your life? Insert your name, respond with a question, rephrase the promise – whatever it takes to absorb what God's saying to you and stand firmly on it as you take the next steps.

Live It. God doesn't intend for us to only fill our heads with knowledge about his Word. He desires us to let it seep into every crevice of our lives. Let him guide you through challenges and encouragements of how you'll apply a verse into your daily life. Write a note about your plan – and then revisit this page to record your progress.

Let's get started!

The One whom God sent speaks the words of God, because God gives him the Spirit fully. John 3:34
Speak It.

Personalize It.

Live It.

We encouraged you, we urged you, and we insisted that you live good lives for God, who calls you to his glorious kingdom. Also, we always thank God because when you heard his message from us, you accepted it as the word of God, not the words of humans. And it really is God's message which works in you who believe. 1 Thessalonians 2:12-13

Speak It.

Personalize It.

Live It.

Blessed is the one who reads the words of God's message, and blessed are the people who hear this message and do what is written in it. Revelation 1:3

Speak It.

Personalize It.

Live It.

The Lord is my light and the one who saves me. So why should I fear anyone? The Lord protects my life. So why should I be afraid? Psalm 27:1

Speak It.

Personalize It.

Live It.

God's word is true, and everything he does is right. Psalm 33:4
   Speak It.

   Personalize It.

   Live It.

Give me back the joy of your salvation. Keep me strong by giving me a willing spirit. Psalm 51:12
   Speak It.

   Personalize It.

   Live It.

Love and truth belong to God's people; goodness and peace will be theirs. Psalm 85:10
   Speak It.

   Personalize It.

   Live It.

Our guilt overwhelms us, but you forgive our sins. Psalm 65:3
   Speak It.

   Personalize It.

Live It.

If you declare with your mouth, "Jesus is Lord," and if you believe in your heart that God raised Jesus from the dead, you will be saved. We believe with our hearts, and so we are made right with God. And we declare with our mouths that we believe, and so we are saved. As the Scripture says, "Anyone who trusts in him will never be disappointed." Romans 10:9-11

Speak It.

Personalize It.

Live It.

Make It Personal #5: *Facing the (Not So) Easy Stuff*

Before we end our first week together, let's spend a little more time addressing some of the traps we can get into concerning our emotions. Perhaps you don't struggle with each of these. That's okay, but I encourage you not to skim over any of them. You might not initially relate with one area, but as we study specific emotions in later weeks, one of these might pop into your mind. Be willing to be honest with yourself and tweak – or drastically change – the way you think of, respond to, and rationalize emotional responses. Remember, we're on a journey to see and experience our emotions the way God intends – the way that best glorifies him. That's going to take some honesty, so take off your rose-colored glasses.

Hormones. You knew it was coming, because this is a women's study. And those hormones – well, they're a part of daily living! We all have them, but we experience them differently. What are your experiences with hormones?

What do people commonly accept as connections between hormones and emotions – whether you accept them or not?

Perhaps you know someone who uses emotions and hormones interchangeably. They've tied their hormonal changes and emotional responses so tightly together, where one ends and another begins is indistinguishable. Hormones excuse emotions. Emotions reflect hormones. And of course, there is a connection. Our emotions are impacted by many factors, including hormones. I'm encouraging you to separate the two – not because there is no connection but because we might be making some connections that aren't true. Once we understand the connections between our hormones and emotions, we can gather tools to cope with the responses we have. But if we don't know what connections are true and what connections we've wrongly assumed, we're not able to fix any faulty connections.

If this is an area of tightly knotted connections for you, be sure to ask yourself regularly:
- Am I using the terms hormones and emotions interchangeably when expressing or explaining myself?
- Is there an actual connection?
- Do I feel like a victim as I tie the two together?
- How does God want me to see the situation?
- How can I reflect God in my response?

If these questions strike a chord for you, write them on an index card or sticky note and move it through this book as you study. You'll be reminded and challenged to ask yourself the questions consistently and seek God's guidance and will. He'll give you the honesty and tools you need to grow!

Avoidance. "I'm not an emotional person." Have you heard yourself say this? Or perhaps you've admitted to being an emotional person. Either way, consider what makes us identify ourselves as emotional or unemotional?

It's not that we're emotional or not emotional. We're all emotional, because we all have emotions. What's different among us is how we express our emotions. Those who say they're not emotional typically mean they don't express their emotions to others often, and those who say they're emotional "wear their emotions on their sleeves." In general, those who declare they're not emotional don't like the out-of-control feeling emotional responses give them. Those who express their emotions aren't necessarily out of control, but some might consider emotional expressions as weakness. Expressing weakness can be seen as not being in full control, so if someone expresses excessive emotion (and who defines what is excessive?), she's seen as weak and out of control.

Have you ever apologized for an emotion? While you're crying, you apologize to someone? While you're complaining about an injustice, you apologize? While you're sharing a fear, you apologize? I'm not saying you should never apologize to people, but what's your motivation for apologizing? Is it because you're sorry for the emotion itself – and therefore, the apology indicates your wish to not have the emotion at all, assuming it's a bad thing – or for the impact the emotion is having or has had on someone or a situation?

Be clear on what you're doing and saying and how emotions are impacting your decisions. We can avoid emotions and reality in the process. Lack of emotion or guilt over emotions might indicate an attempt to avoid emotion. Sure, we don't want to foster unhealthy emotions, but avoiding emotions isn't healthy either!

Early in my marriage, when my husband and I would get into a serious discussion that involved something we were passionate about or disagreed on, I would sometimes begin to cry. I was offended, hurt, angry, or frustrated what I was trying to say wasn't coming out as I wanted it to. As soon as the tears flowed, Tim took pity on me – even when we were in a heated disagreement – and that infuriated me. I didn't want pity. I didn't want to be crying. I just wanted to finish the discussion or argument. I'd get angry with myself and frustrated with him, and the situation rarely turned out well. The more I tried to force back the tears, the worse it became.

Now, Tim knows the drill. He knows my tears don't necessarily mean I need comfort. They're just an overflow of some sort of emotion…the specific emotion varies. I often attribute it to a dam break in my tear ducts. Whatever it is, I don't avoid it (as much), and the funny thing is…I don't cry as much either! Sometimes when we're honest and accept our emotional expressions for what they are in context, we give ourselves permission to express ourselves, and we don't need to express ourselves as much or not in the same way.

Stupid. Yes, I know it's not the best word to use, but if it's stupid, it's stupid, and sometimes, when it comes to dealing with our emotions, we're just plain stupid. Here's one of the most common stupid statements we make concerning our emotions:

I don't know what's wrong with me...

Really? I venture to challenge you on this one. You might not *understand* everything that's going on, but you're not completely clueless. You're smarter than that. You can start somewhere. Say it like it is.

I'm totally stressed out, and I feel like I'm in a cyclone. I need to do something to make it stop.

I feel all this anxiety, and I know it's not healthy. I'm not sure where to begin, but I need to start somewhere!

I thought I had let it go, but I'm really still irritated...and probably more now than when it all happened.

I feel stuck, and it's depressing. I get so angry that this keeps coming up again and again. I'm tired of it!

Get the idea? Say it like it is to the best of your ability. We rarely "don't know," especially when it has to do with our own lives, experiences, and emotions. And when we already feel out of control, "I don't know what's wrong with me." sinks us deeper into a victim or no-hope mentality. Think about it before you say it...then say it like it is.

Throughout the next several weeks, listen for yourself saying "I don't know..." and use your mental muscles to determine whether or not you know more than you're admitting.

Identity Crisis. Many times we say we don't know what's wrong with us, we're talking to someone else, but sometimes we're talking to ourselves. The damage can be the same. Damage also comes from another source – others. We believe things people have said about us.

Think about messages you've received from others as well as things you've believed about yourself because of situations, relationships, or moments of intense emotions.

Complete the following statement. Add more lines if you need them.

I am (a) _____.
I am (a) _____.
I am (a) _____.
I am (a) _____.
I am (a) _____.

It often helps to identify where a message originated. If you know, write a note to the side of each statement to identify whether the message comes from yourself, a particular person, an experience, etc.

Next step: Is it true? Is that really who you are? If it's not, let's start stomping it out today! Use the space below to declare the truth. You might not be ready to declare the opposite if you have deeply-engrained negative messages running through your mind and heart, but if you know it's not the truth, you've taken the first step. You can at least declare that it's *not* true. You can rewrite the same statements, declaring a large "I AM NOT...!"

I know there are some tender hearts working through this page right now. I see the tears of pain and struggle flowing into the words. I want to assure you: God will not condemn you, speaking negative messages over you. He doesn't tear you down. It's not who he is. He is a builder, not a destroyer. Sure, he wants to weed out the sin, but he wants to replace it with redemption. He will never challenge you to grow without giving you all you need through him to grow. He will never lie to you. God is Truth. You can stand firmly on him. Let him speak his truth over you throughout the coming weeks of study.

Jesus answered, "I am the way, and the truth, and the life. The only way to the Father is through me." John 14:6

You have the gift that the Holy One gave you, so you all know the truth. I do not write to you because you do not know the truth but because you do know the truth. And you know that no lie comes from the truth. 1 John 2:20-21

Brothers and sisters, think about the things that are good and worthy of praise. Think about the things that are true and honorable and right and pure and beautiful and respected. Philippians 4:8

Week Two: *What's A Pure Emotion?*

Starter Session

What is pure emotion? We've been exploring emotions, but what's *pure*?

Pure is free from what vitiates, weakens, or pollutes. Pure contains nothing that doesn't properly belong.

Pure emotions are emotions that contain nothing that does not properly belong. Emotions that only contain what *does* belong. Emotions not diluted, polluted, or weakened. *Vitiate* means to impair, make faulty or defective. If our emotions are pure, they're not impaired, faulty or defective.

What are your biggest obstacles to having pure emotions?

*What's one emotion you'd particularly like to strip off all impurities and experience as pure? *Why?

God's emotions are pure emotions. We'll be studying specifics about God's emotions of fear, jealousy, anger, anxiety, peace, frustration, guilt, shame, and joy as we continue our journey together, but let's explore the generalities of God's emotions this week. Let's explore God's character and declare who he is. When we stand on the truth of declaring who God is, we believe and trust him for who he is, including claiming who he created us to be.

*Where do you experience the most struggle in trusting God?

God is trustworthy.

Lord God All-Powerful, who is like you? Lord, you are powerful and completely trustworthy. Psalm 89:8

The issue isn't whether or not God is trustworthy. The issue is whether or not we trust God's trustworthiness. Most of us would nod our heads when asked if we trust God, but *do* you... really...all the time...in *all* circumstances...for *all* his promises?

Okay, I'll go first. I don't. I love God. I believe he is the one and only God. I believe he created the world and is Father, Son, and Holy Spirit. I have a relationship with Jesus, and I believe my salvation is secure. I believe the Holy Spirit guides me in daily life. But...

…there are situations in which my response doesn't reflect my trust in God. I don't doubt who God is, but I respond in doubt sometimes when giving him control, relying on his strength, guidance, provision. It's not that I'm consciously doubting God; usually (I think) I'm just responding, and because all the habits I have don't come out of my disciplined relationship with God, I don't always respond out of my relationship with God. As much as I seek him and want him to be the priority in my life, I look at my feelings, attitudes and behavior and have to admit… it certainly doesn't appear as if I trust him 100% of the time!

It seems I'm not the only one. *What do you learn from the following verse?

Immediately the father cried out, "I do believe! Help me to believe more!" Mark 9:24

To give you a bit of context, this father pleads Jesus to rid his son of an evil spirit. The father gives Jesus some background of his son's behavior and then says, *"If you can do anything for him, please have pity on us and help us." Jesus said to the father, "You said, 'If you can!' All things are possible for the one who believes."* Mark 9:22-23

I can relate to this man! Oh, how many times I've declared I BELIEVE! and in the next breath pleaded "Help me believe more!" Are you with me?

*Share a couple examples of (a) when God has proven himself trustworthy and (b) when God has proven himself untrustworthy.

We need to look closely at the situations in which we think God has been untrustworthy. We're usually…

- *Projecting a person's untrustworthiness onto God.* We're in a situation or relationship we're confident God led us into and yet we're betrayed or hurt in some way. We assume the betrayal and hurt comes from God. How can we possibly trust him in the future?
- *Misconstruing God's promise to us.* We assume and claim something about God that isn't true. It might be rooted in truth; for example, a misinterpreted or misapplied verse or characteristic. Or, we're using our own definition of a God-given characteristic and provision. We read God's desire to give us joy, and if we don't feel full of joy, we think God let us down.
- *Giving up before the completion of a plan or promise.* God works all things together for our good. If we stop anywhere along the journey but expect to fully receive the promises of completion, we'll be disappointed. We can give up and miss out on God's completion of promises, or we can stick to the journey and appreciate the glimpses of promises along the way.

God doesn't ask us to trust our own ability to be faithful. He doesn't ask us to believe in his trustworthiness out of our own strength. He asks us to trust him for who he is - because of who he is. He asks us to trust because he says we can trust him. He wants us to be authentic in our belief and unbelief. We will be weak, but what do we do in that weakness?

How do you most often respond in weakness?
- ❑ I get down on myself for being weak. I punish myself and question my faith.
- ❑ I dig in and rely on my own strength.
- ❑ I try to figure out what went wrong.

All three options have one thing in common; they turn the focus away from God and toward self. We might rationalize that we're just trying to regroup and get back to a place where we trust God after a moment of not trusting God. It won't work. The only way to trust God is to move forward in trust. God desires for you to rely on and trust him. He'll provide you with opportunities along your journey, and even when you doubt or react out of your own habits instead of God's guidance, he'll walk the next steps with you. But you have to rely on him instead of sinking into yourself – your own strength, reasoning, weakness, or doubt.

God provides everything he promises…but we have to yield to him in order to receive. It's not as if he can't provide, but he gives us choice, and that means he'll usually wait for us to yield. Think of it this way: when you're filled up with yourself (messages from culture, untruthful teachings, logic and head knowledge), there's no room to be poured into. Where's the extra space?

You have to sacrifice yourself in order to be filled. God will keep filling you as you yield space to him.

For example, when you give up your own strength, he pours in his. *What other examples of yielding can you brainstorm?

In order to trust God more, you must trust yourself less. In order to be humble, you must be willing to sacrifice yourself. We want to receive God's gift of humility, but we have to be humble to receive it. Now, that seems odd, doesn't it? But it's consistent with God's world.

So those who are last now will someday be first, and those who are first now will someday be last. Matthew 20:16

Those who try to hold on to their lives will give up true life. Those who give up their lives for me will hold on to true life. Matthew 10:39

Not everything makes logical sense. That's where faith comes in. Faith doesn't mean God doesn't want you to think about things. He made you in his image. You're a thinking person, capable of logic and reasoning. He gave you the capacity to think…but just like so many other aspects of ourselves made in his image – including emotions – what he blessed us with can get in the way. We can build a wall between us and God with the exact characteristics and gifts he intends for us to build a bridge with. Our faith is the bridge, and when we trust God's promises, the bridge is firm and strong. Trustworthy. God desires for you to trust his trustworthiness.

Use the space below to declare your belief…and unbelief. Trust God to meet you right where you are – and not be content to leave you there.

"The greatness of a man's power is the measure of his surrender." William Booth
Place a X on the line to indicate your surrender.

•——•

No surrender. I'm holding on to what I have and know.   Complete surrender. None of me; it's all about God.

Now place a * on the line to indicate where you want your level of surrender to be.

•——•

No surrender. I'm holding on to what I have and know.   Complete surrender. None of me; it's all about God.

Your power is the measure of your surrender because your surrender is the humbling of yourself and giving up of your own power. So "your" power is actually not yours at all – it's God's.

God created you in his image but gave you choices to seek and follow his will – or not. As you yield to him, surrendering yourself, he fills you up with more of himself. You become more familiar with him, and as you know him more, you can discern his will more. You become more like him, including godly emotions.

Let's explore one more truth about God before launching into Week Two of *Pure Emotion*. God is both organized and creative.

*In everyday life, how do you see organization and creativity at odds with each other?

*How do you see organization and creativity complementing each other?

As you read through Genesis 1:1-2:3, mark or make notes to indicate the organization and creativity of God.

In the beginning God created the sky and the earth. The earth was empty and had no form. Darkness covered the ocean, and God's Spirit was moving over the water.

Then God said, "Let there be light," and there was light. God saw that the light was good, so he divided the light from the darkness. God named the light "day" and the darkness "night." Evening passed, and morning came. This was the first day.

Then God said, "Let there be something to divide the water in two." So God made the air and placed some of the water above the air and some below it. God named the air "sky." Evening passed, and morning came. This was the second day.

Then God said, "Let the water under the sky be gathered together so the dry land will appear." And it happened. God named the dry land "earth" and the water that was gathered together "seas." God saw that this was good.

Then God said, "Let the earth produce plants—some to make grain for seeds and others to make fruits with seeds in them. Every seed will produce more of its own kind of plant." And it happened. The earth produced plants with grain for seeds and trees that made fruits with seeds in them. Each seed grew its own kind of plant. God saw that all this was good. Evening passed, and morning came. This was the third day.

Then God said, "Let there be lights in the sky to separate day from night. These lights will be used for signs, seasons, days, and year. They will be in the sky to give light to the earth." And it happened.

So God made the two large lights. He made the brighter light to rule the day and made the smaller light to rule the night. He also made the stars. God put all these in the sky to shine on the earth, to rule over the day and over the night, and to separate the light from the darkness. God saw that all these things were good. Evening passed, and morning came. This was the fourth day.

Then God said, "Let the water be filled with living things, and let birds fly in the air above the earth."

So God created the large sea animals and every living thing that moves in the sea. The sea is filled with these living things, with each one producing more of its own kind. He also made every bird that flies, and each bird produced more of its own kind. God saw that this was good. God blessed them and said, "Have many young ones so that you may grow in number. Fill the water of the seas, and let the birds grow in number on the earth." Evening passed, and morning came. This was the fifth day.

Then God said, "Let the earth be filled with animals, each producing more of its own kind. Let there be tame animals and small crawling animals and wild animals, and let each produce more of its kind." And it happened.

So God made the wild animals, the tame animals, and all the small crawling animals to produce more of their own kind. God saw that this was good.

Then God said, "Let us make human beings in our image and likeness. And let them rule over the fish in the sea and the birds in the sky, over the tame animals, over all the earth, and over all the small crawling animals on the earth."

So God created human beings in his image. In the image of God he created them. He created them male and female. God blessed them and said, "Have many children and grow in number. Fill the earth and be its master. Rule over the fish in the sea and over the birds in the sky and over every living thing that moves on the earth."

God said, "Look, I have given you all the plants that have grain for seeds and all the trees whose fruits have seeds in them. They will be food for you. I have given all the green plants as food for every wild animal, every bird of the air, and every small crawling animal." And it happened. God looked at everything he had made, and it was very good. Evening passed, and morning came. This was the sixth day.

So the sky, the earth, and all that filled them were finished. By the seventh day God finished the work he had been doing, so he rested from all his work. God blessed the seventh day and made it a holy day, because on that day he rested from all the work he had done in creating the world.

*As a final thought, how do you think God's creativity and organization are reflected in emotions?

I look forward to continuing our study together this week! Remember and declare…

Do not be shaped by this world; instead be changed within by a new way of thinking. Then you will be able to decide what God wants for you; you will know what is good and pleasing to him and what is perfect. Romans 12:2

WEEK TWO

Make It Personal #1: *Our Emotional God*

We ended the Starter Session by looking at the creativity and organization of God. Because God is creative and organized, and because God possesses and created emotions, we must assume God's emotions (and ours, since we're created in his image) are creative and organized. You'll have your own reaction to this realization, but here are two things that come to mind for me.

1. There is a reason behind emotions (organization).
2. There is expression in emotions (creativity).

I don't know about you, but those two things seem diametrically opposed at times. But God is who he says he is, so let's start exploring what that means when it comes to his – and our – emotions.

Emotions don't make up or define God. Let's be careful in what direction we're transferring qualities of emotions. Because we deal with people, situations, and emotions as humans on earth, when we're trying to comprehend God's characteristics, we often search for the closest thing we can relate to. That's not necessarily a bad thing unless we're assuming some things about God that aren't true.

Let's look for a few examples. You'll likely not have responses to every one of the following questions, but look through the complete list and consider times you've projected qualities or experiences with other people onto God.

Here's how I've projected what I know and have experienced about my dad onto what I believe about God...

Here's how I've projected what I know and have experienced about my friends onto what I believe about God...

Here's how I've projected what I know and have experienced about my pastor/priest onto what I believe about God...

Here's how I've projected what I know and have experienced about my boss or mentor onto what I believe about God...

Here's how I've projected what I know and have experienced about my husband onto what I believe about God...

Here's how I've projected what I know and have experienced about _____ onto what I believe about God...

God is who he says he is...not who we assume he is. When we're seeking pure emotions, the same concept applies. Our emotions are what God says they are, because of who he is, not what we assume they are, because of who we are.

Emotions are one aspect of God. His emotions are never out of control, unbalanced, or unjust. His emotions are consistent with who he is. His emotions are true because he is true.

Many of our emotional experiences aren't true, so it's difficult for us to comprehend the truthfulness and trustworthiness of the pure emotions God gave us. We can believe emotional truthfulness and trustworthiness because of who God is, but we have to seek his promises and his character and set our own perspectives and experiences aside. Once we come to know and declare the truth, we can discern between our own perspectives and experiences and God's, standing on the truth of God's emotions and trusting his emotions instead of our own.

When we make God in our own image, despair will always follow. How have you made God in your image?

How have you experienced others making God into their own images?

We briefly touched on how we project our human experiences, relationships and emotions onto God in the last section. Now let's explore what happens as a result.

Consider a time you experienced despair. What was the situation?

How did you feel?

What did you do?

We experience despair when our expectations don't match reality. In some less significant situations, our response might be disappointment. Despair is deep disappointment. It's a loss of confidence or hope. When God doesn't measure up to our expectations, our confidence and hope in him can be shaken.

But God isn't supposed to measure up to our expectations. We don't make God. He measures up to his expectations, because he *is* the expectations. When we're honest with ourselves, it's not despair over God not measuring up to our expectations that we experience at all – it's despair over our own expectations not being a realistic reflection of the expectations we should have about God!

Let God be God. You might experience uncertainty, but you won't experience despair.

There's a difference between godly and healthy emotions. What emotions do you view as unhealthy? (We're dealing in generalities, but you can make additional notes if you think there are exceptions.)

What emotions do you view as healthy? (Again, we're dealing with generalities, but you can make additional notes about exceptions.)

Revisit both lists and place a "G" beside any emotion you see as godly and "U" beside any emotion you see as ungodly.

Keep in mind our lists might be different, because our experiences have been different, but because God is God, what's godly and ungodly doesn't change. God doesn't waver in who he is.

All godly emotions are healthy.

All ungodly emotions are unhealthy.

At first glance, the reverse statements may seem to be true (All healthy emotions are godly. All unhealthy emotions are ungodly.) But here's the problem: defining healthy and unhealthy can be subjective. We define godly and ungodly by who God is. And God is who he says he is, so whether something is godly or ungodly is unquestionable. (Of course, I'm sure we can find something to argue about, but let's keep the main thing the main thing and not get off on a tangent, trying to find a dividing point. I'm sure there's more that we agree upon than disagree upon.) Whether something is healthy or unhealthy is questionable. We tend to rationalize healthy and unhealthy based on varying standards: our experiences, medicine, biology, ethics, morality, etc.

Of course, it's important to consider what's healthy or unhealthy about your emotions, but we can't trust our own rationale. We *can* trust God, so let's commit to seeking godly emotions, knowing what's godly will also be healthy. Whenever we refer to healthy emotions or relationships throughout the remainder of our study together, assume we're identifying godly emotions or relationships.

We often experience God in the darkness. Just a reminder that all godly emotions aren't going to be light, warm, and fuzzy. God's love is compassionate and corrective. His love is convicting. Living by God's standards isn't easy. Remember, God can bless the difficult.

What differences have you experienced between growing toward God through the easy times versus growing toward God through the difficult times?

When I visited Yad Vashem, Jerusalem's Holocaust History Museum, I knew it would be an emotional experience…but I didn't expect how personal it became.

I listened to our Jewish guide introduce us to the various memorials and features of Yad Vashem. We stood at the entrance of the Children's Memorial. I stared at rows of white pillars, resembling children lined up for a class photo. But this photo is different. Every pillar – child – is cut off.

Each life cut short.

As I walked into the exhibition area, my eyes adjusted to the darkness – or so I thought. I stood in front of a large wall of photos and stared into the eyes of children who didn't live through the Holocaust. I heard my breath. I felt my heart beat. I was alive, yet the dead children's eyes bore into me. For a moment, I died within the life in the children's eyes.

I turned and walked into an even darker room – so dark that my eyes couldn't adjust this time. I listened to names being read in Hebrew, Yiddish and English. Each name was a child who didn't live through the Holocaust. My feet shuffled through the darkness. Our group was in a single file, and as our feet shuffled in the blinding darkness, I thought of those who shuffled into railroad cars, barracks, and incinerators, blinded by the lack of light, lack of choice, lack of compassion. The difference? I stepped out of the darkness and into the light.

A brief respite and then it was time to continue through the main museum. I lingered near the entrance, watching old movie footage and letting the group get ahead of me. I sensed the need to be alone in the crowd. I walked a few steps and stood in front of a large photo somewhat hidden behind a display of smaller photos: photos of people enjoying everyday life, smiling, connecting, laughing. My eyes were drawn to the large wall photo. As my mind made sense of the pile of entangled, distorted bodies, I stared into one person's eyes. Not eyes exactly, but undistinguished sockets. I strained to see a hint of life – like I saw in the children's eyes.

Nothing.

And I thought: That could be me.

I reluctantly turned away. I thought by standing there a bit longer, I'd pay more tribute. Then I realized there was nothing I could do about the reality of the past…except continue to move into the future, remembering the past to let it make a difference as the future unfolds.

I walked through several displays, letting the words and photos seep into me. I turned a corner and stood before a wall splattered with red…a display of Hitler and his Nazi regime. I realized I stood in a red shirt and army green pants, reflecting the vibrant and painful colors on display.

I thought: That could be me.

Here's what I learned in my walk through the darkness: I'm one step from hatred. One step from persecution. One step from judgment – giving or receiving it. One step away from misunderstandings, sacrifice, kindness, love. One step.

Walking through Yad Vashem was a journey I will not soon forget. As I exited, I was overwhelmed by the beauty of the natural scenery. I exited displays of life among the darkest of humanity and entered the brightness of God's creation. I savored the view but realized I wouldn't have experienced it without the journey through the darkness.

I was reminded that each choice impacts the next. I was also reminded that God has a beautiful view waiting for me on the other side of the darkness.

I realize the darkness I walked through was symbolic, not a devastating trial of life, but it's still a reminder to me that we can learn in the darkness. We can experience God in the darkness.

The light we experience as we emerge from the darkness is more vibrant and revealing than it would have been without the experience of darkness.

You must give your whole heart to him and hold out your hands to him for help. Put away the sin that is in your hand; let no evil remain in your tent. Then you can lift up your face without shame, and you can stand strong without fear. You will forget your trouble and remember it only as water gone by. Your life will be as bright as the noonday sun, and darkness will seem like morning. You will feel safe because there is hope; you will look around and rest in safety. Job 11:13-18

WEEK TWO

Make It Personal #2: *Faith in a Faithful God*

In tomorrow's Make It Personal session, we'll dig into how our emotions and faith impact each other. Today let's explore what God's Word has to say about faith and God's faithfulness so we have a firm foundation to build on tomorrow. Read each verse, aloud if possible. Then, either rewrite it or briefly journal the truths you hear God speaking to you through each verse.

So know that the Lord your God is God, the faithful God. He will keep his agreement of love for a thousand lifetimes for people who love him and obey his commands. Deuteronomy 7:9

He is like a rock; what he does is perfect, and he is always fair. He is a faithful God who does no wrong, who is right and fair. Deuteronomy 32:4

Barnabas was a good man, full of the Holy Spirit and full of faith. When he reached Antioch and saw how God had blessed the people, he was glad. He encouraged all the believers in Antioch always to obey the Lord with all their hearts, and many people became followers of the Lord. Acts 11:23

The Good News shows how God makes people right with himself—that it begins and ends with faith. As the Scripture says, "But those who are right with God will live by faith." Romans 1:17

Since we have been made right with God by our faith, we have peace with God. This happened through our Lord Jesus Christ, who through our faith has brought us into that blessing of God's grace that we now enjoy. And we are happy because of the hope we have of sharing God's glory. Romans 5:1-2

My teaching and preaching were not with words of human wisdom that persuade people but with proof of the power that the Spirit gives. This was so that your faith would be in God's power and not in human wisdom. 1 Corinthians 2:4-5

That is why we always pray for you, asking our God to help you live the kind of life he called you to live. We pray that with his power God will help you do the good things you want and perform the works that come from your faith. 2 Thessalonians 1:11

Let us come near to God with a sincere heart and a sure faith, because we have been made free from a guilty conscience, and our bodies have been washed with pure water. Let us hold firmly to the hope that we have confessed, because we can trust God to do what he promised. Hebrews 10:22-23

Without faith no one can please God. Anyone who comes to God must believe that he is real and that he rewards those who truly want to find him. Hebrews 11:6

God's power protects you through your faith until salvation is shown to you at the end of time. 1 Peter 1:5

WEEK TWO

Make It Personal #3: *Relating to God*

You're sticking with it, my friend! As I begin today's study, my heart is sensitive to you. I'm trusting God to take care of you today. Whether you're meeting difficult situations and challenges or celebrating great milestones in your life, God is *for* you. Trust him will every emotion you experience. He won't let you down.

Some of our emotions are horizontally-prompted by the situations and relationships of life. Some are vertically-prompted by our relationship with God.

What emotions have you experienced out of your vertical relationship with God?

What emotions have you experienced out of your horizontal relationships and situations?

Our emotions prompted by our horizontal relationships and situations reflect something in our relationship with God.

If the last sentence didn't sink it, reread it. It's not the most comfortable statement to read. If you're like me, you might think about some emotional moments that weren't pretty. And *that* reflects something in my relationship with God? Yes, it does.

The connection isn't always obvious. If you're angry with your spouse, you're not necessarily angry with God. If you feel guilty, it's not necessarily a guilt prompted by God. Be careful about hasty generalizations. Sometimes the connection is that simple, but often times it isn't.

Sometimes the connection is not so much a direct connection but an opportunity to rely on God, seeking the truthfulness of the situation, realizing the appropriateness (or lack) of the response, and trusting God's guidance of next steps. It's about obedience – just like so many things in life!

All horizontally-provoked emotions are connected to your vertical relationship with God, because…everything we experience and every response we have either draws us closer or distances us from God. It's all about God, which means nothing has nothing to do with God. You might not realize what something has to do with God, and you might not even *want* something to have to do with God, but it's not about what you want or understand. It's all about God.

Many authors have expressed in various arrangements of words that the definition of futility is thinking without ever thinking about God. It's also futile to live without ever (realizing you're) living for God and feeling without ever feeling in the context of your relationship with God.

Who are you? Identify your identity. How do you identify yourself when someone asks? What would your heart-answer be?

We are the first people who hoped in Christ, and we were chosen so that we would bring praise to God's glory. Ephesians 1:12

God has made us what we are. In Christ Jesus, God made us to do good works, which God planned in advance for us to live our lives doing. Ephesians 2:10

Know that the Lord is God. He made us, and we belong to him; we are his people, the sheep he tends. Psalm 100:3

You are who you are…in Christ. Behind every word or phrase you listed above when identifying yourself, now write "in Christ." For example, here are a few of mine…

- Wife…in Christ.
- Mom…in Christ.
- Teacher…in Christ.
- Speaker…in Christ.
- Writer…in Christ.
- Daughter…in Christ.

You get the idea.

Are there any identities on your list that feel awkward with the phrase "in Christ" behind it? Sometimes it's difficult to reconcile some of our roles as being in the context of who we're created to be in Christ. Or writing those words is a reminder of how we haven't been living. We often compartmentalize our lives. There's the spiritual and the practical…but the truth is, it's all spiritual. It's all about God. There's nothing in our lives that isn't spiritual. We might not want it to be. We might not be comfortable with it. We might not understand how it is. But it's all spiritual. There have been times in my life I could have won a major award for my ability to compartmentalize. During those times, I would have said I loved God with all my heart, soul, mind, and strength. In some twisted (or naïve) way, I believed I did. The truth was I loved God with all my heart, soul, mind, and strength in specific areas of my life. Other areas were shoved into the corners of the closet. Out of sight, out of heart, soul, and mind – as far as I was concerned. I was kidding myself. My award in compartmentalizing was really an award in incomplete surrender.

Is God bringing to your mind or heart any areas of compartmentalizing? Now is a good time to break down the walls.

You are who are you in Christ. When you're in his will, when you're looking at your identity through his lens instead of your own, you can firmly claim who you are in Christ. No one can take your identity in Christ away from you. No one else defines you, including yourself. That includes tearing you down or building you up. Your worth comes from God and God alone. Own it. He longs for you to realize and have the freedom of your true identity in him!

For the remainder of today's study, I urge you to make yourself vulnerable in who you are in Christ. I know it's not comfortable at times, but he's going to pour into you. Remember you need to humble yourself, emptying yourself of you in order to fully receive his filling.

I'm keeping today's study brief because I want to allow you the opportunity to richly engage with God. I encourage you to spend time exploring several questions. Dialogue with God. Listen to him. Talk with him. Commit to him. I've provided space for you to journal your conversations with him. If you're not comfortable writing down everything, key words that will prompt you to remember later will work just fine. Or perhaps you want to creatively express your thoughts and commitments with drawings. Make it personal, because that's what your relationship with God is.

What is the most dominating power driving your life right now?

How high would you go with God if you knew you wouldn't fall?

How are you participating with God right now?

I've prayed over you as I stare at the spaces below each question. I know your heart might be tender right now. I can assure of you this, my friend: God wants you to participate. He wants more for you than to sit and soak. He wants you to respond.

What will you put your whole heart into today for God?

Make It Personal #4: *Planting Seeds of Truth*

In the beginning there was the Word. The Word was with God, and the Word was God. He was with God in the beginning. All things were made by him, and nothing was made without him. John 1:1-3

Remember, God wants you to know his Word. God's Word is who he is, so being familiar with the Word is being familiar with God. The more intimate you are with what's in Scripture, the more intimate you'll be with God himself. We need to spend time in God's Word on a regular basis.

Again, I caution you not to become legalistic in this time you spend with God. You don't need to fill all the blanks on a page, but it's critical for you to fill all the spaces of your heart! Let God guide you as you interact with his Word.

Just in case you need a reminder...

Speak It. Say it out loud – several times if you prefer. God's spoken Word has power. Plus, you'll be using several senses to experience God's Word. You're taking it in with your eyes, forming the words with your mouth, and hearing the words. It's like a double exclamation point!

Personalize It. What is God specifically saying to you in this season of your life? Insert your name, respond with a question, rephrase the promise – whatever it takes to absorb what God's saying to you and stand firmly on it as you take the next steps.

Live It. God doesn't intend for us to simply fill our heads with knowledge about his Word. He desires us to let it seep into every crevice of our lives. Let him guide you through challenges and encouragements in how you'll apply a verse into your daily life. Write a note about your plan – and then revisit this page to record your progress.

Here we go!

Lord, listen to my words. Understand my sadness. Listen to my cry for help, my King and my God, because I pray to you. Lord, every morning you hear my voice. Every morning, I tell you what I need, and I wait for your answer. Psalm 5:1-3

Speak It.

Personalize It.

Live It.

Because of your great love, I can come into your Temple. Because I fear and respect you, I can worship in your holy Temple. Lord, since I have many enemies, show me the right thing to do. Show me clearly how you want me to live. Psalm 5:7-8

Speak It.

Personalize It.

Live It.

But let everyone who trusts you be happy; let them sing glad songs forever. Protect those who love you and who are happy because of you. Lord, you bless those who do what is right; you protect them like a soldier's shield. Psalm 5:11-12

Speak It.

Personalize It.

Live It.

I am tired of crying to you. Every night my bed is wet with tears; my bed is soaked from my crying. My eyes are weak from so much crying; they are weak from crying about my enemies. Psalm 6:6-7

Speak It.

Personalize It.

Live It.

I look at your heavens, which you made with your fingers. I see the moon and stars, which you created. But why are people even important to you? Why do you take care of human beings? You made them a little lower than the angels and crowned them with glory and honor. You put them in charge of everything you made. You put all things under their control: all the sheep, the cattle, and the wild animals, the birds in the sky, the fish in the sea, and everything that lives under water. Lord our Lord, your name is the most wonderful name in all the earth! Psalm 8:3-9

Speak It.

Personalize It.

Live It.

WEEK TWO

Make It Personal #5: *Emotions of Faith*

Emotions enhance faith but aren't the cornerstone of faith. Let's keep emotions in perspective. Anytime we place something or someone as the cornerstone of our faith that doesn't belong, we're literally on shaky ground.

What's the cornerstone of your faith? What's the nonnegotiable? Strip everything else away. What's the one person or relationship you can't do without?

_____ **is the cornerstone of my faith.**

I encourage you not to give the "Sunday School answer." I rarely use fill-in-the-blanks during Bible studies because I don't want you to fill in blanks as a reaction without thinking about it. Even though Jesus is the "right," true answer, it's more important to know how you'd currently complete the statement. In other words, be completely honest and choose one of the following variations of the above statement. Perhaps you'll need to cross out or add a few words to precisely express yourself.

- ❑ I want Jesus to be the cornerstone of my faith, but I've been building so long without him, I don't know how to get back to a place of basics.
- ❑ Jesus is the cornerstone of my faith. I know him to be true, and I'm passionate about my relationship. But I need to remember to lay every other stone in alignment with him.
- ❑ I know a lot about Jesus, but I don't have a relationship with him.
- ❑ I cling to the idea that Jesus is my cornerstone, but when my world is falling around me, I'm uncertain that he's enough.

The following verses might reveal more about cornerstones and challenge you as you consider Jesus as the cornerstone of your faith.

You also are like living stones, so let yourselves be used to build a spiritual temple—to be holy priests who offer spiritual sacrifices to God. He will accept those sacrifices through Jesus Christ. The Scripture says:

"I will put a stone in the ground in Jerusalem. Everything will be built on this important and precious rock. Anyone who trusts in him will never be disappointed." - Isaiah 28:16

This stone is worth much to you who believe. But to the people who do not believe, "the stone that the builders rejected has become the cornerstone." - Psalm 118:22

Also, he is "a stone that causes people to stumble, a rock that makes them fall." - Isaiah 8:14

They stumble because they do not obey what God says, which is what God planned to happen to them. But you are a chosen people, royal priests, a holy nation, a people for God's own possession. You were chosen to tell about the wonderful acts of God, who called you out of darkness into his wonderful light. 1 Peter 2:5-9

The cornerstone was laid by priest as the first stone of a foundation. The cornerstone was the reference point for the rest of the structure. Every other stone was laid in relation to the cornerstone. It determines the solidity or shakiness of the entire building.

Consider what God is revealing to you through these verses. Reflect on Jesus as the cornerstone of your faith. Use the space below to journal your thoughts, questions, and commitments.

Wherever you are right now, know that God wants you to draw close to him. Isaiah 30:18-19 says, *"The Lord wants to show his mercy to you. He wants to rise and comfort you. The Lord is a fair God, and everyone who waits for his help will be happy."* And in John 6:28-29: *"The people asked Jesus, 'What are the things God wants us to do?' Jesus answered, 'The work God wants you to do is this: Believe the One he sent.'"*

God desires Jesus to be the cornerstone of your faith – nothing and no one else.

Emotions are not the cornerstone of our faith. We don't build everything else around our emotions. We don't measure everything else *by* our emotions. Yet emotions can and do *enhance* our faith.

Emotions are like bright highlighters, calling attention to something about our faith.

How can emotions call attention to faith in a positive way?

How can emotions call attention to faith in a negative way?

When emotions highlight something not so attractive about faith, don't assume it's negative. It can be, but it can also be positive. It depends on what you do with it. Your emotions reflect something about your faith. The important thing is (1) recognize it and (2) respond to it. I probably use the highlighter analogy because I have a borderline office supply addiction, but go with me for a minute. God is highlighting things about your life that are telling of your relationship with him. In our context, we're referring to emotions, but there are so many other facets of life he highlights. He does the highlighting to call attention to something at a particular time or season, which is why you can have two nearly identical experiences or read the same Scripture at different times of your life and respond in completely different ways.

Even though he does the highlighting, he still gives us a choice. You can highlight an entire textbook in preparation for a test, but what's actually going to make a difference is studying what you highlight. What's really going to make a difference in your relationship with God is whether or not you pay attention and respond to what he's highlighting – through emotions and more.

Perhaps you choose to study on your own, ignoring God's highlighting. You just try to soak up everything you can about emotions without discerning what's true and godly and what's not. Or you prefer to keep the book shut and think about it all from your own perspective, not considering reality at all. It all sounds so much better – or worse for those who prefer the doomsday approach – without digging into reality. Or perhaps you ignore all emotions. *What* emotions?

Ask yourself: Who/what do you seek?

Your answer reflects your longing and ambition.

We're safe with God. He's full of grace.

After Adam sinned once, he was judged guilty. But the gift of God is different. God's free gift came after many sins, and it makes people right with God. One man sinned, and so death ruled all people because of that one man. But now those people who accept **God's full grace** *and the great gift of being made right with him will surely have true life and rule through the one man, Jesus Christ. So as one sin of Adam brought the punishment of death to all people, one good act that Christ did makes all people right with God. And that brings true life for all.* Romans 5:16-18

The thing about God's grace is this: we must accept it. And God's grace comes at a price. Grace requires we give up our self-sufficiency. Self-sufficiency is a little god. It includes the assumption that we can do or make something better on our own. We often *believe in* God's grace while living out of our self-sufficiency. You can't fully grasp both.

We don't lessen God's grace. We don't have that much power. But we choose not to access his full grace. It's as if we cling to trying life partially on our own and see ourselves falling short and think God has fallen short.

Where have you considered God as "falling short" in your life? Even in your belief that God cannot and will not fall short, consider the disappointments you've experienced throughout your life and any assumptions you've made about what God could have or didn't do. Don't worry. God can handle it. He already knows anyway, but he wants you to be honest with yourself, so you can move forward in his relationship with you.

God doesn't fall short. He is God. We fall short. We're human. God isn't diminished by our shortcomings. But because we know we're to reflect God's glory, and our reflections don't completely match up to God, we look in the mirror and distort the reality of God's image. God is not dependent on our obedience and our image to determine his image.

No matter how close we are to God, we'll struggle to fit into God's image. It's like trying to back up a vehicle using only the rear view mirror. Sure, backing up a short distance along a straight road might not be difficult, but what if you had to drive to work, school or the grocery store in reverse using only your rearview mirror? My dad regularly pulls trailers and other equipment and impresses me with his ability to turn the wheel just enough in the proper direction to slightly turn the trailer in just the right direction. He's had years of practice. But even with his extensive experience, I doubt he'd get far driving backward with a trailer on the interstate at the speed limit.

We simply cannot function well with our limited vision and awkward navigation. At best, that's what we're trying to do as we seek to know and reflect God's image. We're a reflection; we're not God. We can't become God. Revisit Adam and Eve's attempt in Genesis if you need a reminder.

We meet God in reality. When we listen to our emotions as God intends – as a reflection of who he is and his emotions – we face and step into reality. When we ignore our emotions or view them out of the context of who God is, we turn our backs on reality. We miss meeting with God.

We desire to know God. He created us for a craving for him. We'll fill that craving with strange concoctions our world offers, but only God can fulfill it. When we fully seek him out of the desire to know him, we don't worry as much about our emotions. They don't consume us. We don't try to figure every out every small aspect of them. We don't make decisions based on them. We don't want to get rid of any emotions we experience as undesirable and stick with the ones we experience as desirable. The point isn't about our emotions. It's about our relationship with God. We want to know God.

We struggle with emotions. Why? Because we struggle with our relationship with God. At least I do. It's not a constant struggle, but it's a journey of struggle. I wrestle and I learn and I draw closer to God as I rely on him for answers and guidance. Struggling with emotions isn't bad, but let's consider why we're wrestling. What problems are we trying to solve? What answers are we trying to find, and where are we searching for those answers?

It's all about your relationship with God.

We're not always going to see our emotions as *pure* emotions – how God intends us to see them – but we need to understand our perspective of our emotions and God's perspective of emotions, as well as how one impacts another, in order to mature emotionally and yield to God through our emotional experiences, allowing him to highlight, teach, guide, and provide.

"...for God all things are possible." Matthew 19:26

You might believe all things are possible, but are you willing to yield and be obedient to let God work out the possible in you and your life?

Week Three: *Fear*

Starter Session

When asked with what emotions women struggled the most, fear had the second highest response in the *Pure Emotion* survey. We all experience fear. Even though our experiences will differ, we'll find commonalities.

Complete the following sentence with as many descriptive words that come to mind.

*Fear is…

I'll add one to the list.

Fear is complex. Consider the many situations in which you've experienced fear. At first glance, you might recall the times you've been most afraid. Continue to search. Sometimes there are fleeting moments of fear. Perhaps fear helped you escape something. Perhaps you later laughed about something you feared. Consider the myriad of responses you've had in fear and jot down several to realize the variety of fearful experiences in your life. I've given you a few prompts to get you started, but I encourage you to be creative.

Paralyzing fear…_____

Warning fear…_____

Fleeting fear…_____

Silly fear…_____

_____

Remember the story I shared about my sisters and the trolls? Of course, I laugh at myself now, but my fear was real at the time. I wanted to hide or escape. I had trouble sleeping. My imagination wildly soared. My fear was real. The *reason* for my fear was not.

*When have you experienced a fear that was real but the reason for the fear was not?

Fear is complex. We rarely experience fear by itself. We mix it up with a variety of other emotions: anxiety, worry, uncertainty, apprehension. We toss in a little of this and a little of that with no recipe until the dish we feast on is a casserole of jumbled and often indiscernible ingredients. We're not sure what we're eating. We're not sure how we created it. We doubt anyone else could replicate it. We place it in the center of the table as our main dish of the day. Fear Casserole.

Just as we compare our menus and recipes with other women, we do the same with our fear. We wish we had less to fear. We wish we could deal with fear better. We're glad we don't have the same fear as someone else. We can always find someone who seems more fearful and less fearful, comparing ourselves in similar situations or widely varying situations. We'll look for affirmation in whatever direction we want to most find it. If we're feeling badly about our fear, we look for people who are more fearful than we are and we feel better – or we look for people who are less fearful and we feel worse. Either helps us feel better or worse about ourselves just as we prefer. The opposite is also true. We can listen to someone express their fears and be glad – even proud – that we're not as fearful or that we don't have the same circumstance. We're sure we'd deal with something better – or worse – and in the process judge those around us.

That's not the worst of it. In the process of comparing ourselves to others, we lose the reality of our own experiences. We start with a mixed up casserole of fear, anxiety, worry, uncertainty, and apprehension. We already aren't clear on the authenticity and accuracy of what we're experiencing and instead of focusing on discernment, we complicate matters further. No wonder we often experience fear as a quagmire!

This week we'll gather some practical tools for stopping the process before it's so messy and assessing our fears for what they truly are – in the context of God and what he says about fear. We'll declare his truths and determine to stand on them from this day forward. God has a lot to say about fear. And we have a lot of misconceptions. We'll explore both so we're able to tell the difference between godly and ungodly fear.

Untwisting worry and fear. As mentioned before, fear is usually mixed with anxiety, worry, uncertainty, and apprehension. Perhaps even more emotional seasonings will come to mind. Worry seems to be an especially close cousin to fear. *How have you experienced worry and fear together?

My cousin Melissa and I lived only a couple miles from each other, and we could walk through the woods and hills to each other's houses. We were two years apart and enjoyed many adventures together. We built tents, created imaginary families and communities, played games, and spent countless hours and days together. We also spent a lot of time with the grandparents we shared, especially Grandma Hacke, who showered us with gifts. Not extravagant gifts, but they were extravagant to us. Each Christmas – or any other holiday involving gifts – we each had the exact same amount of gifts. It was easy to see from the outside that they were pretty much the exact gifts. Grandma wrapped everything individually, so we'd open up a package of underwear, an outfit, socks, another outfit, pajamas, etc. We opened our gifts at the same time, finding the matching paper or size and shape, because we didn't want to ruin the surprise for the other. Well, it was probably more that we each didn't want our own surprises revealed *by* the other.

Melissa's mom and dad – my aunt and uncle – invited me to go along on their family vacation one year. Melissa and I planned our wardrobes, packing all the similar outfits Grandma had given us over the past year. One of my very favorites was the "ice cream" outfit with a large ice cream appliqued to the front of the shirt. We wore the same outfits, even pajamas, every day of that vacation. Many people asked if we were twins. Funny. With her dark long hair and my short blonde hair, we looked more like two strangers than twins. Except for our clothes.

We can put clothes on that make us look more connected than we are. And that's how fear and worry are connected. We've dressed them in similar clothes for so long that it's difficult to tell them apart. But when we take a discerning look, we see they are separate emotions. Let's spend the time it takes to unknot them from one another, so we can deal with worry as worry and fear as fear.

Finding the source of fear. As we untwist fear from the other emotions that encase it, we're able to see it for what it is. We must also find out what our fear really is. Not what we're fearful of but what the source of the fear is.

Revisit the earlier lists you made of your experiences with fear. Search for the source of fear in one or more of your experiences. Ask yourself "What is it about this that prompts fear in me?" When you answer that question, take your answer and apply the same question again: "What is it about this that prompts fear in me?" Take that answer and ask the question again. Over and over. Show your work. Remember math class – when the teacher instructed you to show your work? It's important to do the same as you get to the bottom of your fears. I've provided some space for you.

Math teachers instructed us to show our work because even if we ended up with an incorrect answer, she could see where we'd taken a wrong step. Yes, the final answer is still wrong, but because there are a lot of steps toward the final answer, there are many opportunities to mess up. If we don't show our work, all we know is we're wrong. We have no idea where we went wrong or how to correct what we've done without starting all over again. And from my own experiences, we'll likely repeat the same mistakes again. That's why it's so helpful to have someone else look at a bank account when you can't find the $2 (or $200) error.

Showing your work – exposing the process – isn't so that you'll be able to figure everything out. It's about exposing the mistakes. Just as your math teacher was able to find errors, as you expose the process of your fear, you expose your irrational assumptions and conclusions to God. He absolutely already knows every step of your work and your thinking, but he invites you into a relationship, where everything you do – in public or in secret, spoken or unspoken – welcomes him into the process. Let him find fault. God doesn't seek to find fault to condemn you. He desires for you to excel in life and defeat ungodly fear. When you're in relationship with him, exposing yourself – including your fears – to his mercy, wisdom, and guidance, he not only pours his heart into teaching you, but with his grace, he grades on a curve.

God is a patient teacher. *When have you experienced God's patience?

I was on an airplane recently and overheard a conversation between a mother and son. She was explaining url addresses. She explained what www means. Http. The difference between .org, .net, .com, and .edu. After every explanation, she asked, "Does that make sense?" The son's answer of yes or no drove her next words. Sometimes she would restate what she'd already said. Other times she'd shift the focus, leaving something incompletely understood. I assume she had insight into what her son could and couldn't understand, and that familiarity guided her explanations.

God is patient with you as you're learning – about fear and every other emotion you experience. God is patient with you as you're learning about him. God is patient as you listen to his teaching. He's patient when you don't listen. He's patient when you don't understand. He's patient because he understands. He knows your learning process better than you do. He knows your emotions better than you do. He knows your life better than you do.

The following verses speak of patience. *How do they speak to you?

Since we have been made right with God by our faith, we have peace with God. This happened through our Lord Jesus Christ, who through our faith has brought us into that blessing of God's grace that we now enjoy. And we are happy because of the hope we have of sharing God's glory. We also have joy with our troubles, because we know that these troubles produce patience. And patience produces character, and character produces hope. And this hope will never disappoint us, because God has poured out his love to fill our hearts. He gave us his love through the Holy Spirit, whom God has given to us. Romans 5:1-5

Everything that was written in the past was written to teach us. The Scriptures give us patience and encouragement so that we can have hope. May the patience and encouragement that come from God allow you to live in harmony with each other the way Christ Jesus wants. Romans 15:4-5

The Lord makes us feel sure that you are doing and will continue to do the things we told you. May the Lord lead your hearts into God's love and Christ's patience. 2 Thessalonians 3:4-5

Commit to accepting God's teaching. Commit to his challenges and to his patience. Know how you usually meet God's teachings. Each approach has its own challenges you will need to overcome as we continue the honest look at our emotions in the context of God's holy emotions.

- ❑ To be honest, I sometimes take advantage of God's patience. I can be complacent, putting off the changes I know he'd rather I make today.
- ❑ To be honest, I don't fully accept God's patience. I'm hard on myself and distance myself from God. I can't fathom why he'd continue to extend patience toward me.

Set yourself and your assumptions aside. It's not about you. Don't make it about you. Accept who God says he is and who he says he created you to be. Listen to him. Become more familiar with him. He desires nothing less.

It is better to finish something than to start it. It is better to be patient than to be proud. Ecclesiastes 7:8

WEEK THREE

Make It Personal #1: *Godly Fear*

All fear is not created equal. When have you experienced unproductive fear?

When have you experienced godly fear?

Godly fear is constructive. Fear that is destructive isn't godly. There's a difference between constructive, godly fear and destructive, anxious fear. The difference is…one is constructive and one is destructive!

Sounds easy enough, but it's a bit more difficult to pull apart in our daily lives. Let's dig into what God's Word says about fear. When we learn what godly fear is – and isn't – we're more likely to recognize destructive fear.

Sometimes our English words don't quite capture the essence of an original Hebrew or Greek word of Scripture. Even if you examine the use of words across versions of the Bible, you'll find differences. In some cases, the differences can be attributed to whether or not original manuscripts or later translations and interpretations were used in finalizing a version, but in many cases, original manuscripts were used and there are still differences in word usage. The Hebrew and Greek languages are rich in tenses and derivatives, so we sometimes struggle with choosing just the right English word to capture the true expression and intended meaning.

Let's keep it fairly simple and focus on a couple versions. The New Century Version is used throughout *Pure Emotion*, so the verses that follow will be from NCV. I'll then give you some input about the original Hebrew and Greek according to the *Hebrew-Greek Key Word Study Bible*.[2] Finally, I'll let you know when the word choice differs in another translation, primarily the New American Standard Bible.

Set aside your conclusions and assumptions about the word *fear* and let's dig into Scripture for God's truth about fear. We're going to dig deep here, so put your thinking caps on and tie them tightly! I've provided you some space to write your responses. Are you learning anything about fear as you read and study each verse? I hope so. Sometimes as we learn, we have more questions. It's great to jot those as well.

Yare – verb, meaning to fear, to respect, to reverence, to be afraid, to be awesome, to be fearful, to make afraid, to frighten. It's most commonly used as to be afraid, to fear, or to fear God.

---

2   Zodhiates, Spiros. <u>Hebrew-Greek Key Word Study Bible</u>. Chattanooga TN: AMG, 2009

The Lord is my light and the one who saves me. So why should I fear anyone? The Lord protects my life. So why should I be afraid? Psalm 27:1

Even those people at the ends of the earth fear your miracles. You are praised from where the sun rises to where it sets. Psalm 65:8 (NASB uses the word *awe*.)

Those who go to God Most High for safety will be protected by the Almighty.

I will say to the Lord, "You are my place of safety and protection. You are my God and I trust you." God will save you from hidden traps and from deadly diseases.

He will cover you with his feathers, and under his wings you can hide. His truth will be your shield and protection.

You will not fear any danger by night or an arrow during the day. Psalm 91:1-5 (NASB uses the word *afraid*.)

Yare – adjective from the verb yare, meaning fearing, afraid.

How great is your goodness that you have stored up for those who fear you, that you have given to those who trust you. You do this for all to see. Psalm 31:19

But the Lord looks after those who fear him, those who put their hope in his love. Psalm 33:18

You have raised a banner to gather those who fear you. Now they can stand up against the enemy. Psalm 60:4

God, you have heard my promises. You have given me what belongs to those who fear you. Psalm 61:6

Yirah – feminine of yare, adjective, meaning moral reverence, fear of God. This fear is viewed as a positive quality, acknowledging God for who he is, complete with good intentions.

Jehoshaphat commanded them, "You must always serve the Lord completely, and you must fear him. Your people living in the cities will bring you cases about killing, about the teachings, commands, rules, or some other law. In all these cases you must warn the people not to sin against the Lord. If you don't, he will be angry with you and your people. But if you warn them, you won't be guilty." 2 Chronicles 19:9-10

Obey the Lord with great fear. Be happy, but tremble. Psalm 2:11 (NASB uses the word *reverence*.)

Knowledge begins with respect for the Lord, but fools hate wisdom and discipline. Proverbs 1:7 (While NCV uses the word *respect*, NIV uses *fear*. Specifically in this verse, the word is used to indicate a fear that makes a person receptive to knowledge and wisdom.)

Mowra – from yare, meaning a sense of fear or awe that causes separation or respect

Then God blessed Noah and his sons and said to them, "Have many children; grow in number and fill the earth. Every animal on earth, every bird in the sky, every animal that crawls on the ground, and every fish in the sea will respect and fear you. I have given them to you. Everything that moves, everything that is alive, is yours for food. Earlier I gave you the green plants, but now I give you everything for food." Genesis 9:1-2

Lord, rise up and judge the nations. Don't let people think they are strong. Teach them to fear you, Lord. The nations must learn that they are only human. Psalm 9:19-20

Pachad – meaning to be startled, be afraid, stand in awe, be in fear, make to shake. This is a form of fear that anyone who worships and trusts God does not need to have.

Everything I feared and dreaded has happened to me. Job 3:25

Great fears overwhelm me. They blow my honor away as if by a great wind, and my safety disappears like a cloud. Job 30:15 (NASB uses the word terrors.)

This word can also be used to indicate a fear, or dread, caused by God, as in Psalm 91:5, which we also looked at under *yare*:

You will not fear any danger by night or an arrow during the day. (In the NASB, *terror* is used instead of *danger*, which is connected fear.)

The feminine form, *pachdah*, of this same word means religious awe; specifically, when the proper respect and reverence due to God is lacking because someone forsakes God and his commands. This word only appears once in Scripture:

This is what the Lord said: "We hear people crying from fear. They are afraid; there is no peace." Jeremiah 30:5 (NASB uses the word *terror*.)

Mgowrah – meaning a fear, terror. It only occurs once in Scripture and reflects the fate of wickedness, as opposed to righteousness.

Evil people will get what they fear most, but good people will get what they want most. Proverbs 10:24

Pallatsuwth – meaning fearfulness, horror, trembling.

I am worried, and I am shaking with fear. My pleasant evening has become a night of fear. Isaiah 21:4

Chared – meaning fearful, reventual, afraid, trembling.

"My hand made all things. All things are here because I made them," says the Lord. "These are the people I am pleased with: those who are not proud or stubborn and who fear my word." Isaiah 66:2 (NASB uses the phrase "trembles at my word."

Another form of the word, *charadah*, means fear, anxiety, quaking and trembling often brought on by acts of God.

All the Philistine soldiers panicked—those in the camp and those in the raiding party. The ground itself shook! God had caused the panic. 1 Samuel 14:15 (NASB uses *trembling* instead of *panic*.)

Being afraid of people can get you into trouble, but if you trust the Lord, you will be safe. Proverbs 29:25 (NASB uses the phrase *the fear of man* where NCV uses *afraid of people*.)

What variety! No wonder we can become confused about fear! Let's take a look at one more to emphasize the variety in word usages. It's a familiar passage portraying the morning of Jesus' resurrection.

*The women entered the tomb and saw a young man wearing a white robe and sitting on the right side, and they were **afraid**.*

*But the man said, "Don't be **afraid**. You are looking for Jesus from Nazareth, who has been crucified. He has risen from the dead; he is not here. Look, here is the place they laid him. Now go and tell his followers and Peter, 'Jesus is going into Galilee ahead of you, and you will see him there as he told you before.'"*

*The women were confused and shaking with **fear**, so they left the tomb and ran away. They did not tell anyone about what happened, because they were **afraid**.* Mark 16:5-9

- The first two occurrences of afraid are *ekthambeo*, meaning amaze. The NASB uses *amazed*.

- The word fear is *ekstasis*, meaning amazement or astonishment. The NASB uses the word *astonishment*.
- The last use of the word *afraid* is *phobeo*, meaning to frighten, be alarmed, be in awe.

Take a deep breath. You just took in a lot! I don't want to overwhelm you, but I want you to experience the richness of God's Word. The problem is we hear so many conflicting messages and interpretations of how we should feel about or experience fear. Now that you've dug into Scriptures concerning fear, are there any misconceptions that are being exposed or truths you're realizing?

Here's the truth. God doesn't have an ego issue. He doesn't want you to fear him because he's bigger than you and needs your respect to prove how powerful he is. He wants to be in a relationship with you, and no matter what your relationships here on earth have been like, I can assure you…someone who truly wants to be in a relationship with you for healthy reasons is not going to instill some sort of destructive fear in you.

Godly fear is balanced with godly love. You can't fully appreciate the fear of God referred to in Scripture – the awe, reverence and honor for God – without grasping the love of God.

God loved the world so much that he gave his one and only Son so that whoever believes in him may not be lost, but have eternal life. God did not send his Son into the world to judge the world guilty, but to save the world through him. John 3:16-17

If we don't recognize God as someone in a position to be revered, awed, honored, and yes, feared, can we truly embrace the idea – the fact – that he sent his Son to live on earth to be humiliated and brutally treated and to die an excruciating death for us? For you. For me. When we say God is a God of love and we shouldn't have to fear him, we're misconstruing the true meaning of love and the true action of God through his sacrifice.

Basically, it comes down to the perspective of your position in relation to God. Reflect on the next couple questions and answer them truthfully.

Who do I believe God is?

Who am I in relation to God?

Keep seeking, my friend. As you continue to grow in understanding and acceptance of who God is, you'll begin to see the love of God as the only truthful emotion completely entwined with the fear of God.

WEEK THREE

Make It Personal #2: *Planting Seeds of Truth*

In the beginning there was the Word. The Word was with God, and the Word was God. He was with God in the beginning. All things were made by him, and nothing was made without him. John 1:1-3

Yesterday was a heavy day as we dug into God's Word, so let's keep today a bit lighter. I've provided less verses for you to dig into, but I challenge you to stretch yourself by using at least two of the challenges under each verse. Need a reminder?

Speak It. Say it out loud – several times if you prefer! God's spoken Word has power. Plus, you'll be using several senses to experience God's Word. You're taking it in with your eyes, forming the words with your mouth, and hearing the words. It's like a double exclamation point!

Personalize It. What is God specifically saying to you in this season of your life? Insert your name, respond with a question, rephrase the promise – whatever it takes to understand what God is saying to you and stand firmly on it as you take the next steps.

Live It. God doesn't intend for us to only fill our heads with knowledge about his Word. He desires us to let it seep into every crevice of our lives. Let him guide you through challenges and encouragements of how you'll apply a verse into your daily life. Write a note about your plan – and then revisit this page to record your progress.

You are great and you do miracles. Only you are God. Lord, teach me what you want me to do, and I will live by your truth. Teach me to respect you completely. Lord, my God, I will praise you with all my heart, and I will honor your name forever. Psalm 86:10-12

Speak It.

Personalize It.

Live It.

Thank the Lord because he is good. His love continues forever. Let the people of Israel say, "His love continues forever." Let the family of Aaron say, "His love continues forever." Let those who respect the Lord say, "His love continues forever." Psalm 118:1-4

Speak It.

Personalize It.

Live It.

He is not impressed with the strength of a horse or with human might. The Lord is pleased with those who respect him, with those who trust his love. Psalm 147:10-11

Speak It.

Personalize It.

Live It.

This is how love is made perfect in us: that we can be without fear on the day God judges us, because in this world we are like him. Where God's love is, there is no fear, because God's perfect love drives out fear. It is punishment that makes a person fear, so love is not made perfect in the person who fears. 1 John 4:17-18

Speak It.

Personalize It.

Live It.

WEEK THREE

Make It Personal #3: *Fear of Sacrifice*

Perhaps you've read or heard the account of Abraham and Isaac several times. I urge you to read with fresh eyes, ears, and heart as you fully embrace what God is saying to you.

After these things God tested Abraham's faith. God said to him, "Abraham!"

And he answered, "Here I am."

Then God said, "Take your only son, Isaac, the son you love, and go to the land of Moriah. Kill him there and offer him as a whole burnt offering on one of the mountains I will tell you about."

Abraham got up early in the morning and saddled his donkey. He took Isaac and two servants with him. After he cut the wood for the sacrifice, they went to the place God had told them to go. On the third day Abraham looked up and saw the place in the distance. He said to his servants, "Stay here with the donkey. My son and I will go over there and worship, and then we will come back to you."

Abraham took the wood for the sacrifice and gave it to his son to carry, but he himself took the knife and the fire. So he and his son went on together.

Isaac said to his father Abraham, "Father!"

Abraham answered, "Yes, my son."

Isaac said, "We have the fire and the wood, but where is the lamb we will burn as a sacrifice?"

Abraham answered, "God will give us the lamb for the sacrifice, my son."

So Abraham and his son went on together and came to the place God had told him about. Abraham built an altar there. He laid the wood on it and then tied up his son Isaac and laid him on the wood on the altar. Then Abraham took his knife and was about to kill his son.

But the angel of the Lord called to him from heaven and said, "Abraham! Abraham!"

Abraham answered, "Yes."

The angel said, "Don't kill your son or hurt him in any way. Now I can see that you trust God and that you have not kept your son, your only son, from me."

Then Abraham looked up and saw a male sheep caught in a bush by its horns. So Abraham went and took the sheep and killed it. He offered it as a whole burnt offering to God, and his son was saved. So Abraham named that place The Lord Provides. Even today people say, "On the mountain of the Lord it will be provided."

The angel of the Lord called to Abraham from heaven a second time and said, "The Lord says, 'Because you did not keep back your son, your only son, from me, I make you this promise by my own name: I will surely bless you and give you many descendants. They will be as many as the stars in the sky and the sand on the seashore, and they will capture the cities of their enemies. Through your descendants all the nations on the earth will be blessed, because you obeyed me.'" Genesis 22:1-18

What stands out to you from these verses?

Jot any other thoughts that God brought to mind as you were reading. What is he highlighting for you?

It's tempting for us to stand in awe of (1) why God would ask such a thing of Abraham and (2) how Abraham could have a faith strong enough to answer "yes." But let's not get caught up in comparing ourselves and our faith to Abraham. God doesn't expect us to mimic. He expects us to obey. And he wants you to learn something about sacrifice.

What has or is God asking you to sacrifice or set aside?

What do you fear most that he would ask you to sacrifice or set aside? If your first response is "family," go ahead and jot it down but also stretch yourself to look for the "next" thing. I want to challenge you to look beyond Abraham's experience.

Something strikes me about the account of Abraham and Isaac – the fear involved. Oh, I know it doesn't expressly refer to fear, but it's there. Think about the godly fear we've been studying. God called to Abraham. Abraham declared, "Here I am." Basically, he was saying, "Yes, God?" And because of what happened next, I think that his "Yes, God?" was more of a "Here I am, ready to serve you without question, God." After all, Abraham received God's instructions, and as far as we know, didn't hesitate in obedience. He got up the next morning, gathered everything and everyone he needed for the day and went.

There's only one reason behind that extent of an obedient response. Fear. Not the human-driven fear. That kind of fear wouldn't (1) drive Abraham to action the way godly fear did, and (2) be honored by God the way it was. Abraham revered God. He honored him with obedience. We have little insight into Abraham's frame of mind as he was lying in bed that night, preparing for the journey the next morning, and walking with Isaac toward the mountain. What we do know is this – Abraham was willing to sacrifice for God because God asked.

Sometimes we don't ask God what he wants for us, because we have a fear of the level of sacrifice it will entail. Or we only listen to the demands we think we can handle. We define what we can handle and what we can't. But if God demands it of you, you can handle it. Not on your own strength, but with God's.

We're not sure our faith is as strong as Abraham's. Do we immediately respond when God whispers our names? Do we unquestioningly say, "Yes"? Do we trust him to provide the strength to walk the next steps? Or do we think through the possibilities of the sacrifice and reason our way out of obedience?

There's fear in sacrifice to be sure, but which fear overrides the other?

What can happen when we let the human fear of the sacrifice dominate?

What can happen when we let the godly fear dominate?

What do you learn about sacrifice from Romans 12:1?

So brothers and sisters, since God has shown us great mercy, I beg you to offer your lives as a living sacrifice to him. Your offering must be only for God and pleasing to him, which is the spiritual way for you to worship. Romans 12:1

In case you haven't realized, this is the verse that leads into our theme verse of *Pure Emotion*: *Do not be shaped by this world; instead be changed within by a new way of thinking. Then you will be able to decide what God wants for you; you will know what is good and pleasing to him and what is perfect.* Romans 12:2

Personalize it. Place your name in the blanks and then speak it aloud. Let God speak it over you.

So _____, since God has shown us great mercy, I beg you, _____, to offer your life as a living sacrifice to him. Your offering must be only for God and pleasing to him, which is the spiritual way for you to worship. Do not be shaped by this world, _____; instead be changed within by a new way of thinking. Then you will be able to decide what God wants for _____; you will know what is good and pleasing to him and what is perfect. Romans 12:1-2

What do you fear most, and to whom do you cling through the fear?

Our human fear ties us to the junk of this world. Of course, we have to live in it, and we can't completely withdraw from it. After all, God placed us here. He doesn't want us to be consumed by the world, but he wants us to be his light and salt in it so that others can see and experience him. When we fear him, we're able to keep our earthly fears in perspective. We're able to replace withdrawing from the world with carrying God throughout it.

Whether that involves your family, neighbors or people around the world, you need to listen to what God is asking you to sacrifice. Set aside your human fear of sacrifice. He always provides just want you need. Embrace a godly fear of sacrifice – the part of your relationship with God that doesn't hesitate when he says your name, when he says "Go! or "Stay!" or "Wait!" You don't have to be giddy about your response. Don't confuse one emotion for another. We're commanded to fear God. He's a powerful God. He's our Creator.

He's Lord *and* Savior. That means he's not just giving you eternal life. He's also the boss of your life. It's part of the relationship. Jesus paid a high price for you. Your sacrifice for him pales in comparison. Yield. Your obedience will be totally worth it.

I am the good shepherd. The good shepherd gives his life for the sheep. The worker who is paid to keep the sheep is different from the shepherd who owns them. When the worker sees a wolf coming, he runs away and leaves the sheep alone. Then the wolf attacks the sheep and scatters them. The man runs away because he is only a paid worker and does not really care about the sheep. I am the good shepherd. I know my sheep, and my sheep know me, just as the Father knows me, and I know the Father. I give my life for the sheep. I have other sheep that are not in this flock, and I must bring them also. They will listen to my voice, and there will be one flock and one shepherd. The Father loves me because I give my life so that I can take it back again. No one takes it away from me; I give my own life freely. I have the right to give my life, and I have the right to take it back. This is what my Father commanded me to do. John 10:11-18

WEEK THREE

Make It Personal #4: *Emotional Check-Up*

How can you apply what you're learning into daily life? After all, if I give you a challenge to deal with fear this week but you don't encounter a situation involving fear, how can you practice what you're learning about godly fear?

I can assure you God will provide opportunities to challenge you – to rely on him. You'll be able to try out the truths you're learning to help you get and stay out of emotional ruts. It doesn't take one swerve of the wheel to get and stay out of a rut. It takes practice. Your current emotional responses didn't happen overnight. You've been learning and practicing for years. It's going to take time to relearn and then solidify godly, healthy responses.

For the remainder of *Pure Emotion*, you'll spend one day answering several key questions. The questions will remain the same, so (1) you can check progress you're making and (2) you'll remember the questions better as you're faced with situations throughout each week. As we study an additional emotion each week, you'll see it added to the list. You'll get the opportunity to reflect and report on each emotion every week.

Here we go!

How might fear be distorting reality?

Is my fear serving me – is it enhancing my life – or am I serving it – have I become enslaved to it?

Is fear generally temporary or chronic for me?

Fear

How is my past experience with fear affecting today?

How is fear affecting my future?

Is fear drawing me to or separating me from God?

Week Three

Make It Personal #5: *Fear and Faith*

"The remarkable thing about fearing God is that when you fear God you fear nothing else, whereas if you do not fear God you fear everything else." Oswald Chambers

God can take care of you. He created you. He isn't going to leave you now. No matter what you fear. Let's make what we've been studying stick and apply it into our daily lives. God's Word – his truths – makes a difference in our lives. But we have to proclaim them and stand firmly on them.

There's a difference in our fears. On one end of the spectrum is the human fear that is accompanied by anxiety and worry. On the other end is godly fear accompanied by reverence and awe. Make no mistake; there is overlap. We shouldn't humanize godly emotions. Let's not compartmentalize and believe that all respect is godly and all quaking fear is not. We can certainly respect someone or something that is not godly, and the fear – a trembling fear – of God is real. For those who trust God completely, imagining standing face to face to him prompts fear…along with anticipation and excitement. Those who acknowledge God but are distant in their relationship experience fear because of the distance. And those who don't acknowledge God? Well, they might not attribute any fear to their (lack of) relationship with God, but God is still a God to be feared. I just pray they catch of glimpse of who he is, complete with the mercy and love he extends, even though they might need to walk through some dark trials and wrath along the way. And don't we all experience darkness? We live in a sinful world, after all!

Where do you fall on the following spectrum?

My fear is mostly of human-based things.   My fear is mostly God-driven.

Now put an asterisk (*) where you'd like to be.
One more step: starting at your first mark, draw an arrow, stopping at your asterisk.

This is the direction in which you're moving. Remember, it's a process. You can't wish yourself into growth. God wants you to be an overcomer. *Could* he deliver you to another place along the spectrum? Sure! But if he always delivered us with one fell swoop, we wouldn't step closer to him with each opportunity to be obedient to him, trusting him for all guidance and provision. We'd be really thankful to him in that moment, but I'm positive our relationship with him becomes stronger as we develop a routine of gratitude and dependence on God. He knows what we need, and he's willing to work patiently to develop a thriving relationship with us. He loves you too much to make faith easy.

Faith is like a well-fitted wetsuit. We struggle and squirm to get into it, thinking it will never fit. It's tight and uncomfortable as we wiggle into it. We'd rather give up and walk away at times. But when we finally pull up that zipper and enter the water, we know it's the perfect fit and just what we need. It's worth the struggle!

How has faith and fear impacted each other in your experiences?

How do you believe God wants faith and fear to impact each other based on this week's study?

Faith isn't the absence of fear. Faith encompasses godly fear. We can embrace anything that comes our way when we discern the difference between godly and human fear. In godly fear, God will always provide, guide, and challenge us each step of the way. Our response is to trust, obey, and interact with God in a constant, significant, relevant way.

We're instructed to *Pray continually, and give thanks whatever happens. That is what God wants for you in Christ Jesus. Do not hold back the work of the Holy Spirit.* 1 Thessalonians 5:17-19

What's this look like in your everyday life?

Look at the first statement.

Pray continually, and give thanks whatever happens.

There are two verbs. Write them below. (If you need a reminder, a verb is an action word.)

_____   _____

God wants you to pray and give. List what those demands involve and require below each word.

I hope your responses include areas you're already doing pretty well in, areas you feel like you fall short in, and some that you know are the "right" answers but you either don't see how they fit or you just haven't been challenged to apply them quite yet. Stretch yourself! If you don't, how can you expect to grow?

Go ahead and set your study aside for a moment. Spend time in prayer, asking God to equip you to meet the challenges he's giving you.

Let's dig into the same verse a bit further. What about the word *continually*? How can you possibly pray continually?

Remember, we often need to widen our perspective. It's not about how we define continually. It's how God defines it. Praying continually is about communicating with him about everything going on in your life.

When I walked into a hotel room recently, I was drawn to the windows. This was one of those really nice "why-did-they-give-this-to-me" rooms. I hadn't booked it. I was a guest, and when I walked into the room, I felt like royalty. Nearly the entire outside wall was glass, hidden by shutter-style sliding doors. I could glimpse the city lights through the tilted slats of the doors, but it wasn't until I slid the doors open that I saw the vastness of the view. My room overlooked a valley full of city lights; a myriad of colors and patterns filled the darkness. And I could see the outline of the mountains in the distance. When I stepped onto one of the terraces, there were less obstructions, and I could see even more. I stepped onto the terrace several times during my stay, watching the sunset one evening. I would have missed a lot had I only glimpsed through the slats.

You can let God in through the slats, or you can throw open the doors and live life fully with him. That's what praying continually is all about. It's not about being on your knees or having your eyes closed. It's not about where you are. It's about inviting God into every single aspect of your life. Every moment.

I don't know about you, but I pick and choose when I want those blinds open and when I don't, when I think I have time and when I don't. Perhaps I need to redesign the room and just take out the blinds altogether!

God doesn't waste words, does he? There's another important phrase in the same verse: *whatever happens*. Give thanks for whatever happens? Really? Surely this conjures up some questions for you. Feel free to get them out of your mind by jotting them down. God already knows them so you might as well admit them and put them on the table so you can deal with them.

This is a difficult one. Life is hard. We don't like everything that happens. But that's okay! We can easily misinterpret this verse. It doesn't say we have to like everything that happens or be happy about everything that happens. It says to *give thanks* whatever happens. It's about having an attitude of gratitude. It's about acknowledging that we don't always understand, but we know that God does. And we appreciate that he's God – the all-knowing, all-powerful, all-sufficient God. We're accepting our position in relationship with him. He understands. We don't. But we can trust him. And give thanks that he is who he is. We might not be able to fully embrace what's going on in our lives, but we can certainly fully embrace who God is and thank him for being who he is – complete with his mercy, grace, and strength.

When you fully embrace who God is, you can fully embrace your relationship with God in his fullness. Consider another part of these verses:

That is what God wants for you in Christ Jesus. Do not hold back the work of the Holy Spirit.

God exists in relationship: Father, Son, and Holy Spirit, and he's not going to hold back any part of himself from you. He wants you to throw back those shutters to fully reveal your life to him so he can reveal himself to you. He will pour the Holy Spirit into you and secure your relationship with him through Jesus. He wants you to know him intimately…he already knows you much more intimately than you can imagine, but he'll let you expose your life in perfect timing.

God wants you to experience the fullness of joy. We'll learn more about joy in a later section of *Pure Emotion*. For now, simply consider fullness of joy as God's will for you. Be sure you're only allowing godly fear into your life, because there's no room for anything else when you're experiencing God's fullness of joy.

I am the door, and the person who enters through me will be saved and will be able to come in and go out and find pasture. A thief comes to steal and kill and destroy, but I came to give life—life in all its fullness. I am the good shepherd. The good shepherd gives his life for the sheep. John 10:9-11

Week Four: *Jealousy*

Starter Session

Before beginning this week, let's remember and commit:

Do not be shaped by this world; instead be changed within by a new way of thinking. Then you will be able to decide what God wants for you; you will know what is good and pleasing to him and what is perfect. Romans 12:2

You're dealing with some big challenges, looking at the patterns of your emotions and holding them up to godly emotions so you can develop godly emotional habits. Don't be lazy. It's worth the work! Before we get started with studying jealousy this week, I want to challenge you to expose some situations in which people might use emotions to get what they want. *Dig in and brainstorm.

It happens all the time. In fact, I doubt you can go through a single day without encountering someone who is justifying behavior with emotions…perhaps it's even you! Have you ever said these statements or something like them?

- ❑ I'm eating because I'm sad (mad, angry…).
- ❑ I wouldn't have done it, but she made me so angry!
- ❑ I just wouldn't be good company.
- ❑ She makes me so nervous I can't do my best.
- ❑ I'm so happy…I'm not going to do anything to ruin it.
- ❑ It's okay. I love him.
- ❑ I would do anything for a moment of peace.
- ❑ If you love me, you'll…
- ❑ You owe me.
- ❑ I'll do what I want; I'm the one who has to live with myself.

We use emotions as excuses even in broad-sweeping generalizations such as "I'm just menopausal" or "She's just a teen with raging hormones" or "It's just the terrible twos." Anytime we use the word "just" we're likely making some sort of excuse for behavior, and in many cases, the behavior we want to excuse is in some response to an emotion. When a young girl breaks down, throwing herself on the floor as she cries over hurt feelings or what she experiences as an enormous injustice, we sometimes remark, "She's such a sensitive girl." instead of helping her deal with what's going on. I'm not saying we should have a rational discussion every time we experience someone's excessive behavior because of emotions, but we can certainly make every effort not to perpetuate the cycle.

Making decisions based on our emotions can be disastrous. It usually ends up resulting in more emotions – and not the healthy ones! Pity, anger, frustration, guilt, pride. When we were little, we threw temper tantrums. We got over them fairly quickly, and we didn't have a lot of guilt, pity or pride afterward. We typically just moved on. As we grow up – and "mature" – our temper tantrums look a lot less severe – hopefully – but we don't get over them as quickly. We might look like we get over them, but oh, the grudges and hurts can deepen for days and weeks and sometimes years.

Without betraying anyone's trust, recall a situation or relationship that you've seen a longstanding grudge or hurt impact a relationship or individual. We don't want to condemn anyone through this process. We simply want to recognize the long-term ramifications unrecognized and unheeded emotions can have. We're learning and moving forward, not getting stuck in the mud of the past.

Longstanding grudges and hurts and short-term temper tantrums typically end in selfishness. Think about it. When you feel pity, it's about you. When you feel guilt, it's about you. (We'll cover more about guilt and shame later in *Pure Emotion*. We're not talking about godly guilt here.) When you're frustrated, it's about you. When you feel anger – in this context of temper tantrums and grudges – it's about you. Oh, you can justify that it's all about the other person. They *made* you feel this way. They *made* you behave a certain way.

You aren't powerless. You have a choice in how you respond. Choose an inwardly-focused response or choose a God-focused response. Any inwardly-focused response is going to be based on pride. Again, you can justify it's not pride at all. You can rationalize it's the opposite, because you feel pity for yourself. You feel guilty. But even when we feel horrible about ourselves, it's about us. Ask yourself…is this about me, or is it about God? Your answer will help you determine where you are and your next steps. If you don't think it's about either, ask again. Every reaction you have will either take you one step away from or one step toward God.

It's like driving a car up a hill. If you do nothing, you're going to end up at the bottom. You have to exert effort by putting pressure on the gas pedal in order to move. At the very least, you'll need to put pressure on the brake pedal to keep the car from rolling backward. You're not going to develop godly emotions by doing nothing to change them. If you want to mature emotionally, you're going to have to exert some effort. Working through *Pure Emotion* will definitely help…but you'll need to apply what you're learning. So apply the pressure and let's continue up the hill.

*Let's start by digging into what comes to mind when you consider jealousy.

Now put a "G" beside anything you'd identify as godly jealousy and a "U" for anything you'd identify as ungodly jealousy.

God is a jealous god.

Don't worship any other god, because I, the Lord, the Jealous One, am a jealous God. Exodus 34:14

I'd say God takes jealousy pretty seriously. After all, he named himself Jealous One. Giving himself a name means it's an important part of his identity!

Just as fear can be destructive or constructive, so can jealousy. Destructive, ungodly jealousy is envy. And just like fear, it can be knotted and twisted with other emotions such as fear and insecurity. Constructive jealousy is zealous. God is zealous for you. Zealous is a fervent passion. Oh, I'm liking this. If there's anything I want God to feel for me, it's a fervent passion!

We might be tempted to separate godly and ungodly jealousy to the extent that we think only God can have godly jealousy, and we must settle for ungodly, human jealousy. Not so. Remember, God created us in his image. When we reflect anything other than his jealousy (or any other godly emotion), we're twisting the emotion he created within us. He wants us to be zealous, too…for him and for everything he wants for you. He wants to pull up all the weeds of ungodly jealousy – envy that doesn't reflect him at all.

God's jealousy can't be unholy. Nothing about God's emotions can be unholy. We often project our own experiences with jealousy – and other emotions – onto God. And our jealousy can be ugly to say the least. All we need is contact with other people, and ta-da! – jealousy and all sorts of other messy emotions spring up! Life might be a lot easier if we didn't have to do it with other people…but people *are* the point. We're created to be in relationship with and reach others for God's glory and honor!

Growing in relationship with God is a journey, which means growing in godly emotions is a journey as well. We don't outgrow our ungodly emotions. But as we mature spiritually, we grow toward God, allowing us to define our emotional responses more in the context of who God is. We cope with our emotions differently. Be sure not to confuse spiritual maturity with human maturity. I know many people who are mature in age who are still in spiritual infancy. And I know some very spiritually mature people who are in their twenties and early thirties. With age, hopefully, we mature spiritually, but it's not a given – it's an effort and commitment.

Before we launch into our study of jealousy for the week, let's take a look at Asaph's psalm concerning wealth and wickedness.

God is truly good to Israel, to those who have pure hearts.
But I had almost stopped believing; I had almost lost my faith
because I was jealous of proud people. I saw wicked people doing well.
They are not suffering; they are healthy and strong.
They don't have troubles like the rest of us; they don't have problems like other people.
They wear pride like a necklace and put on violence as their clothing.
They are looking for profits and do not control their selfish desires.
They make fun of others and speak evil; proudly they speak of hurting others.
They brag to the sky. They say that they own the earth.
So their people turn to them and give them whatever they want.
They say, "How can God know? What does God Most High know?"
These people are wicked, always at ease, and getting richer.
So why have I kept my heart pure? Why have I kept my hands from doing wrong?
I have suffered all day long; I have been punished every morning.
God, if I had decided to talk like this, I would have let your people down.
I tried to understand all this, but it was too hard for me to see
until I went to the Temple of God. Then I understood what will happen to them.
You have put them in danger; you cause them to be destroyed.
They are destroyed in a moment; they are swept away by terrors.
It will be like waking from a dream. Lord, when you rise up, they will disappear.

When my heart was sad and I was angry,
I was senseless and stupid. I acted like an animal toward you.
But I am always with you; you have held my hand.
You guide me with your advice, and later you will receive me in honor.
I have no one in heaven but you; I want nothing on earth besides you.
My body and my mind may become weak, but God is my strength. He is mine forever.
Those who are far from God will die; you destroy those who are unfaithful.
But I am close to God, and that is good. The Lord God is my protection. I will tell all that you
have done. Psalm 73

*What examples of ungodly emotions – including jealousy – do you recognize?

*What examples of godly emotions – including jealousy – do you recognize?

Let's take one more look at godly versus ungodly jealousy.

I realized the reason people work hard and try to succeed: They are jealous of each other. This, too, is
useless, like chasing the wind. Ecclesiastes 4:4

"You must not make for yourselves an idol that looks like anything in the sky above or on the earth
below or in the water below the land. You must not worship or serve any idol, because I, the Lord your
God, am a jealous God." Exodus 20:4-5

Throughout this week's study, I'll try to discriminate between godly and ungodly jealousy by using zeal to indicate godly jealousy and envy to indicate ungodly jealousy.

Who are you seeking? When you can identify who you are seeking – or serving – you'll identify your ambition, longing and yearning.

I hope it's for God, my friend!

WEEK FOUR

Make It Personal #1: *Envy*

What does envy look like when we want something for ourselves or others? Remember, we're using envy for ungodly jealousy. This isn't a zeal for something, a desire for something that deeply affects someone else. This is the destructive side of jealousy.

Recall your own experiences with envy.

Envy has been around for a very long time. In fact, you'll find it in the first book of the Bible (in more places than one). Let's take a look at what happened in the Garden of Eden.

Now the snake was the most clever of all the wild animals the Lord God had made. One day the snake said to the woman, "Did God really say that you must not eat fruit from any tree in the garden?"

The woman answered the snake, "We may eat fruit from the trees in the garden. But God told us, 'You must not eat fruit from the tree that is in the middle of the garden. You must not even touch it, or you will die.'"

But the snake said to the woman, "You will not die. God knows that if you eat the fruit from that tree, you will learn about good and evil and you will be like God!"

The woman saw that the tree was beautiful, that its fruit was good to eat, and that it would make her wise. So she took some of its fruit and ate it. She also gave some of the fruit to her husband who was with her, and he ate it.

Then, it was as if their eyes were opened. They realized they were naked, so they sewed fig leaves together and made something to cover themselves. Genesis 3:1-7

Where do you find envy in these verses?

I wonder…is a desire to be God always at the root of envy? Isn't that what we're doing when we make something about us? That's what envy does. It directs all focus on us. We don't have. We want. We were wronged. We, we, we. Me, Me, Me. Envy is rooted in selfishness. I see it all over Genesis 3, because jealousy is definitely Satan's issue. He can't be God, but he's going to do everything he can to make us think we can be. He's going to distract us away from God and get us as inwardly focused as he can. If he can't get us to disbelieve, he'll settle for distraction, because he'll do whatever it takes to disable us from doing God's work.

When have you been distracted from your relationship with God?

Complete the following statements.

If I had _____, I could be happy, too.
If I didn't have _____, I could be happy, too.

We look at others and say, "I want…," but do we want everything that goes along with it? We really have no idea what that "want" entails. And if we're not supposed to have it, do we *really* want it after all?

When the answer is "yes," when we continue to pursue something out of envy, we're dipping our toes (or sometimes diving headfirst) into covetousness and deception. Here's what God says about both:

You desire but do not have, so you kill. You covet but you cannot get what you want, so you quarrel and fight. You do not have because you do not ask God. James 4:2 (NIV)

"You live in the midst of deception; in their deceit they refuse to acknowledge me," declares the LORD. Jeremiah 9:6 (NIV)

The NIV even uses the word *deceive* in a verse following those we just read in Genesis: *Then the LORD God said to the woman, "What is this you have done?" The woman said, "The serpent deceived me, and I ate."* Genesis 3:13

What connections do you see between envy, covetousness and deception?

The next question might step on a few toes, but let's be authentic. We women are frequently jealous of each other. It can be little things like hair style or color, new shoes, or weight. It can be families, houses, or jobs. It can be ministry positions, respect, or spiritual gifts. Whether it's big or small, we need to call it what it is: envy. We want what someone else has. And we're not sure we want what we have!

God gives us a gift, and we're thrilled with it…at first. Then we see what he gave someone else. Humph. We want that because, in our opinion, it's better, bigger, more important. We complain about it even though we know God loves us and gave us our own gift to exactly fit who we are and what we need as we live out the life he intends for us, but envy seeps in, and we start to question, "So does my gift mean that I'm not as important as her? Am I not as worthy? Does he not love me as much? Did I do something wrong?" Even if God switched out your gift to give you someone else's, a third person would come along, and you'd start the whole process over again!

What have you seen in someone else's life – a talent, skill, or gift – that you've thought "I wish I could do that."? Make a list of what you admire in the women around you, particularly women of faith in your life. If you could have what they have, what would it be?

Envy is a vicious cycle. When we're not satisfied, we're usually determined not to be satisfied no matter what's going on around us.

I don't think it's the actual gift that stirs up envy in us. I've thought about the qualities in the women I look up to spiritually. The truth is I actually have some of the same gifts they have. Or I've seen people with the same gifts they have but it looks a lot different. What sets them apart aren't the gifts; it's the fruit of their lives.

I am the true vine; my Father is the gardener. He cuts off every branch of mine that does not produce fruit. And he trims and cleans every branch that produces fruit so that it will produce even more fruit. You are already clean because of the words I have spoken to you. Remain in me, and I will remain in you. A branch cannot produce fruit alone but must remain in the vine. In the same way, you cannot produce fruit alone but must remain in me. John 15:1-4

The fruit in people's lives is appealing. It attracts people because it radiates the glory of God. And guess what? You, having a relationship with God, can have fruit! There's no reason for envy. The fruitfulness of a godly life comes from faithfulness, and that's something each and every person can have. Choose it – not because you want to measure up to someone else, not because you want others to admire you, but because it's what God wants most for you. He wants to be in a thriving relationship with you. He's zealous for you!

What else does God's Word have to say about envy?

Patient people have great understanding, but people with quick tempers show their foolishness. Peace of mind means a healthy body, but jealousy will rot your bones. Proverbs 14:29-30

Anger is cruel and destroys like a flood, but no one can put up with jealousy! Proverbs 27:4

All these evil things begin inside people, in the mind: evil thoughts, sexual sins, stealing, murder, adultery, greed, evil actions, lying, doing sinful things, jealousy, speaking evil of others, pride, and foolish living. All these evil things come from inside and make people unclean." Mark 7:21-23

I hope you've been challenged through today's study, seeing yourself and your emotions with a fresh perspective. When we take an honest look at our emotions, they can allow us to see things in ourselves that we might not otherwise see, because as we compare our emotions to God's intentions for our emotions, we'll see gaps and opportunities for growth.

WEEK FOUR

Make It Personal #2: *Planting Seeds of Truth*

In the beginning there was the Word. The Word was with God, and the Word was God. He was with God in the beginning. All things were made by him, and nothing was made without him. John 1:1-3

Let's get right to it today!

Change your heart! Turn away from this evil thing you have done, and pray to the Lord. Maybe he will forgive you for thinking this. I see that you are full of bitter jealousy and ruled by sin. Acts 8:22-23

Speak It.

Personalize It.

Live It.

The teaching I gave you was like milk, not solid food, because you were not able to take solid food. And even now you are not ready. You are still not spiritual, because there is jealousy and quarreling among you, and this shows that you are not spiritual. You are acting like people of the world. 1 Corinthians 3:2-3

Speak It.

Personalize It.

Live It.

I wish you would be patient with me even when I am a little foolish, but you are already doing that. I am jealous over you with a jealousy that comes from God. I promised to give you to Christ, as your only husband. I want to give you as his pure bride. But I am afraid that your minds will be led away from your true and pure following of Christ just as Eve was tricked by the snake with his evil ways.

You are very patient with anyone who comes to you and preaches a different Jesus from the one we preached. You are very willing to accept a spirit or gospel that is different from the Spirit and Good News you received from us. 2 Corinthians 11:1-4

Speak It.

Personalize It.

Live It.

But if you are selfish and have bitter jealousy in your hearts, do not brag. Your bragging is a lie that hides the truth. That kind of "wisdom" does not come from God but from the world. It is not spiritual; it is from the devil. Where jealousy and selfishness are, there will be confusion and every kind of evil. But the wisdom that comes from God is first of all pure, then peaceful, gentle, and easy to please. This wisdom is always ready to help those who are troubled and to do good for others. It is always fair and honest. James 3:14-17

Speak It.

Personalize It.

Live It.

They used things that are not gods to make me jealous and worthless idols to make me angry. So I will use those who are not a nation to make them jealous; I will use a nation that does not understand to make them angry. Deuteronomy 32:21

Speak It.

Personalize It.

Live It.

Don't be upset because of evil people. Don't be jealous of those who do wrong, because like the grass, they will soon dry up. Like green plants, they will soon die away. Trust the Lord and do good. Live in the land and feed on truth. Psalm 37:1-3

Speak It.

Personalize It.

Live It.

They made God angry by building places to worship gods; they made him jealous with their idols. Psalm 78:58

Speak It.

Personalize It.

Live It.

Make It Personal #3: *Zealousy*

Today we're turning our attention toward godly jealousy: zeal. Even though my spell-check argues with me, I like the word *zealousy*. I might just rebel and use it from time to time! Zeal is fervent passion. It's intense pursuit.

Let's take a look at biblical zeal.

When it was almost time for the Jewish Passover, Jesus went up to Jerusalem. In the temple courts he found people selling cattle, sheep and doves, and others sitting at tables exchanging money. So he made a whip out of cords, and drove all from the temple courts, both sheep and cattle; he scattered the coins of the money changers and overturned their tables. To those who sold doves he said, "Get these out of here! Stop turning my Father's house into a market!" His disciples remembered that it is written: "Zeal for your house will consume me." John 2:13-17 (NIV)

What do you learn from the word *zeal* in this verse?

The Greek word for zeal is translated into English as both favorable and unfavorable. In other words, zeal and envy are both words that mean...jealousy. Same word, different context. What that tells me is that the two are so closely related that we particularly need to pay attention to our responses concerning this emotion. It's easy to slip from one to the other, and it's difficult to discern our motives.

But we can be certain of one thing: God's jealousy, his zeal, is holy and true. Jealousy involves relationship. We're only jealous in relationship. Yes, we can be jealous about a thing, but the jealousy grows out of our comparisons of ownership; it involves us. We relate one thing – or person – to another, and we're discontent. If you water discontent that's been planted in comparison, you'll grow jealousy, or to clarify, *envy*.

God's zeal for us is similar. He wants exclusivity in our relationship with him. Remember, when God mentions his name, Jealous One, he's commanding us not to worship idols. He knows that for us to give anything more attention than him weakens our relationship with him. He's zealous for us because he's protective of our exclusive relationship with him. He doesn't need his relationship with us to complete him. He knows we need our relationship with him to complete us. It's how he created us.

There's a fine line, starting with a comparison in a relationship and moving toward either zealousy, a fervent passion to protect an exclusive relationship, and envy, a resentment about a difference and desire to conquer that difference. Before we go any further, I want to be very clear about something. "A fervent passion to protect an exclusive relationship" can never describe an unhealthy relationship. I was once in a relationship in which the other person would have said he had "a fervent passion to protect an exclusive relationship," and it had nothing to do with godly zeal or godly love. Just because someone says it's so doesn't make it so. Just because *you* say it's so doesn't make it so. It's only God who can say it's so. Don't deceive yourself. Let God reveal the truth.

As humans, just with any other emotion, we can twist everything into tight knots that mix a little bit of truth with a lot of untruths, and before we know it, we're tied to chairs like a babysitter who thought it was a good idea to play good guy/bad guy with the kids. Handing the rope over to someone who isn't responsible enough to have the rope isn't a good idea – while babysitting or in your everyday life.

We can assume a threat in a relationship where there is no threat. We can create envy where there needs to be no envy. If you don't believe me, observe the details of how you respond to people in the next couple days. When you're standing in line, do you begin to look at other people – in line or on the magazine covers – and compare yourself to them? Do you notice where your husband, children, or friends' eyes roam and assume you know what they're thinking? Do you make assumptions because of something you hear? I'm not saying we shouldn't pay attention to the clues around us that are giving us valid caution. I'm encouraging you to be aware of when one assumption leads to another with little basis for connections. Most of our ungodly emotions grow one step at a time – little increments that are barely noticeable until we're consumed by them. In this case, the green-eyed monster takes control!

On the other hand, God's zealousy is pure. What do you learn from the following verses?

We are a joke to the other nations; they laugh and make fun of us. Lord, how long will this last?

Will you be angry forever? How long will your jealousy burn like a fire?

Be angry with the nations that do not know you and with the kingdoms that do not honor you.

They have gobbled up the people of Jacob and destroyed their land.

Don't punish us for our past sins. Show your mercy to us soon, because we are helpless!

God our Savior, help us so people will praise you. Save us and forgive our sins so people will honor you. Psalm 79:4-9

Be careful. Don't forget the Agreement of the Lord your God that he made with you, and don't make any idols for yourselves, as the Lord your God has commanded you not to do. The Lord your God is a jealous God, like a fire that burns things up. Even after you have lived in the land a long time and have had children and grandchildren, don't do evil things. Don't make any kind of idol, and don't do what the Lord your God says is evil, because that will make him angry. Deuteronomy 4:23-25

God's zealousy is pure...and purifying.

Using the gift God gave me, I laid the foundation of that house like an expert builder. Others are building on that foundation, but all people should be careful how they build on it. The foundation that has already been laid is Jesus Christ, and no one can lay down any other foundation. But if people build on that foundation, using gold, silver, jewels, wood, grass, or straw, their work will be clearly seen, because the Day of Judgment will make it visible. That Day will appear with fire, and the fire will test everyone's work to show what sort of work it was. If the building that has been put on the foundation still stands, the builder will get a reward. But if the building is burned up, the builder will suffer loss. The builder will be saved, but it will be as one who escaped from a fire. Philippians 3:10-15

God's refining fire is both destructive and cleansing. Just as a forest fire destroys, it also prepares an area for new growth. I recently watched a television show documenting growth of trees and other vegetation in a large national park. People have tried to stop all fires in the area for many years, thinking they were preserving the vegetation, but the natural fires that regularly burn – even though they can have massively destructive consequences – produce lush, beautiful, balanced vegetation in the long run. The fire isn't comfortable. It's terrifying, but it's also necessary for growth.

Your life is the same. The benefit we have in relationship with God is that he's not going to devastate us in the process. Yes, we'll be uncomfortable. We'll think we can't bear any more heat. We'll want to run for our lives…but the fire is part of our lives, and when we walk out on the other side, having stayed close by God's side, we can walk out in victory, prepared for fresh growth on the other side. Like Shadrach, Meshach and Abednego.

They're the three men who refused to bow down to King Nebuchadnezzar. They adamantly – and very bravely – demanded they'd only bow to God. They knew God was zealous for them, and they weren't going to betray their relationship with him.

So they were thrown into the furnace.

What happened?

The king said, "Look! I see four men walking around in the fire. They are not tied up, and they are not burned. The fourth man looks like a son of the gods."

Then Nebuchadnezzar went to the opening of the blazing furnace and shouted, "Shadrach, Meshach, and Abednego, come out! Servants of the Most High God, come here!"

So Shadrach, Meshach, and Abednego came out of the fire. When they came out, the governors, assistant governors, captains of the soldiers, and royal advisers crowded around them and saw that the fire had not harmed their bodies. Their hair was not burned, their robes were not burned, and they didn't even smell like smoke!

Then Nebuchadnezzar said, "Praise the God of Shadrach, Meshach, and Abednego. Their God has sent his angel and saved his servants from the fire! These three men trusted their God and refused to obey my command. They were willing to die rather than serve or worship any god other than their own." Daniel 3:25-28

Not only were they not killed, but they're weren't burned and they didn't smell like smoke! When God describes his jealousy as a burning fire, keep these verses in Daniel in mind. He's not trying to destroy you, my friend. He's just trying to destroy the parts of you that are coming between you and him. He's purifying you, and while it's a frightening process, it's essential for your thriving relationship with him. Don't let your own discomfort get in the way of your spiritual growth.

What is God speaking to you today? Pour your heart out to him and soak up all of his encouragements and challenges. He's pouring into you!

Week Four

Make It Personal #4: *Emotional Check-Up*

Remember, God provides opportunities to challenge you to rely on him. Try out the truths you're learning to get and stay out of emotional ruts. Be patient. It's going to take time to relearn and then solidify godly, healthy responses.

This week you'll answer questions about both jealousy and fear. You can check your progress with fear and get started assessing jealousy. Let's go!

Jealousy

How might jealousy be distorting reality?

Is my jealousy serving me – is it enhancing my life – or am I serving it – have I become enslaved to it?

Is jealousy generally temporary or chronic for me?

How is my past experience with jealousy affecting today?

How is jealousy affecting my future?

Is jealousy drawing me to or separating me from God?

How might fear be distorting reality?

Is my fear serving me – is it enhancing my life – or am I serving it – have I become enslaved to it?

Is fear generally temporary or chronic for me?

Fear

How is my past experience with fear affecting today?

How is fear affecting my future?

Is fear drawing me to or separating me from God?

Make It Personal #5: *Pursuing Purpose*

God's zeal, his passionate pursuit of an exclusive relationship with you, is the path by which he'll accomplish his purpose in your life and throughout the lives of communities of believers. God's zeal is also the path, or instrument, of his wrath in the judgment of those who choose to distance themselves from him. We can experience God's zeal as positive or negative, but I can assure you, as it's rooted in his love, God has your best interest and personal spiritual growth in mind. He's passionate about you; he zealous for you!

Earlier this week we talked about how we can be jealous, envious, of others' gifts and talents. We can twist our perspective of God's perfect gifts into objects of envy even though God is zealous for us and will prune and produce fruit in us if we're willing. Godly zeal can stir up human envy if we're not careful.

What do you learn from the following verses?

One time Joseph had a dream, and when he told his brothers about it, they hated him even more. Joseph said, "Listen to the dream I had. We were in the field tying bundles of wheat together. My bundle stood up, and your bundles of wheat gathered around it and bowed down to it."

His brothers said, "Do you really think you will be king over us? Do you truly think you will rule over us?" His brothers hated him even more because of his dreams and what he had said.

Then Joseph had another dream, and he told his brothers about it also. He said, "Listen, I had another dream. I saw the sun, moon, and eleven stars bowing down to me."

Joseph also told his father about this dream, but his father scolded him, saying, "What kind of dream is this? Do you really believe that your mother, your brothers, and I will bow down to you?" Joseph's brothers were jealous of him, but his father thought about what all these things could mean. Genesis 37:5-11

I love that Joseph's father, Jacob, questioned Joseph verbally but quietly pondered the truth. How often do we say one thing with assurance but waver in our thoughts about it?

Joseph's brothers acted on their jealousy. They plotted to killed him but sold him into slavery instead. God's plan prevailed and through the gift of dreams and interpreting dreams – the same gift that was the "last straw" for the brothers' jealousy – Joseph ended up in a well-respected appointed position and many years later extended generous grace and provision to the same brothers who mistreated him:

Joseph could not control himself in front of his servants any longer, so he cried out, "Have everyone leave me." When only the brothers were left with Joseph, he told them who he was. Joseph cried so loudly that the Egyptians heard him, and the people in the king's palace heard about it. He said to his brothers, "I am Joseph. Is my father still alive?" But the brothers could not answer him, because they were very afraid of him.

So Joseph said to them, "Come close to me." When the brothers came close to him, he said to them, "I am your brother Joseph, whom you sold as a slave to go to Egypt. Now don't be worried or angry with yourselves because you sold me here. God sent me here ahead of you to save people's lives. No food has grown on the land for two years now, and there will be five more years without planting or harvest. So God sent me here ahead of you to make sure you have some descendants left on earth and to keep you alive in an amazing way. So it was not you who sent me here, but God. God has made me the highest officer of the king of Egypt. I am in charge of his palace, and I am the master of all the land of Egypt." Genesis 45:1-8

What challenges you about Joseph's life?

What encourages you about Joseph's life?

Aren't you thankful God works through all of our circumstances? Even when it seems we're in the darkest pit, we can trust God's plan. We might not like where we are. We might not understand. But we can trust – trust that God is pursuing us. And he sees your life from a perspective that only he can see. He's passionate about you; he's zealous for you…and he's not going to let you down!

No matter where you are, no matter what your background is, you can fulfill your God-ordained purpose. Why? Because it's God-ordained! How? By staying close to God, growing in him every moment of every day. Yes, it *is* hard work! It takes discipline, commitment, and perseverance…but we don't have difficulty committing to other work even when we don't feel like it. We're disciplined about the things we want to be disciplined about. We're committed to the things we want to be committed to. We persevere in situations we want to persevere through. We work a lot in our daily lives. Our work in God is work, too, but it involves grace! God shares the load with us. He requires much of us: faith, and that can make us more uncomfortable than a desk full of files and forms. The difference between our earthly work and eternal work is that our eternal work actually requires a different perspective on work. By accepting God's grace, we yield a significant part of our workload so that we accept God's grace and make every effort within that grace to know and fulfill God's will.

All the other apostles are greater than I am. I am not even good enough to be called an apostle, because I persecuted the church of God. But God's grace has made me what I am, and his grace to me was not wasted. I worked harder than all the other apostles. (But it was not I really; it was God's grace that was with me.) So if I preached to you or the other apostles preached to you, we all preach the same thing, and this is what you believed. 1 Corinthians 15:9-11

We learn to yield to the Spirit. We accept God's grace and forgiveness through Jesus, and we receive the Holy Spirit, but yielding is a process. Paul addresses the duality in the verse above as well as earlier in his letter to Corinth. These verses are rich in God's grace and provision and our yielding. Pour over them. Don't just skim. Let yourself sink into these verses, listening to what God would have you hear. Interact with God through these verses, conversing with and committing to him through your notes.

Dear brothers and sisters, when I came to you, I did not come preaching God's secret with fancy words or a show of human wisdom. I decided that while I was with you I would forget about everything except Jesus Christ and his death on the cross. So when I came to you, I was weak and fearful and trembling. My teaching and preaching were not with words of human wisdom that persuade people but with proof of the power that the Spirit gives. This was so that your faith would be in God's power and not in human wisdom.

However, I speak a wisdom to those who are mature. But this wisdom is not from this world or from the rulers of this world, who are losing their power. I speak God's secret wisdom, which he has kept hidden. Before the world began, God planned this wisdom for our glory. None of the rulers of this world understood it. If they had, they would not have crucified the Lord of glory. But as it is written in the Scriptures:

"No one has ever seen this, and no one has ever heard about it. No one has ever imagined what God has prepared for those who love him." - Isaiah 64:4

But God has shown us these things through the Spirit.

The Spirit searches out all things, even the deep secrets of God. Who knows the thoughts that another person has? Only a person's spirit that lives within him knows his thoughts. It is the same with God. No one knows the thoughts of God except the Spirit of God. Now we did not receive the spirit of the world, but we received the Spirit that is from God so that we can know all that God has given us. 1 Corinthians 2:1-12

Commit to sifting through the junk of your own will and your own emotions to get to God's will and the truth of his emotions. Get to know who he created you to be – not who you want him to have created you to be or who the distortion of who you think he wants you to be. God's truth survives every refining fire, and his truth in you will survive as well.

Week Five: *Anger*

Starter Session

I hope you've experienced some uncomfortable moments through *Pure Emotion* so far. It's not that I want to see you squirm. It's that I know if we're always comfortable, we're not growing. Challenges take struggle and effort. If you're choosing comfort, you're also choosing stagnancy. I'm not saying everything in life has to be painful in order to be worthwhile. That's not the case at all. We experience the highs and lows within the movement between the two.

It's natural to avoid being uncomfortable. Most of us aren't going to seek pain and turmoil. There's a balance. It's called reality. But what we sometimes do is skew our perspective of reality to make it seem more like we want it to be.

One emotion we often handle in a similar way is anger. Many believe there is no room for anger in the Christian faith. We'll explore that this week, but before we get started, share a time when you've experienced volcanic anger. You know the one. It starts with a slight bubbling and heats and expands until it spews all over the place. *When have you unjustly spewed?

Mine was at a fast food restaurant. (Truth be told, I've had many. This is just the one I'm sharing today. Catch me in a vulnerable moment, and I'll share enough stories to fill this book!) The local high school girls' basketball team was in the state tournament in a city a couple hours away, and Tim and I decided to take our young girls. It was quite a splurge for us to spend money on tickets and a hotel room, but we were excited about the last minute adventure. After the first late night game, we went to a fast food drive through to get some food before going to the hotel.

We were the third car back from the order screen. We waited…and waited…and waited. Okay, it was probably only five minutes, but in a fast food line, five minutes feels like a long time. Add two hungry and tired young girls, and timing felt critical. We finally inched forward so we were the next ones to order. The car in front of us was a television crew from our area's major station. After they'd waited another ten minutes, people in other cars started asking them if they should start filming, hoping to speed up the line with the attention. They entertained the idea but decided not to. As they ordered and it was our turn to move forward – fifteen minutes after we'd started the process – we wavered. Should we stay in line or get out? We couldn't think of anything else that would still be open in the area, and by the time we got to another area of town, we weren't guaranteed anything would be open there either. We'd waited this long. So we ordered.

To spare you the painstaking details, imagine how long it took us to continue to move through the line at the pace we started. We weren't gaining speed at all. Somewhere between placing our order and getting to the window, I'd had enough. I got out of the car and went inside. The people inside were no happier than the people outside. I hung back from the mayhem for a couple minutes. I'm not sure if I was assessing the situation or planning my attack.

101

I tried to sound calm when I approached the manager, but when he starting blaming his employees, customers and even his own managers, I'd had enough. I refrained from throwing obscenities at him, but that's about all I refrained. I wanted to let him know what a horrible job he was doing as a manager. I spewed. He walked away. A couple people gave me "atta-girls," and I left.

We found a convenience store and bought junk food close to midnight.

Please don't tell me I was justified. Erupting anger is uncontrolled anger. It's not productive. Every week we've been talking about the constructive and destructive sides of emotions. Volcanic anger is not constructive.

I think that's why Christians think they can't express anger. We make the assumption that all anger is explosive. Not so.

Avoiding anger is like shutting off all electricity to your house because you're worried about being electrocuted. Oh, you might be safe from electrocution inside your house, but you're going to miss out on a lot of benefits of electricity. Anger – as God intends – is holy. If it's part of who God is and how he expresses himself – and God is definitely angry sometimes – an emotion is holy, as long as we're not messing it up. We can sin in anger, but God can't, which means anger doesn't have to be sinful.

Rank the following reasons for avoiding anger in the order you think you personally apply them. I've included a few spaces for you to add other reasons if you have them.

_____ Fear of repeating your own past patterns of anger.
_____ Fear of repeating past patterns of anger from someone else.
_____ Fear of an intense emotion. The power of passion is discomforting.
_____ Fear of being out of control.
_____ Fear of misapplying anger; being angry over the "wrong" things.
_____ Fear of isolation of relationships.
_____ Fear of being labeled as "angry."
_____ _____
_____ _____
_____ _____

Once again, one emotion gets entwined with another.

The truth is Christians are often seen as angry, judgmental and narrow-minded. And in a society that reveres tolerance, taking a stand against anything – especially sin, because we're then encroaching on someone's behavior and "rights" – attracts critics. (Critics who judge, I might add. Ironic, isn't it, how the cycle is unending?)

The fact is that when you stand *for* God, you'll stand *against* anything against God! Romans 12:9 says *Your love must be real. Hate what is evil, and hold on to what is good.*

We must be careful not to mishandle anger. After all, we can easily become more discontent and angry about someone else's issues than our own.

Why do you notice the little piece of dust in your friend's eye, but you don't notice the big piece of wood in your own eye? How can you say to your friend, "Friend, let me take that little piece of dust out of your eye" when you cannot see that big piece of wood in your own eye! You hypocrite! First, take the wood out of your own eye. Then you will see clearly to take the dust out of your friend's eye. Luke 6:41-42

In the survey leading into *Pure Emotion,* women identified anger as the emotion most frequently experienced as negative. Anger takes discernment – just like any other emotion – between what is godly and what isn't. Godly anger is an assault against injustice. When we refuse to wait for justice and take matters into our own hands, we can easily slip into ungodly anger.

*How do you think issues with control affect the discernment between godly and ungodly anger?

Yielding to God's control takes something everyone struggles with. I don't make broad-sweeping statements often, but I'm confident – while some of us struggle with it more intensely and often – we all have issues with patience. When we take justice into our own hands instead of waiting on God's timing, we not only have potential anger issues but also patience issues. And even for those who don't see themselves as having anger issues, there are likely patience issues.

Waiting doesn't signify we're denying what's going on around us. It's not sticking our heads in the sand to reality. It's a holding pattern. When an airplane is put into a holding pattern, it doesn't land and doesn't reprogram it's route to another location. The plan is to complete the trip it started, but it's put on hold. In the meantime, the flight is up in the air longer and covers some areas it wouldn't have covered if it had flown directly to the airport.

*What's your response to the following verse?

Wait and trust the Lord. Don't be upset when others get rich or when someone else's plans succeed. Don't get angry. Don't be upset; it only leads to trouble. Psalm 37:7-8

*How do you typically respond to a holding pattern?

We struggle with patience because patience signifies dependence. We're dependent on God. Yes, we have choices…and one of those choices – applied on a daily basis – is whether or not to acknowledge our dependence on God. Whether or not to accept our position as the created, acknowledging God as the Creator. Without settling the dependence issue, we're not going to settle the patience issue.

Please don't misconstrue what I'm saying. Being dependent doesn't mean we're lazy and uninvolved. Just the opposite. God seeks active relationship with us. He invests in relationship and demands that you be invested, too – if you want the relationship to thrive and grow. That's why he gives you boundaries, choices, and consequences.

Let's peel back one more layer before continuing with our study of anger. To review, anger is twisted with control, which is twisted with patience, which is twisted with dependence. And our dependence on God…provides hope. Hope is what we find in patience.

Wait for the Lord's help. Be strong and brave, and wait for the Lord's help. Psalm 27:14
So our hope is in the Lord. He is our help, our shield to protect us. Psalm 33:20
I wait for the Lord to help me, and I trust his word. Psalm 130:5

When we have hope in our dependent relationship with God, we don't struggle (as much) with control, which means we also won't struggle (as much) with ungodly anger. I'm not willing to take out the "as much" qualifiers, because it's simply not realistic to think we're never going to struggle. Perhaps you're not going to struggle as much as the person next to you on a particular issue, but I'm sure there's something else you struggle with more, so be careful in your complacency and pride.

Before launching into this week's study of anger, let's brainstorm one more – very human – experience of anger. *List every physical symptom or effect of anger you can think of whether you personally experience it or you know it to be generally experienced when people are angry.

Circle the top 1-3 symptoms you personally experience when you're angry. List them below the far right end of the line.

Dormant Volcano   Active, Erupting Volcano

What happens right before the explosion? For me, it's a tension in my head and tightness in the back of my neck. Just as people who study volcanoes determine and watch for signs of erupting volcanoes, you need to watch for signs of erupting anger.

Write those "just before" signs to the left of the symptoms of anger you've written to the far right below the line.

Your challenge is to be sensitive to when you experience those warning signs. That's your signal to run to God, take a time out, or do whatever you need to in order to squelch that bubbling mess of lava about to spew all over the people closest to you at the time. It's going to take practice, but as you stop the spewing earlier and earlier in the process, you'll decrease the likelihood of massive, destructive explosions.

One more thing. Put a big "X" through the end identified as *Dormant Volcano*. Your goal isn't to be dormant. Dormant means sleeping, and if you're sleeping, you're not active. God didn't create you with emotions so you can ignore them. No matter how much you deny your anger, it's going to bubble and seep out somewhere, because at the very least, you're going to experience the godly anger, or assault on injustice, to glorify him. Let God's anger reside in you. Let him guide you every step of the way. Stand with him in truth, and you'll know just when and what to stand against.

WEEK FIVE

Make It Personal #1: *Let's Define It*

As I sifted through Bible commentaries and dictionaries, I found many words trying to capture the meaning of anger.

Enraged	Provoked	Displeasure
Displeased	Vexed	Abhor
Divine anger	Wrath	Violent passion
Indignation	Outburst	Vengeance
Wrath	Fury	Fierceness
Trouble	Furious	
Grieve	Rage	

These aren't all synonyms to replace the word *anger*. Some portray more of the godly emotion and some ungodly. Let's start to dig into the differences so we can stretch beyond understanding the meaning of anger and discern how best to express it and when.

When a person's anger is unjustified. When the anger of men is portrayed in the Bible, it is almost always negative.

I said, "I will be careful how I act and will not sin by what I say. I will be careful what I say around wicked people." So I kept very quiet. I didn't even say anything good, but I became even more upset.

I became very angry inside, and as I thought about it, my anger burned. Psalm 39:1-3

Just as stirring milk makes butter, and twisting noses makes them bleed, so stirring up anger causes trouble. Proverbs 30:33

In your past, evil life you also did these things. But now also put these things out of your life: anger, bad temper, doing or saying things to hurt others, and using evil words when you talk. Do not lie to each other. You have left your old sinful life and the things you did before. Colossians. 3:7-9

What's the danger of responding in ungodly anger?

When you are angry, do not sin, and be sure to stop being angry before the end of the day. Ephesians 4:26

Ungodly anger can't reflect God because it's sinful, which means it separates us from God. It misses the mark of what God wants for us.

When a person's anger is justified. There are instances in the Bible when man's anger is portrayed as positive. What do you discover about anger in the following verses?

When Moses came close to the camp, he saw the gold calf and the dancing, and he became very angry. He threw down the stone tablets that he was carrying and broke them at the bottom of the mountain. Exodus 32:19

When Saul heard their words, God's Spirit rushed upon him with power, and he became very angry. 1 Samuel 11:6

One question to ask in discerning whether or not anger is godly is "Will it connect people to God more intensely than they're connected now?" If anger is God-driven, it will always have at the center of its purpose the drawing of people into a closer relationship with him. As we've already mentioned, growth doesn't equal comfort. If you search Exodus 32 further, you'll find the Israelites weren't happy as they lived ramifications of the godly anger poured onto them through Moses and by God. It wasn't a pleasant experience. Consequences that involve anger rarely are. But it was a positive outcome in the sense that people grew in their knowledge – their faith and familiarity – with God.

When God's anger seems overwhelming. Another word used to describe God's anger is wrath. I've bolded the word *anger* where it has been translated *wrath* in the NASB.

Remember this and do not forget it: You made the Lord your God angry in the desert. You would not obey the Lord from the day you left Egypt until you arrived here. At Mount Sinai you made the Lord **angry**—*angry enough to destroy you.* Deuteronomy 9:7-8

"Go and ask the Lord about the words in the book that was found. Ask for me, for all the people, and for all Judah. The Lord's **anger** *is burning against us, because our ancestors did not obey the words of this book; they did not do all the things written for us to do."* 2 Kings 22:13

God's breath destroys them, and a blast of his anger kills them. Job 4:9

His anger will blow them away alive faster than burning thorns can heat a pot. Psalm 58:9

Pour your anger out on them; let your anger catch up with them. Psalm 69:24

People praise you for your **anger** *against evil. Those who live through your* **anger** *are stopped from doing more evil.* Psalm 76:10

He has been very kind and patient, waiting for you to change, but you think nothing of his kindness. Perhaps you do not understand that God is kind to you so you will change your hearts and lives. But you are stubborn and refuse to change, so you are making your own punishment even greater on the day he shows his **anger***. On that day everyone will see God's right judgments. God will reward or punish every person for what that person has done.* Romans 2:4-6

We could isolate these verses and have a distaste for who God is. After all, who wants to have a relationship with someone who is so intensely angry? Well, he's not. What stirs God's anger?

God's anger is righteous. He abhors anything that pulls us away from him. It's the same with jealousy and many other emotions we twist. We know that if we're expressing an emotion that pulls us away from God, it's not godly. If anger or any other emotion draws us closer to God, we're headed in the right direction. God isn't a needy God. He's a wanting God. And he wants you. He wants righteousness for you, but he'll give you repeated choices, so when you're his, you're his because you chose to be, and you're willing to yield to him – a small price to pay for the sacrifice he paid for you.

When God's anger is tempered. God's anger is never out of control and is never unjustified. His anger is just and righteous. He will often withhold his anger in mercy – but only if it is best for us in the long run.

The Lord passed in front of Moses and said, "I am the Lord. The Lord is a God who shows mercy, who is kind, who doesn't become angry quickly, who has great love and faithfulness." Exodus 34:6

The Lord is kind and shows mercy. He does not become angry quickly but is full of love. Psalm 145:8

Still God was merciful. He forgave their sins and did not destroy them. Many times he held back his anger and did not stir up all his anger. Psalm 78:38

You forgave the guilt of the people and covered all their sins. You stopped all your anger; you turned back from your strong anger. Psalm 85:2-4

We need all the pieces about God's emotions and characteristics in order to know him better and reflect his image most effectively. We can easily take any of these emotions and blow one aspect or incident out of proportion. It's like making our own god, which we know God abhors! We're not going to be able to fully comprehend God, but when we seek him and empty ourselves of ourselves as we yield to him, we become transparent so that people see more of God and less of us. That's spiritual maturity.

Consider the four points we've studied today and rank them in the order that you think you live by them. In order to keep them balanced, we need to see how imbalanced they are in our minds.

_____ When a person's anger is justified.

_____ When a person's anger is unjustified.

_____ When God's anger seems overwhelming.

_____ When God's anger is tempered.

Now that you've ranked them, assign each one a percentage of how much it makes up your current view of God and anger. Make sure all numbers add up to 100%. This step gets more specific than a simple ranking because one person might take up 80% with her #1 statement and have little left for the remaining statements. Someone else might give 35% for the #1 statement and be fairly close all the way through. Recognizing the weight you're giving each takes you one step closer in your familiarity with God's anger.

When have you personally experienced God's anger, and in what category would you place it? You can list more than one experience.

I've shared with you many words I found that have been used to describe and explain anger. I've told you *wrath* is often used in translations instead of *anger*. (Other commonly used words in the Bible are burning indignation, fury, and provocation.) Something else intrigued me. It's not necessarily an "a-ha" of a sudden leap in knowledge or insight, but I thought you might be interested.

You're likely familiar with the book (and account) of Esther.

I found it interesting – and a bit ironic – to find the word anger used in several contexts in Esther.

- *The eunuchs told Queen Vashti about the king's command, but she refused to come. Then the king became very angry; his anger was like a burning fire.* Esther 1:12
- *Today the wives of the important men of Persia and Media have heard about the queen's actions. So they will speak in the same way to their husbands, and there will be no end to disrespect and anger.* Esther 1:18
- *But he controlled his anger and went home. Then Haman called together his friends and his wife, Zeresh.* Esther 5:10

First, King Xerxes is angry. The use of the word indicates an anger arising out of someone's failure to properly perform duties.

Second, the anger is generalized to married couples. It's coupled with disrespect and is a related form of the word indicating the failure to properly perform duties.

Third is Haman's anger. This is what made me chuckle, because of all people, Haman actually *controlled* his anger! In case you don't recognize the name, I can assure you Haman is considered the "bad guy" throughout Esther. Interestingly, the New American Standard Bible doesn't use the word anger. Instead, it says, "he controlled himself." The New International Version says, "he restrained himself."

You might be asking, "so what?" at this point. What struck me – besides the irony of Haman being the one who restrained his anger – is that we're all susceptible to anger! It doesn't matter if you're a king or a commoner, man or woman, white-collar or blue-collar. Anger does not discriminate!

So, what we must do is be discriminatory in what is godly anger and what is unrighteous. We're off to a great start. Hang in there. Your perseverance through the journey is worth it!

WEEK FIVE

Make It Personal #2: *Planting Seeds of Truth*

In the beginning there was the Word. The Word was with God, and the Word was God. He was with God in the beginning. All things were made by him, and nothing was made without him. John 1:1-3

It's time to dig into God's Word again. Remember, the more intimate you are with what's in Scripture, the more intimate you'll be with God himself. In case you're beginning to get stuck in a rut, because you're taking a similar approach week after week during our *Planting Seeds of Truth* times, be sure to stretch yourself. God is a creative God, and he'll direct you to search him completely through a variety of lenses. When we get used to the same old routine, we can become hearing and sight impaired in our faith journey!

Remind yourself of the possible approaches:

Speak It. Say it out loud – several times if you prefer. God's spoken Word has power. Plus, you'll be using several senses to experience God's Word. You're taking it in with your eyes, forming the words with your mouth, and hearing the words. It's like a double exclamation point!

Personalize It. What is God specifically saying to you in this season of your life? Insert your name, respond with a question, rephrase the promise – whatever it takes to absorb what God is saying to you and stand firmly on it as you take the next steps.

Live It. God doesn't intend for us to simply fill our heads with knowledge about his Word. He desires us to let it seep into every crevice of our lives. Let him guide you through challenges and encouragements of how you'll apply a verse into your daily life. Write a note about your plan – and then revisit this page to record your progress.

My dear brothers and sisters, always be willing to listen and slow to speak. Do not become angry easily, because anger will not help you live the right kind of life God wants. So put out of your life every evil thing and every kind of wrong. Then in gentleness accept God's teaching that is planted in your hearts, which can save you. James 1:19-21

Speak It.

Personalize It.

Live It.

I am a man who has seen the suffering that comes from the rod of the Lord's anger. He led me into darkness, not light. He turned his hand against me again and again, all day long. Lamentations 3:1-3

Speak It.

Personalize It.

Live It.

But God shows his great love for us in this way: Christ died for us while we were still sinners. So through Christ we will surely be saved from God's anger, because we have been made right with God by the blood of Christ's death. While we were God's enemies, he made us his friends through the death of his Son. Surely, now that we are his friends, he will save us through his Son's life. Romans 5:8-10

Speak It.

Personalize It.

Live It.

On the day that God will show his anger, neither their silver nor gold will save them. The Lord's anger will be like a fire that will burn up the whole world; suddenly he will bring an end, yes, an end to everyone on earth. Zephaniah 1:18

Speak It.

Personalize It.

Live It.

The Father loves the Son and has given him power over everything. Those who believe in the Son have eternal life, but those who do not obey the Son will never have life. God's anger stays on them. John 3:35-36

Speak It.

Personalize It.

Live It.

God's anger is shown from heaven against all the evil and wrong things people do. By their own evil lives they hide the truth. God shows his anger because some knowledge of him has been made clear to them. Yes, God has shown himself to them. There are things about him that people cannot see—his eternal power and all the things that make him God. But since the beginning of the world those things have been easy to understand by what God has made. So people have no excuse for the bad things they do. Romans 1:18-20

Speak It.

Personalize It.

Live It.

Week Five

Make It Personal #3: *Slow to Anger*

Patient people have great understanding, but people with quick tempers show their foolishness. Proverbs 14:29

The literal translation of patience is "long of nose." Anger has a lot more to do with the nose than I ever realized! I found something interested when digging into the different root meanings of *anger* in the Bible.

For example, *God's breath destroys them, and a blast of his anger kills them.* (Job 4:9) The word used for anger, according to the *Hebrew-Greek Key Word Study Bible*[3], means "nose, nostril, snout, face, angry, wrath." Anger in the following two verses includes a reference to breath or breathing, particular through the nose.

Remember this and do not forget it: You made the Lord your God angry in the desert. You would not obey the Lord from the day you left Egypt until you arrived here. At Mount Sinai you made the Lord angry—angry enough to destroy you. Deuteronomy 9:7-8

And then another angel, who has power over the fire, came from the altar. This angel called to the angel with the sharp sickle, saying, "Take your sharp sickle and gather the bunches of grapes from the earth's vine, because its grapes are ripe." Then the angel swung his sickle over the earth. He gathered the earth's grapes and threw them into the great winepress of God's anger. Revelation 14:18-19

Consider how the face changes as someone becomes angry. List all the changes you can think of in the space below.

Hebrew often uses figurative language to express difficult concepts. The idiom "his nose became hot" is the literal wording used to express "he became angry" nearly 80 times in the Old Testament[4]. A literal translation *of quick tempers* or *anger* in Proverbs 14:29 – the verse beginning today's study – is "shortness of nose."

So what's up with all the nose references?

When a person gets angry, nostrils contract or flare, making them draw up, hence, making the nose a bit shorter. Someone who is relaxed and patient with no tension in her nose is going to be "long of nose." Shortness of nose, long of nose – it's beginning to make sense.

Let's take a look at a few more verses concerning the length of our noses. (I've given you some space to interact with God through these verses. What's he telling you? How is he encouraging or challenging you?)

---

3   Zodhiates, Spiros. <u>Hebrew-Greek Key Word Study Bible</u>. Chattanooga TN: AMG, 2009
4   Carpenter, Eugene, and Comfort, Philip. <u>Holman Treasury of Key Bible Words</u>. Nashville TN: Broadman and Holman Publishers, 2000.

My dear brothers and sisters, always be willing to listen and slow to speak. Do not become angry easily. James 1:19

When you are angry, do not sin, and be sure to stop being angry before the end of the day. Ephesians 4:26

This makes you very happy, even though now for a short time different kinds of troubles may make you sad. 1 Peter 1:6

But the Spirit produces the fruit of love, joy, peace, patience, kindness, goodness, faithfulness, gentleness, self-control. There is no law that says these things are wrong. Those who belong to Christ Jesus have crucified their own sinful selves. They have given up their old selfish feelings and the evil things they wanted to do. Galatians 5:22-24

If you haven't already, spend some time in Galatians 5:22-24. Here are several highlights to explore:

- Fruit is produced by the Holy Spirit. What significance does that have to you right now?

- Love, joy, peace, patience, kindness, goodness, faithfulness, gentleness, and self-control – as the fruit of the Spirit – aren't wrong. Another example of what's godly is that it's always right and good and just. How can we twist our concept or portrayal of these good things of God and make them into something negative?

- We let go of the sinful part of our selves when we belong to Jesus. Is there a difference between accepting who Jesus is as your Savior and belonging to him?

- We give up the selfish feelings and evil things we wanted to do as the Holy Spirit works in us. What part of this has been a struggle for you?

I don't know about you, but I want to be long-nosed! We often warn each other about praying for patience. I wonder if we start praying for having a long nose if we'd feel differently about it? I'm glad I'm not on a video call right now. I can feel myself contorting my nose in all sorts of strange directions. I'm noticing a secondary benefit to having a long nose. As I'm moving my nose around, I'm thinking of the wrinkles I'm likely causing! But when I relax, as if in a state of patience, my face isn't stressed. Less stress = less wrinkles?

Sorry for the tangent, but I can let my imagination take me down the tangent road in the middle of serious study time! Let's get back to application that makes a difference in our lives.

As I mentioned earlier, the meaning of anger can also involve breath or breathing. What does breath have to do with anger?

We tend to breathe more rapidly and shallow as anger escalates. It's a side effect of anger. But relaxation and patience can in turn be a side effect of controlled breathing. Anger and breathing can become a vicious cycle or a calming cycle.

What do you learn from breath in the following verses

Then the Lord God took dust from the ground and formed a man from it. He breathed the breath of life into the man's nose, and the man became a living person. Genesis 2:7

People are like a breath; their lives are like passing shadows. Psalm 144:4

Let everything that breathes praise the Lord. Praise the Lord! Psalm 150:6

After he said this, he breathed on them and said, "Receive the Holy Spirit." John 20:22

This God is the One who gives life, breath, and everything else to people. He does not need any help from them; he has everything he needs. Acts 17:25

Breath is God-given. It's life-sustaining. We can use all kinds of relaxation breathing techniques, but there's one that is above all others. Anything that draws us to God, emptying ourselves of ourselves and allowing him to fill him with himself, is desirable.

Fully access God. As a follower of Christ, you've been blessed with the Holy Spirit.

The word for spirit comes from a word that means breath, air, or life. Perfect, isn't it? The Holy Spirit *is* breath, air and life! We need air to live, and the Holy Spirit equips us to live our faith on a daily basis. We can't live on stale air. Our bodies use oxygen and get rid of waste through the carbon dioxide. We use what we need and get rid of the rest. If we don't access fresh air, we can't live for long.

The Holy Spirit is always fresh. He only pours into us what we need. There's no waste in what he gives us. He's completely nourishing.

But we have to inhale.

In the New Testament (for example, see Jesus' words in John 20:22), the Greek root of *Holy Spirit* includes "wind." Air that's active and moving. The Holy Spirit is active. When we yield to him, we will move. We'll grow. We can also be tossed in wind, and to be honest, living a life of faith can feel like being tossed in the wind at times. But I can assure you God doesn't aimlessly toss us in the air. He knows exactly where the winds are carrying us and at what rate.

As always, God invites us to be active in faith. Breath isn't nourishing unless we breathe. We must inhale. In the same sense, we must yield to the Holy Spirit to get the full nourishment and guidance.

When you're feeling angry, take in a slow breath. As you do, pray for God to fill you with his Spirit. Slowly exhale, asking God to rid yourself of yourself. Inhale God. Exhale self.

Yes, if you have a relationship with Jesus, the Holy Spirit already resides in you…but are you *filled* with the Holy Spirit? We can *all* stand to grow in our relationships of faith.

Of course, our entire lesson today has concerned ungodly anger, but I assure you God will guide you as you need to experience and express godly anger, too. As you fully rely on him, trusting him to fill and equip you and setting aside yourself, your breaths might be calming, but your anger won't be appeased. The injustice against God stirring your anger will simply become more clear in both direction and intensity.

Trust God with each breath. He will always nourish you.

Peter said to them, "Change your hearts and lives and be baptized, each one of you, in the name of Jesus Christ for the forgiveness of your sins. And you will receive the gift of the Holy Spirit." Acts 2:38

Week Five

Make It Personal #4: *Emotional Check-Up*

Remember, God provides opportunities to challenge you – to rely on him. Try out the truths you're learning to get and stay out of emotional ruts. Be patient. It's going to take time to relearn and solidify godly, healthy responses.

This week we're adding anger to your questions. Don't forget to watch your progress with fear and jealousy!

Anger

How might anger be distorting reality?

Is my anger serving me – is it enhancing my life – or am I serving it – have I become enslaved to it?

Is anger generally temporary or chronic for me?

How is my past experience with anger affecting today?

How is anger affecting my future?

Is anger drawing me to or separating me from God?

Jealousy

How might jealousy be distorting reality?

Is my jealousy serving me – is it enhancing my life – or am I serving it – have I become enslaved to it?

Is jealousy generally temporary or chronic for me?

How is my past experience with jealousy affecting today?

How is jealousy affecting my future?

Is jealousy drawing me to or separating me from God?

Fear

How might fear be distorting reality?

Is my fear serving me – is it enhancing my life – or am I serving it – have I become enslaved to it?

Is fear generally temporary or chronic for me?

How is my past experience with fear affecting today?

How is fear affecting my future?

Is fear drawing me to or separating me from God?

WEEK FIVE

Make It Personal #5: *Effects of Anger*

I just got home from a basketball game. At the end of the first quarter, the score was 16-10. The opposing team's coach was off the bench yelling and waving his arms until…"technical foul!" On the bench he sat. At the end of the second quarter, the score was 38-12. Apparently, the anger approach didn't work.

What effects have you experienced or observed when leaders express (ungodly) anger?

Ungodly anger can definitely have some damaging and lasting effects, yet we often justify it. On the other hand, God's anger *is always* justified.

Explore a few instances of God's expressions of anger for just cause.

This is what we must do. We must let them live. Otherwise, God's anger will be against us for breaking the oath we swore to. Joshua 9:20

The people of Judah have left me and have burned incense to other gods. They have made me angry by all that they have done. My anger burns against this place like a fire, and it will not be put out. 2 Kings 22:17

Lord, rise up in your anger; stand up against my enemies' anger. Get up and demand fairness. Psalm 7:6

Destroy them in your anger; destroy them completely! Then they will know that God rules over Israel and to the ends of the earth. Psalm 59:13

Who knows the full power of your anger? Your anger is as great as our fear of you should be. Psalm 90:11

Look, the punishment from the Lord will come like a storm. His anger will be like a hurricane. It will come swirling down on the heads of those wicked people. The Lord's anger will not stop until he finishes what he plans to do. When that day is over, you will understand this clearly. Jeremiah 23:19-20

When we only express God's just anger, we're justified. When we're not in God's will in anger, we're never justified.

We need to understand God's anger more fully if we're going to reflect him. What qualities of godly anger do you discover in each of the following verses?

When Rehoboam was sorry for what he had done, the Lord held his anger back and did not fully destroy Rehoboam. There was some good in Judah. 2 Corinthians 12:12

His anger lasts only a moment, but his kindness lasts for a lifetime. Crying may last for a night, but joy comes in the morning. Psalm 30:5

I never sat with the crowd as they laughed and had fun. I sat by myself, because you were there, and you filled me with anger at the evil around me. Jeremiah 15:17

Just as with many other emotions, we struggle to separate our own experiences and assumptions of anger with godly anger. We must get rid of the destructive aspect of our emotions in order to accurately reflect God's emotions – and his character.

When I think of a reflection, I often think of looking into water. But it's not the way we should strive to reflect God's emotions. After all, when you look at a reflection in water, the image isn't accurate. The size, colors, and lines are all distorted.

When we reflect God's anger – or any other emotion – it's more like a photograph negative. It's not the actual image, but it has every detail of the image recorded in accurate dimension and proportion. Someone can take the negative and reveal the truth about God. Your life becomes a series of snapshots of God for all around you to see.

God isn't fearful of anger. Remember, he created you in his image. He's blessed you with anger – to use it to his glory. How can you use anger to glorify God?

Is there an injustice against God that you're passionate about? God's blessing of anger energizes a passion to confront and uproot sin. There are injustices all around us – in our backyards and on the other side of the world. Whether you've been fighting for a cause or you're uncertain if you've ever felt or will ever feel a strong passion to fight for an injustice, take a few moments to let God guide you as you explore and act on your passion for injustice.

You might feel a nearly oppressive burden for injustice, or you might sense a tiny seed has been planted. Either way, keep your mind, heart and eyes open. Choose what will honor God. We can sometimes start with a God-driven passion and somewhere along the way slide into the drivers' seat and end up somewhere God didn't intend for us to go. It doesn't mean you're doing a bad thing. You can still be positively impacting lives. But if you're not in the center of God's will, it's not the *right* thing. Good and right aren't always equal. Right is always greater than good.

Seek God. Choose God. Yield to God.

When I was a child, I talked like a child, I thought like a child, I reasoned like a child. When I became a man, I stopped those childish ways. It is the same with us. Now we see a dim reflection, as if we were looking into a mirror, but then we shall see clearly. Now I know only a part, but then I will know fully, as God has known me. 1 Corinthians 13:11-12

Week Six: *Anxiety and Peace*

Starter Session

Do not be shaped by this world; instead be changed within by a new way of thinking. Then you will be able to decide what God wants for you; you will know what is good and pleasing to him and what is perfect. Romans 12:2

We're halfway through *Pure Emotion*. Difficult to believe! Let's take a moment to consider where we have been, are, and are going.

*How are you experiencing "a new way of thinking?"

*What have you learned about what God wants for you?

*How are you being challenged?

I pray what you're learning as you study each day is seeping into your everyday life. I know it's not easy. In addition to the ruts we've become accustomed to journeying along, we're bombarded by messages contradictory to what God's Word says about who he is and how we're supposed to live.

I was at my husband's office a few days ago and picked up a chocolate – you know, the kind that has a message inside the wrapper? I was about to toss the wrapper in the trash when the message caught my eye: "Do what feels right." I sighed. No wonder we struggle with our emotions. We're disoriented!

During a women's trip to Israel, our guide Abi led us through a section of Jerusalem's Old City. As we studied a reconstructed painting of the city, he explained the directional orientation of the artwork. The top of the painting wasn't north, as we're accustomed with our maps. It was east. Well, that just didn't make sense, but as he taught (and he was a phenomenal teacher, asking us questions and helping us learn with discovery instead of spoon-feeding us), we learned that at the time of the painting, the Orient was considered to be the epitome of developed society. It was where the best trade markets were, so the goal was to take and get goods in the Orient. Plus, the sun rises in the east. It's the first sign of each new day that can help people see where they are – and where they're going.

Because the east was seen as the most significant reference point, it was positioned at the top of maps, and we began using the words orient, orientation, disoriented, etc.

We're disoriented when it comes to our emotions. Our reference point is often our own emotions and experiences instead of God's. We need to make sure our reference point is correctly aligned before building a map – making judgments and reactions.

Our reference point spurs our judgments. Our subsequent reactions become habitual. Do your habits drive your emotional responses? To say the least, your habits will have a significant impact, because when we react, we're responding based on what's already in place. Until we change our habits – and that takes time and effort – our responses won't change. We won't hunger for new passions while feeding the old.

We often let "feeling better" become the determining factor of our emotional responses. We want to respond in ways that make us feel better. What if, instead, our determining or driving factor for emotional responses is redemption, or our deepening relationship with God, trusting him to guide every aspect of our lives? *How does life look different between one driven by "feeling better" versus one driven toward redemption?

When it's all about God, and our lives are oriented by him, God works through things *for* us, not *against* us. God is for you, not against you. That doesn't mean you'll get everything you want or everything will go your way. God is for you becoming more like him. If something is for God, he wants you to claim it. If something is against God, we wants you to stand against it. God is always for you – it's sin he's against. He wants to weed out everything sinful in you, but he's for you in the process. In fact, the whole process of redemption is *because* he's for you!

Jesus looked at them and said, "For people this is impossible, but for God all things are possible." Matthew 19:26

All things are possible with God. Are you willing to yield and let God do the possible?

Okay, now it's time to jump into this week's study on anxiety and peace. *Let's start with brainstorming a list of all things that spur anxiety for you.

*What words come to mind when you think of peace?

Be sure to check these lists later in the week to see if you make any adjustments.

How is *anxious* used as a descriptor in the following verses?

God, examine me and know my heart; test me and know my anxious thoughts. Psalm 139:23

When my anxious thoughts multiply within me, Your consolations delight my soul. Psalm 94:19 NASB

Say to those with anxious heart, "Take courage, fear not Behold, your God will come with vengeance; The recompense of God will come, But He will save you." Isaiah 35:4 NASB

Digging into the original languages and meanings, anxious or anxiety can indicate the following:

- To whirl in motion
- To writhe in pain
- Intense, or earnest expectation
- Concern

Circle the one that most closely describes your experiences with anxiety.

*Consider if anxiety is exclusively negative or positive.

*What do you learn about anxiety from the following verses?

For I consider that the sufferings of this present time are not worthy to be compared with the glory that is to be revealed to us. For the anxious longing of the creation waits eagerly for the revealing of the sons of God. For the creation was subjected to futility, not willingly, but because of Him who subjected it, in hope that the creation itself also will be set free from its slavery to corruption into the freedom of the glory of the children of God. Romans 8:18-21 NASB

But you, beloved, building yourselves up on your most holy faith, praying in the Holy Spirit, keep yourselves in the love of God, waiting anxiously for the mercy of our Lord Jesus Christ to eternal life. Jude 1:20-21 NASB

I don't know about you, by my main experiences about anxiety haven't been pleasant. The feelings I've attributed to anxiety have been tense and uncomfortable. And God doesn't want me to entertain unhealthy, consuming anxiety. However, he doesn't want us to rid our lives of anxiety. He just wants us to have anxiety about God-driven things. *What can you imagine being anxious about – godly anxiety?

The biggie for me is heaven. As Mercy Me sings in *Homesick*,
Help me Lord cause I don't understand your ways
The reason why I wonder if I'll ever know
But, even if you showed me, the hurt would be the same
Cause I'm still here so far away from home.

My favorite line is "If home's where my heart is then I'm out of place," and while the focus of the song is mourning the loss of a loved one and longing to see her again in heaven, I long to be where my heart is, in heaven, because God is there, and I'm anxious to spend eternity with him. I want to fully experience his glory. And I want to be rid of the messes of life on earth.

The reality is I'm only ready for heaven when God says I'm ready. I don't want to miss out on a single moment here on earth. I love my family and friends and all the joys life embraces. I want to have every single influence I can possibly have. I want to grow and learn and be challenged. I want to embrace all opportunities.

But my most intense anxiety is my longing to live eternally with God. Anxiety in a longing sense, not debilitating.

When I continue to dig into what I most long for spiritually, or what I'm most spiritually anxious about, I think of fruit of the Spirit.

How intensely do you long for, or are you anxious for, the following? Place an "x" on each line, assuming 1=no anxiety at all and 10=high anxiety. Remember to consider anxiety as longing.

Love	1●————————————————————●10	
Joy	1●————————————————————●10	
Peace	1●————————————————————●10	
Patience	1●————————————————————●10	
Kindness	1●————————————————————●10	
Goodness	1●————————————————————●10	
Faithfulness	1●————————————————————●10	
Gentleness	1●————————————————————●10	
Self-control	1●————————————————————●10	

It strikes me that peace is among the fruit of the Spirit when I'm thinking about being anxious for the full-development of the fruit of the Spirit. Obviously, I can't be (godly) anxious for something that I'm (ungodly) anxious about. It's a "duh" moment for me. I've determined I can quickly uncover whether or not my anxiety is godly or not by asking a simple question about the object of my anxiety.

Is this something I desire more of or less of?

Of course, what I'm defining as desire must be godly in order for this formula to work, but once I pass that hurdle, my yes or no response immediately tells me whether or not I should embrace my anxiousness. If what I'm desiring is godly, of course, I want to embrace my anxiousness. I want to long for what God wants most for me. I'm anxious for my desires to line up with his desires. If what I'm desiring isn't godly, I don't want to long for it, and I don't want to spend my time worrying about it. Simply put, I don't want to spend time and energy on it at all except for the time and energy it takes for me to get rid of it! To desire filling my life with what God wants also assumes emptying my life of everything he doesn't want.

Before we dig into anxiety and peace for this week, I want to plant a seed about peace. There's no peace without grace.

*What do you think this statement means?

I recently heard a story of an inventor who was working on hot air balloons when the Civil War broke out. At some point, the inventor approached President Lincoln about using the technology to take the advantage of observing where the opposing troops were being positioned. It was decided not to use the technology because it was an unfair advantage. Those in charge took the "gentlemanly" approach.

Do you think either team in the Superbowl is going to set aside potential advantages to be the gentlemen? I'm not saying no one on either team is a gentleman, but it's a competition, and as someone admitted on Superbowl Sunday, "I'm going to do what it takes to win."

Now before you start making yourself feel better by claiming you don't take that approach at all with games and sports – that if you play at all, it's just for fun – step outside the sphere of sports and games for a moment. There *is* something in your life you're competitive about. Even for the extreme person who says they'll sacrifice anything for anyone…the extend of sacrifice can be competitive, too. Just because we're competitive about different things doesn't make us better or worse than the next person.

God measures you…as you…against his own measure…no one else's.

Will you win at any cost? What if winning requires surrender?

WEEK SIX

Make It Personal #1: *Peace and Quiet*

Peace. We all seek it. Bubble bath. Candlelight. Sun and sand. A relaxing book. Quiet. Perhaps your sense of peace involves something besides what I listed. But quiet always goes with peace, right? Or is that our own definition of peace? Let's explore what God has to say about it.

Peace is an important part of who God is. Jesus is the Prince of Peace. We'll explore more in the New Testament soon, but let's first turn our attention to Gideon in Judges. Gideon built a place to worship God and called it The Lord is Peace.

The angel of the Lord came and sat down under the oak tree at Ophrah that belonged to Joash, one of the Abiezrite people. Gideon, Joash's son, was separating some wheat from the chaff in a winepress to keep the wheat from the Midianites. The angel of the Lord appeared to Gideon and said, "The Lord is with you, mighty warrior!"

Then Gideon said, "Sir, if the Lord is with us, why are we having so much trouble? Where are the miracles our ancestors told us he did when the Lord brought them out of Egypt? But now he has left us and has handed us over to the Midianites."

The Lord turned to Gideon and said, "Go with your strength and save Israel from the Midianites. I am the one who is sending you."

But Gideon answered, "Lord, how can I save Israel? My family group is the weakest in Manasseh, and I am the least important member of my family."

The Lord answered him, "I will be with you. It will seem as if the Midianites you are fighting are only one man."

Then Gideon said to the Lord, "If you are pleased with me, give me proof that it is really you talking with me. Please wait here until I come back to you. Let me bring my offering and set it in front of you."

And the Lord said, "I will wait until you return."

So Gideon went in and cooked a young goat, and with twenty quarts of flour, made bread without yeast. Then he put the meat into a basket and the broth into a pot. He brought them out and gave them to the angel under the oak tree.

The angel of God said to Gideon, "Put the meat and the bread without yeast on that rock over there. Then pour the broth on them." And Gideon did as he was told. The angel of the Lord touched the meat and the bread with the end of the stick that was in his hand. Then fire jumped up from the rock and completely burned up the meat and the bread! And the angel of the Lord disappeared! Then Gideon understood he had been talking to the angel of the Lord. So Gideon cried out, "Lord God! I have seen the angel of the Lord face to face!"

But the Lord said to Gideon, "Calm down! Don't be afraid! You will not die!"

So Gideon built an altar there to worship the Lord and named it The Lord Is Peace. It still stands at Ophrah, where the Abiezrites live. Judges 6:11-24

What is your impression of Gideon?

What similarities do you see between yourself and Gideon?

Gideon went through a process with God before declaring an altar as The Lord Is Peace. What have you gone through that led you to experience the peace of God?

Peace isn't a static status. You don't arrive at a place of peace and camp under it. Gideon didn't live under or beside or even near the altar he built to worship the God of peace. If you read further in Judges 6, you'll discover Gideon, despite his fear, was obedient to God and did as he was told… he destroyed the altar of Baal and the idol of Asherah. And he didn't destroy it without knowing those who used it. His family used it. Imagine the fear of going against the accepted and expected practice of those around you – *and* having your family among those people. Despite Gideon's experience of the peace of God, he continues to question – in obedience – and God continues to guide and provide, which is peace. Peace is a process.

Suffering on earth is inevitable. We experience peace through suffering – through anxiety. Our suffering (and anxiety) on earth is temporary, not eternal. It's relevant to your everyday life. Nothing goes unused by God. Suffering is understandable. Perhaps *you* don't understand it, but God certainly understands each and every moment of your life.

What do you learn from the following verse? (I've given it to you in two translations to give you a wider breadth to consider.)

They are blessed who work for peace, for they will be called God's children. Matthew 5:9
Blessed are the peacemakers, for they will be called children of God. (NIV)

Peace isn't something we sit back and receive. We're actively involved. Jesus didn't tell us that the peacekeepers are blessed, but we often assume that's what this verse is telling us. What's the difference between a peacemaker and a peacekeeper?

Peacekeeping assumes peace already exists, and you'll do whatever it takes to keep it. First, as mentioned before, peace isn't something we obtain and keep. It's a process, and while it can be any underlying current through our lives, there will be times that are more turbulent than others. Second, if you're willing to keep peace at all costs, you won't have peace! You might brush aside issues that need to be faced. You might be oblivious. Ignorance and avoidance do not equal peace.

Making peace, on the other hand, requires action, and it's not just conflict. God guides us through discernment in when to confront and when to step aside, when to stand up and when to sit down, when to speak up and when to shut up. Consider our earlier study on anger. If we're responding out of godly anger to confront something unrighteous, we're in his will. Our goal isn't to destroy. The goal is to construct and build up. When we respond out of our own anger, not confirmed or convicted by God, we're not making peace. We're likely making a mess.

Like many things in God's kingdom, making peace seems contradictory. To make peace is active, yet it requires surrender. In order to make peace according to God's will, we must surrender our own will. We might think surrender is holding up the white flag, and it's similar as we consider giving ourselves up to God's will. We place ourselves in his hands and are willing to be used by him. However, surrender is not inactive. Surrender isn't possible without a fight or struggle. Surrender comes out of a fight or struggle. In the case of making peace – or setting aside our own emotional responses to any godly emotion – the surrender precedes making peace with any other person or situation. The conflict often happens within ourselves.

How have you experienced a struggle in accepting God's peace or making peace in a situation?

How are we to give up our human anxieties and accept the peace God wants to provide us?

Be anxious for nothing, but in everything by prayer and supplication with thanksgiving let your requests be made known to God. Philippians 4:6 (NASB)

Cast all your anxiety on him because he cares for you. 1 Peter 5:7 (NIV)

You might recognize a popular acronym, P.U.S.H. – Pray Until Something Happens. Yet another case in which we begin to believe something that's not biblical because we see it on a regular basis, and we like the concept. We like to think our persistence pays off, and yes, God wants us to pursue him. However, it's not about the push. It's about pursuing God's will. And it's not about praying until something happens. Something *is* happening. God is present. You are going to him in prayer, seeking him and trusting him. God is listening and he will not let you down. The "something" that happens might not be what you prefer. It might be that the best "something" is the process of you waiting or struggling and how close you grow to God in the process. You might even feel some distance from him through the process because you're questioning when and how he's going to answer. But he *is* answering. He's not walking away. He's pursuing you.

I know the process hurts sometimes. Growing pains are uncomfortable to say the least and sometimes downright excruciating. Pain – or wounds – aren't necessarily bad if your healing is dependent on God.

Consider your reliance on God. Talk to him about it. Commit to him. Pursue him. Be authentic with him. Acknowledge him. Take a break in today's study before we wrap it up. I've provided some space for you to converse with God on paper.

As we close for the day, I want to give you some time to reflect on making peace instead of keeping peace. It's a concept most of us will struggle with.

- Some of us don't withdraw from conflict. Our struggle might be making peace within the confines of God's will instead of taking charge of the situation in our own will and timing.
- Some of us prefer to avoid conflict. Making peace is a struggle because we don't prefer peace to be a constant without effort. We don't want to have to walk through a messy situation to get to a place of peace.
- Some of us are fairly well balanced – if we look across all situations and people. But there are situations and people that seem to consistently pull us to one extreme or the other.

It's important for you to know what your default setting is.

You'll find a list of words below. What is your response to each word? Don't worry about making notes beside every word, but look for the ones that quickly bring something to mind. Perhaps it's a person or a struggle or an experience. Perhaps God is prompting you to resolve something or change your perspective. He'll speak to you personally. Expect to hear from him.

Conflict

Disharmony

Unity

Friction

Infighting

War

Strife

Division

Serenity

Stability

Pacification

Build

Forge

Patch

Refashion

Manufacture

Glancing over your notes, are there words or situations that primarily stand out to you? Circle them…and commit to taking action this week. God expects you to make peace in his will and timing. You will be blessed by your faith and obedience.

WEEK SIX

Make It Personal #2: *Planting Seeds of Truth*

In the beginning there was the Word. The Word was with God, and the Word was God. He was with God in the beginning. All things were made by him, and nothing was made without him. John 1:1-3

Let's jump right in to God's Word. While the verses are short, there are quite a few of them. I want you to explore and claim God's peace, being anxious for him!

Speak It. Say it out loud – several times if you prefer. God's spoken Word has power. Plus, you'll be using several senses to experience God's Word. You're taking it in with your eyes, forming the words with your mouth, and hearing the words. It's like a double exclamation point!

Personalize It. What is God specifically saying to you in this season of your life? Insert your name, respond with a question, rephrase the promise – whatever it takes to absorb what God's saying to you and stand firmly on it as you take the next steps.

Live It. God doesn't intend for us to simply fill our heads with knowledge about his Word. He desires us to let it seep into every crevice of our lives. Let him guide you through challenges and encouragements of how you'll apply a verse into your daily life. Write a note about your plan – and then revisit this page to record your progress.

Do not fear, for I am with you; Do not anxiously look about you, for I am your God I will strengthen you, surely I will help you, Surely I will uphold you with My righteous right hand. Isaiah 41:10 (NASB)

Speak It.

Personalize It.

Live It.

I have no peace or quietness. I have no rest, only trouble. Job 3:26

Speak It.

Personalize It.

Live It.

Obey God and be at peace with him; this is the way to happiness. Job 22:21
Speak It.

Personalize It.

Live It.

The Lord gives strength to his people; the Lord blesses his people with peace. Psalm 29:11
Speak It.

Personalize It.

Live It.

Stop doing evil and do good. Look for peace and work for it. Psalm 34:14
Speak It.

Personalize It.

Live It.

People who are not proud will inherit the land and will enjoy complete peace. Psalm 37:11
Speak It.

Personalize It.

Live It.

Love and truth belong to God's people; goodness and peace will be theirs. Psalm 85:10
Speak It.

Personalize It.

Live It.

Those who love your teachings will find true peace, and nothing will defeat them. Psalm 119:165
Speak It.

Personalize It.

Live It.

A child has been born to us; God has given a son to us. He will be responsible for leading the people. His name will be Wonderful Counselor, Powerful God, Father Who Lives Forever, Prince of Peace. Isaiah 9:6
Speak It.

Personalize It.

Live It.

You, Lord, give true peace to those who depend on you, because they trust you. Isaiah 26:3
Speak It.

Personalize It.

Live It.

I pray that the God who gives hope will fill you with much joy and peace while you trust in him. Then your hope will overflow by the power of the Holy Spirit. Romans 15:13
Speak It.

Personalize It.

Live It.

We do not enjoy being disciplined. It is painful at the time, but later, after we have learned from it, we have peace, because we start living in the right way. Hebrews 12:11
Speak It.

Personalize It.

Live It.

Week Six

Make It Personal #3: *Powerful Peace*

Consider a time you've experienced peace. What was it about that situation or season that provided you with peace?

Consider a time you've longed for peace. What words describe the situation or season?

Reflecting on what we've learned so far about anxiety and peace, do you think your experiences will reflect both godly anxiety and peace? Why or why not?

As a reminder, godly anxiety is anxiousness or longing for God and his will. Ungodly anxiety is worry. There's no such thing as "productive worry." Of course, we've become so accustomed to using the word worry and anxiety interchangeably – and Scriptures use both as well – that it's not the actual word usage we're as concerned about. It's the heartitude. If you want to worry for God and you know it's the godly longing he wants you to have for him, call it worry if you want. It's godly anxiety, and it's more important that you *do* what's right than use a certain word. However, keep in mind our habits dig deep ruts, and calling something by the same name of an emotion you've been mishandling for years might be the a trigger to gently slide you back into old habits.

On the other hand, you can start using the word longing to replace worry – or anxiety – but you might be giving lip service instead of changing behavior and emotional responses. Replacing the word doesn't help much except to get you started down the road of change. Replacing behavior and emotional responses is the key. You might see little growth in yourself. Worry might be a pit for you. You might feel trapped.

I assure you…no matter how deep your pit is and no matter how long you've been in it, you can get out. You're not going to leap out immediately and stay out forever. It's a process. It's as if you're in a pit and need to make footholds in the side of the pit wall to climb out. With each struggle and step, you're closer to the sunshine awaiting you, but with each struggle and step, you're still in the pit. Pit escape takes patience. With each step, you can consider yourself one step closer to the daylight or you can continue to consider yourself as being in the pit. You choose whether you see progress in comparison to the top or the bottom – like a glass half-full or half-empty. It's about progress. Even if you stop digging for awhile after digging the pit deeper for years, you're making progress!

Could God deliver you from the pit all at once? Sure! He's God, and there are situations of instant deliverance in Scripture and in everyday life, but it's not as common as a process of deliverance. I'm confident God allows us to experience the process for a couple reasons: (1) If he instantly delivers me to the top of the pit, I've had one opportunity to rely on and trust him. If it's a lengthy process full of effort, I have many opportunities to rely on and trust him. With each sweaty, messy, mucky step, I rely on him a little bit more. I see the process being made and my trust deepens.

(2) I gain a lot through the process. In addition to relying on and trusting God, he teaches me small (and big) lessons that he'll use later in my life. I'll get to share some of my experiences with someone who needs encouragement. I'll toss out the tactics I tried that didn't work well and ended with me falling flat on my back on the bottom of the pit. God doesn't waste a single opportunity to teach me a lesson. Sometimes I'm just not listening.

Let's turn toward peace again. This is perhaps one of the hardest areas of change to accept – that peace isn't a place to camp under but it's a process in which we're actively involved. Remember the difference between peacekeeping and peacemaking? You might still be struggling with the concept. Use the space below to review what you studied a couple days ago. Renew your commitment toward seeking peace or share your struggles with peace. Take it to God!

Let's return to Scriptures to talk about the name of God with peace in it. The first time we see Prince of Peace in Scripture is Isaiah 9. What do you learn about peace – and God – in these verses?

A child has been born to us; God has given a son to us.
He will be responsible for leading the people.
His name will be Wonderful Counselor, Powerful God, Father Who Lives Forever, Prince of Peace.
Power and peace will be in his kingdom and will continue to grow forever.
He will rule as king on David's throne and over David's kingdom.
He will make it strong by ruling with justice and goodness from now on and forever.
The Lord All-Powerful will do this because of his strong love for his people. verses 6-7

Power and peace go hand in hand. Peace cannot be accomplished without power.

In Jesus', the Prince of Peace, own words: *"Don't think that I came to bring peace to the earth. I did not come to bring peace, but a sword."* Matthew 10:34

Remember, peace isn't that nice quiet place where nothing goes wrong. Peace isn't a fairy tale. Effort is required to make peace, and because we live in a messy, sinful world, we're going to struggle. People around the world are going to struggle. Jesus didn't bring peace to the earth. He *is* peace, so there's peace wherever he goes, but he makes it clear: peace is a messy process. A sword divides something, and in this case, Jesus divided right from wrong. He called out people's sin. He taught people the difference between right and wrong. He – with very sharp cuts – separated godly and ungodly.

He came with a sword.

He continues to do the same in our daily lives even though he's no longer on earth as a man.

But the Helper will teach you everything and will cause you to remember all that I told you. This Helper is the Holy Spirit whom the Father will send in my name.

I leave you peace; my peace I give you. I do not give it to you as the world does. So don't let your hearts be troubled or afraid. You heard me say to you, "I am going, but I am coming back to you." If you loved me, you should be happy that I am going back to the Father, because he is greater than I am. John 14:26-28

Claim all the promises God gives you through these verses.

The Holy Spirit gives us the guidance and wisdom we need to live every moment of every day to glorify God. God's economy isn't the world's economy. God's justice isn't the world's justice. God's peace isn't the world's peace. We can easily become as disoriented as a blindfolded child who has been turned around a dozen times and expected to pin the tail on the donkey when we mix a little of God's truth with a lot of stuff we learn from everyone around us. We can rationalize that it's "kind of truth," because it looks a little like truth. But there's no hybrid truth with God.

But the wisdom that comes from God is first of all pure, then peaceful, gentle, and easy to please. This wisdom is always ready to help those who are troubled and to do good for others. It is always fair and honest. James 3:17

God is. His truth is. His righteousness is.

God pours himself into you because he wants you to fully know him. He wants you to discern what's of him and what's of the world. What's okay to turn away from and what you need to face head on. When you need to speak up and when you need to be quiet. When you need to reach out and when you need to build a relationship.

We've become accustomed to saying "I don't see anything wrong with it" when it's not obvious to us what God thinks about something. Or perhaps we don't think he has interest in something. I can assure you he has an interest. He's invested in your life. Instead of forging ahead if we don't see something wrong with what we're doing or thinking – or feeling, flip the question: What's *right* with it?

It's only when we discern what's right that we can know what's wrong. When we start with the wrong, our orientation is off from the very beginning. Our map is inaccurate, and we're going to make many subsequent decisions based on the first one. Why are we trying to create our own map or read the map upside down or sideways? God has us covered from every angle. He's given us the map – God's Word. And he's given us a personal tour guide – the Holy Spirit. We need to interact with both to get to where we're going – where God wants us to be. And where is he? Everywhere! He's made the map and everything in it! He's the reality of the map.

Peace is living within you. As a follower of Jesus, you have the Holy Spirit, guiding you through every twist and turn. You have to seek him. You have to listen. You have to obey. God created you with free will, which means the Holy Spirit isn't holding puppet strings, tugging and dragging you to and fro. Even when you're listening and obeying, you're going to feel tugged and dragged at times. Remember, peace isn't a constant feeling of tranquility. It's a journey of knowing through the mountains, valleys, wrong turns, dead ends, road construction, traffic, sore feet, hunger and thirst, God knows just where you are and is guiding you through every experience to draw you closer to him.

God is peace. And he wants you to fully access and experience him – and his peace.

Lord, show us your love, and save us.

I will listen to God the Lord.

He has ordered peace for those who worship him.

Don't let them go back to foolishness.

God will soon save those who respect him, and his glory will be seen in our land.

Psalm 85:7-9

WEEK SIX

Make It Personal #4: *Emotional Check-Up*

Even though we're talking about the combination of anxiety and peace this week, your emotional check-up will mainly focus on anxiety. However, keep in mind you can replace peace for anxiety in any of the questions if it makes more sense to you. The important thing is to establish benchmarks so you can listen for God's challenges for growth and check your progress along the way.

Anxiety/Peace

How might anxiety be distorting reality?

Is my anxiety serving me – is it enhancing my life – or am I serving it – have I become enslaved to it?

Is anxiety generally temporary or chronic for me?

How is my past experience with anxiety affecting today?

How is anxiety affecting my future?

Is anxiety drawing me to or separating me from God?

How might anger be distorting reality?

Is my anger serving me – is it enhancing my life – or am I serving it – have I become enslaved to it?

Is anger generally temporary or chronic for me?

Anger

How is my past experience with anger affecting today?

How is anger affecting my future?

Is anger drawing me to or separating me from God?

How might jealousy be distorting reality?

Is my jealousy serving me – is it enhancing my life – or am I serving it – have I become enslaved to it?

Is jealousy generally temporary or chronic for me?

Jealousy

How is my past experience with jealousy affecting today?

How is jealousy affecting my future?

Is jealousy drawing me to or separating me from God?

How might fear be distorting reality?

Is my fear serving me – is it enhancing my life – or am I serving it – have I become enslaved to it?

Is fear generally temporary or chronic for me?

Fear

How is my past experience with fear affecting today?

How is fear affecting my future?

Is fear drawing me to or separating me from God?

Week Six

Make It Personal #5: *Shalom*

Remember Day One of this week, when you brainstormed two lists – all the things that spur anxiety and what comes to mind when you think of peace? Revisit those lists and reflect on them in the space below. Claim the truths you've learned. Share your thoughts and concerns with God. Let him challenge you.

I'm trusting God to pour into you, my friend! I know growth is difficult. It's uncomfortable. But when you're growing in God's will, all the struggle is worth it. Stick with it!

May the Lord show you his kindness and have mercy on you.

May the Lord watch over you and give you peace. Numbers 6:25-26

The word for peace in Numbers 6 is shalom. If you've heard any Hebrew, you likely know shalom. It's commonly used as a greeting, just as we might say "Hello." But shalom means so much more. As a greeting, it also is a "How are you?" of sorts. Literally, it would sound more like "How is your peace?" When spoken as people say farewell to each other, it is a blessing, "Go in peace." Shalom embraces health, prosperity, peace, favor, rest, tranquility, safety. It also means to make amends, finish, make good, recompense, and restore, as in a treaty of peace. This is the specific meaning in Job 22:21:

Obey God and be at peace with him; this is the way to happiness.[5]

Once again, this peace is active. You work with God, who provides peace through the journey. He guides you through the decisions to make peace, not keep peace. Yes, I've brought this up every day this week, but it's central to who God is and what peace means in the context of his character. Our goal is to know God, to know his character, to know his emotions, so we can respond out of that familiarity instead of relying on our own strength, understanding and emotions. We're not going to be perfect, but we can be headed in the right direction along our journey. And we can determine to get to where God wants us to go, savoring the experiences along the way.

I want you to savor today. Today's study looks unusually short. It's because I want you to take a field trip. You've already set aside time for study, so at the very least, take the same amount of time you'd usually use for today's study. If possible, I encourage you to take a larger block of time. I'm praying God will pour peace over you as you share some quiet time with him, soaking in his presence.

You might find a quiet place in your house or go to a local coffee shop to journal in conversation with him. Perhaps you'll sit beside a lake or take a meandering walk. Wherever you go, whatever you do, I want you to go in peace. Experience how God wants you to experience his peace in this season of your life. It might be a calming of worry. It might be an anxiety, or longing, for him. It might be guidance in struggling through a situation where you need to make peace. Whatever it is, I assure you that if you're seeking God, you will experience him.

I'm trusting you to God. You're in good hands. Shalom, my friend!

---

5   Zodhiates, Spiros. <u>Hebrew-Greek Key Word Study Bible</u>. Chattanooga TN: AMG, 2009

Week Seven: *Frustration*

Starter Session

Frustration is the feeling that something is missing in life. Frustration is braided with discontentedness, disappointment, and dissatisfaction. It can be situational or chronic. Sometimes our situational and chronic experiences with frustration differ slightly. Check the words that best describe your personal situational and chronic experiences with frustration.

Situational Frustration:	Chronic Frustration:
❑ afflicted	❑ afflicted
❑ aggravated	❑ aggravated
❑ bothered	❑ bothered
❑ defensive	❑ defensive
❑ exasperated	❑ exasperated
❑ hassled	❑ hassled
❑ headache	❑ headache
❑ inconvenienced	❑ inconvenienced
❑ insecure	❑ insecure
❑ irritated	❑ irritated
❑ joyful	❑ joyful
❑ nuisanced	❑ nuisanced
❑ opportunity	❑ opportunity
❑ options	❑ options
❑ peeved	❑ peeved
❑ ruffled	❑ ruffled
❑ tested	❑ tested
❑ trial	❑ trial
❑ uncomfortable	❑ uncomfortable
❑ understanding	❑ understanding
❑ upset	❑ upset
❑ vexed	❑ vexed
❑ worried	❑ worried
❑ worthwhile	❑ worthwhile

*What are your biggest triggers for frustration...
   ...in friendships?

   ...in daily life?

…at work?

…with family?

…at church?

…when shopping?

…in _____?

…in _____?

Let's not turn this into a gripe session, but it's important to know what frustrates you and how you respond to frustration. You can experience frustration one day and wake up the next morning and declare, "I'm not going to get frustrated today with _____ (my children, coworker, spouse, parent)." but you'll likely fail to meet that expectation without understanding what's feeding the frustration and gathering tools to deal with it when it rears itself.

We're going to dig deeper than surface level. You might be tempted to whine and complain about a specific situation. I challenge you to dig deeper. Get underneath the problem.

When we moved into our current house, there was wallpaper on every surface except the bathroom walls. Every other wall (and ceiling!) was covered in layers upon layers of thick wallpaper from decades of house decorating changes. As soon as my husband left for work each morning, I'd bundle up our young girls and spend the day in the empty house, trying to remove the wallpaper. It wasn't a fun job to say the least. The wallpaper glue of today is not the wallpaper glue of yesterday. I think they used some type of super glue! I filled my spray bottle with warm soapy water more times than I want to know. Small strips of paper fell to the floor in sticky, wet piles as I scraped the putty knife under the paper.

I couldn't scrape off the wallpaper until I got my putty knife under it, one layer at a time. As I removed each layer, I sprayed more water, making the paper soft enough to pry the knife under. It was tedious work, but I got to the bottom of it eventually.

If you're not going to get under your frustrations, you're going to continue to look at the same things that frustrate you and not know what to do except to scrape and claw or give up. There are better ways to deal with it.

Frustration can be multiplied when one situation is exaggerated by other pressures and influences, such as

- ❑ Employment struggles
- ❑ Financial struggles
- ❑ Marital struggles
- ❑ Unfulfilled dreams or goals
- ❑ Health issues
- ❑ Community issues
- ❑ Faith

When you're in a frustrating situation, which of these contribute to your frustration? Add additional influences as you think of them.

You've now admitted some of your frustrations and what contributes to them. I don't want you to get stuck where you are – or in the memory of your frustrations – as if you're glued to your frustrations as securely as the wallpaper was glued to my walls and ceilings. More important, God doesn't want you intricately tied to your frustrations.

The Lord is the Spirit, and where the Spirit of the Lord is, there is freedom. 2 Corinthians 3:17

Freedom is what God wants for you. He longs for you to experience his freedom. And this includes freedom from your frustrations. At the end of this week's study, your life is not going to be free of frustrations. Sorry to disappoint you. My hope is that you will catch a glimpse of the freedom you can have *from* your frustrations – the frustrations bubbling up within your life, feeling as if you have no control and in some cases no hope. The discontentedness, disappointment, and dissatisfaction that gets in the way of daily life.

Remember, God has a purpose for you. He wants to reveal himself to you in a way that sets in stone the truth of who he is and what he has planned for you. We so often ask him questions about ourselves. We ask him to reveal ourselves to us. The truth is, when we seek him, when we know him, we know more of ourselves, because (1) we're created in his image, and (2) we more readily recognize the very ungodly behavior and emotional responses within us.

Remember our *Pure Emotion* key verse…

Do not be shaped by this world; instead be changed within by a new way of thinking. Then you will be able to decide what God wants for you; you will know what is good and pleasing to him and what is perfect. Romans 12:2

*How does this verse apply specifically to the emotion and experience of frustration?

With each emotion, we've determined the godly side and ungodly side of the emotion. We're going to take a slightly different approach with frustration. We've already covered some aspects of frustration in two previous studies; both anxiety and fear are closely related with frustration.

Even anger is related. Remember how our ungodly response to anger is a failure to wait for God's justice? We often take matters into our own hands, unwilling to wait for God's justice or failing to yield to or recognize God's justice or ability and willingness to acknowledge God's sovereignty. Frustration is similar. As we continue to study frustration and gather practical tools for dealing with it, we'll explore a replacement for it: hope.

Before we get started, let's talk about God's frustration.

*What do you learn from the following verses?

When our enemies heard that we were aware of their plot and that God had frustrated it, we all returned to the wall, each to our own work. Nehemiah 4:15

The LORD watches over the foreigner and sustains the fatherless and the widow, but he frustrates the ways of the wicked. Psalm 146:9

The eyes of the LORD keep watch over knowledge, but he frustrates the words of the unfaithful. Proverbs 22:12

One definition of *frustrate* is to thwart or defeat an endeavor. God will frustrate ungodly plans sometimes: that's godly frustration. But there are a couple assumptions we must not make based on this godly emotion:

1. ***God will frustrate, but he's not frustrated.*** To be frustrated is the ungodly side of the emotions. It's responding out of the emotion. God's frustration is different than our frustration. His acts of frustration are a response to other emotions, usually anger. Remember, his anger is righteous and just. God's anger is in response to behavior contrary to his will. Based on this anger, he might frustrate people who are behaving contrary to his will. The frustration of God is different in this way from other emotions we've been studying, because we have to be extremely cautious in applying what godly frustration is.

   We could easily justify taking the liberty to frustrate people's plans because they're not consistent with God. But we really don't have the power to frustrate someone's plans in the same way God does. We can absolutely access God's power when we're within his will, and there might be times when he uses us to thwart something going on that's contrary to his will, but I want to emphasis the fine line we're walking in this area. I think it's much wiser to cease considering how God wants us to frustrate others and defer to what we've learned about godly and ungodly anger in these situations.

   If God is arousing a godly anger in you, asking you to walk alongside him in a battle against evil, he'll guide you every step of the way in your thoughts, responses, and actions. Your actions will only be consistent with his actions. It might involve frustrations, but frustrations are a very small part of how God prompts us to respond in godly anger. We might be prompted to confront, listen, make peace, etc. Keep your perspective wide and exercise your spiritual muscles in godly anger. The details will come along as you're obedient and faithful.

2. ***God will not always frustrate ungodly plans.*** Remember to *frustrate* means to thwart. God doesn't thwart every bad plan. He created us with free will, and there are consequences

for each decision we make. If he controlled every situation and thwarted every bad plan, he'd take our choices off the table. God gave us the Holy Spirit to help us discern right and wrong, good and evil, godly and not, in every situation. He doesn't intend for us to ignore the Holy Spirit, relying on God to then thwart any ungodly plan that gets by us because we didn't take the time to listen and discern and obey. He certainly has his hands in the consequences of our choices – good and bad. I'm certain you can see his fingerprints all through situations in your life.

*For instance, consider a positive situation that you attribute God working through in your life.

*Now consider a negative situation that you attribute God working through in your life. In other words, how did God either thwart something in your life or at least raise caution flags to get your attention – whether you paid attention or not?

Let's take another look at God's use of frustration.

I consider that our present sufferings are not worth comparing with the glory that will be revealed in us. For the creation waits in eager expectation for the children of God to be revealed. For the creation was subjected to frustration, not by its own choice, but by the will of the one who subjected it, in hope that the creation itself will be liberated from its bondage to decay and brought into the freedom and glory of the children of God.

We know that the whole creation has been groaning as in the pains of childbirth right up to the present time. Not only so, but we ourselves, who have the firstfruits of the Spirit, groan inwardly as we wait eagerly for our adoption to sonship, the redemption of our bodies. For in this hope we were saved. But hope that is seen is no hope at all. Who hopes for what they already have? But if we hope for what we do not yet have, we wait for it patiently. Romans 8:18-25

In the Bible I'm using, the heading of this section of Scripture is "Present Suffering and Future Glory." *How is this an accurate heading and where does frustration fit?

God created an orderly world – an orderly world that contains frustration. That doesn't seem to make much sense, does it? But remember, part of the orderly world God created is our free will. We can choose to follow God or not. To live in sin or not. To acknowledge God or not. God's creation includes frustration because man has choice, and God wants a relationship with each of us. If I didn't experience frustration or tension or a void while living without him, what would my motivation be to live *with* him? God doesn't need me, but he wants me. God doesn't need you, but he wants you. God allows the frustration to give us freedom and glory as a child of God.

Remember, I'm not referring to the frustration we started talking about today. I'm not referring to earthly frustration, worry, and anxiety. We're going to address those issues soon, because it's only when we yield to God that we can keep our earthly frustrations in perspective with his will.

As we close today's session, I have two challenges for you. First, read Romans 8:18-25 aloud to emphasize the truth it proclaims about God's character. This time, replace the word frustration with futility. The New American Standard Bible uses futility instead, and it might help separate God's intentions from your own baggage about frustration.

Second, declare the truths from John 16:33. I've provided this verse to you from the Amplified Bible because I think it emphasizes the truths you might need to hear repeatedly, loud and clear. Below the verse, I've given you some space. Rewrite it with personal emphasis. What are the specific words that speak most loudly to you or that you need to hear the most often and most pronounced? Write them in all CAPS, write them BIG...anything you need to do to emphasize them!

I have told you these things, so that in Me you may have [perfect] peace and confidence. In the world you have tribulation and trials and distress and frustration; but be of good cheer [take courage; be confident, certain, undaunted]! For I have overcome the world. [I have deprived it of power to harm you and have conquered it for you.]

WEEK SEVEN

Make It Personal #1: *Biblical Frustration*

We began the Starter Session by identifying frustrations – mainly earthly frustrations. Let's focus more specifically today on spiritual frustrations we have. I anticipate receiving a few emails demanding spiritual frustrations are just wrong and we shouldn't have them and how I shouldn't say such things in a Bible study. Whether that's your stance or not – perhaps especially for those who share that stance – I hope you'll persevere through today's study. I want you to keep today's lesson in the context of the Scriptures we studied at the end of the Starter Session.

I consider that our present sufferings are not worth comparing with the glory that will be revealed in us. For the creation waits in eager expectation for the children of God to be revealed. For the creation was subjected to frustration, not by its own choice, but by the will of the one who subjected it, in hope that the creation itself will be liberated from its bondage to decay and brought into the freedom and glory of the children of God.

We know that the whole creation has been groaning as in the pains of childbirth right up to the present time. Not only so, but we ourselves, who have the firstfruits of the Spirit, groan inwardly as we wait eagerly for our adoption to sonship, the redemption of our bodies. For in this hope we were saved. But hope that is seen is no hope at all. Who hopes for what they already have? But if we hope for what we do not yet have, we wait for it patiently. Romans 8:18-25

God can handle your frustrations. You might do a great job of hiding them from people around you. You might even do a great job at personally ignoring them. You can't hide or disguise them from God. He wants to reveal your spiritual frustrations because he wants you to grow through them. Authenticity is tough, but authenticity with God is absolutely essential if you want to grow. If you're not willing to be authentic about your spiritual frustrations, your spiritual frustrations might just be what deters your spiritual growth.

So let's start identifying what our spiritual frustrations are. You might not answer every question. That's okay. You might be hesitant to ink something onto this page. I encourage you to at least write a code word. It's one step toward recognizing and accepting your experiences and emotions, letting God seep into and heal you. Remember, wounds aren't bad if you allow God to fully heal them.

What frustrates you about your spiritual journey?

What frustrates you about a past or current experience with God?

Have you experienced a BIG moment of frustration with God – even if it didn't last for long? If so, what was the situation?

How could God help you with your frustrations?

What is unhealthy or unproductive about the way you deal with your spiritual frustrations?

Is there anything you sometimes experience as a frustration but at other times embrace and enjoy?

Something that both frustrates and thrills me is the depth and breadth of God's Word. I love to study God through his Word. I appreciate how he reveals truth to me every time I'm studying. Sometimes it's a life-changing a-ha and sometimes it's simply fascinating. Sometimes he takes me deeper in an already familiar area and sometimes he reveals something completely new to me. Sometimes I dig and dig, moving from one verse to another, flipping from one book to another, referring to reference notes and word origins and meanings, and I'm deeply satisfied. But sometimes I have more questions that I can't seem to get answered. Or I don't have time to keep searching. Or I'm just overwhelmed with the fact that there will always be more to learn and know about God! I'll seek and seek and seek…and there will always be more. And while that can be frustrating at times, it thrills me to my very core at other times! I realize the frustration comes out of my need to accomplish something and mark it off my list – whether it's a daily to do list or a lifetime achievement list. I accept and love that my spiritual journey is something I can't check off my list – today or as long as I'm alive. I'm thankful for God for being that big. But I get selfish from time to time in my limitations.

A BIG moment of frustration with God came many years ago when one of my very best friend's young daughter was killed in an accident. After a sleepless night and a hopeless prognosis, I said goodbye…walked out of the hospital room and cried from the depth of my soul, "I don't understand, God!" I didn't question God's sovereignty, and I knew there was eternal hope and promise. In that moment, I clung to God in my frustration. I knew he was the only one I could trust with the intensity of my emotions. I knew I wouldn't offend him. I knew the frustration wouldn't last. I knew he would understand and hold me as I collapsed in his care and comfort.

Tears overflow every time I revisit that moment. I relive it in a small dose…and then move into what I experienced next. I don't remember what actually happened in those next few moments in the hospital, but how I visualize my interaction with God is very clear. It's as if I was a child who ran to my dad for help, and I sank into his lap as deeply as I could and sobbed uncontrollably into his chest, clinging to him tightly. Just as a child will do, once comforted, I looked into the eyes that I trust and jumped off my dad's lap with reassurance. As a final send off, I got a little pat on the rear as if to say, "I love you. You're okay. I gave you what you need. Go get 'em." God gave me what I needed – comfort and strength – and he sustained me for the hours, days, weeks, and months of healing alongside my friend.

Take a deep breath. God wants to fill you. He wants to comfort and encourage you…not so that you'll sit on his lap forever. He's got work for you to do here on earth. Get to it!

He had work for Jonah, too. God told Jonah to go to Nineveh, which was a city filled with sin. God told Jonah to warn the people that if they didn't change their ways, he'd destroy them. That would be God not just frustrating plans but manifesting his anger through wrath. But God provided another option. If the people of Nineveh repented, God would forgive them.

Jonah wasn't happy to say the least. He was frustrated, because God was the God of the Hebrews, and it didn't make sense to Jonah to spend time on such godless people or for God to seek and accept their repentance. You probably know a lot of Jonah's journey of trying just about everything to get out of going to Nineveh. Suffice it to say he not only went to great lengths in his refusal and disobedience but great depths! However, God is persistent, and Jonah finally obeyed God and shared God's message with the Ninevites.

Jonah's worst expectations were revealed. The Ninevites repented, and God spared them. Jonah pouted. He knew it wasn't going to turn out how he thought it should, and that's why he avoided it in the first place. Now he was proven right and was miserable and wanted to die.

I've heard of drama queens, but Jonah was definitely a drama king!

I love how God taught him the next lesson.

Jonah went out and sat down east of the city. There he made a shelter for himself and sat in the shade, waiting to see what would happen to the city. The Lord made a plant grow quickly up over Jonah, which gave him shade and helped him to be more comfortable. Jonah was very pleased to have the plant. But the next day when the sun rose, God sent a worm to attack the plant so that it died.

As the sun rose higher in the sky, God sent a very hot east wind to blow, and the sun became so hot on Jonah's head that he became very weak and wished he were dead. He said, "It is better for me to die than to live."

But God said to Jonah, "Do you think it is right for you to be angry about the plant?"

Jonah answered, "It is right for me to be angry! I am so angry I could die!"

And the Lord said, "You are so concerned for that plant even though you did nothing to make it grow. It appeared one day, and the next day it died. Then shouldn't I show concern for the great city Nineveh, which has more than one hundred twenty thousand people who do not know right from wrong, and many animals, too?" Jonah 4:5-11

What do you learn about your own spiritual frustration through Jonah?

Our natural tendency as humans is to rebel against God. On one extreme, people don't acknowledge he exists, or if they do, they certainly don't think they need him. You might say, "Well, that's not me! I have a relationship with God." But even those who have a thriving relationship with God rebel in subtle (and not so subtle) ways through self-reliance and pride. We rebel because we don't understand, and we don't want to be obedient through the tough stuff. We get angry, disappointed, or frustrated with God.

Sometimes we rationalize that our motives are pure. After all, Jonah just wanted to keep the God of the Hebrews for the Hebrews. That's who Jonah knew him to be, so he couldn't conceive God would want anything else. But God won't be limited. You might get frustrated because you can't imagine how God provided for someone who has been living a life of sin while you're still struggling and you've been faithful. There are all kinds of ways we compare ourselves to others and assume we have enough details to know how God should respond.

What personal experiences come to mind of such "unfairness"?

God will not be limited. Our assumptions and limited understanding do not drive God's ways. And your pity party about a situation is only going to hurt your relationship with God. Is your frustration worth it?

WEEK SEVEN

Make It Personal #2: *Planting Seeds of Truth*

In the beginning there was the Word. The Word was with God, and the Word was God. He was with God in the beginning. All things were made by him, and nothing was made without him. John 1:1-3

You won't find the word frustrate in many of the verses below. Instead, the following verses speak God's truth in spite of your frustration. Claim them so you can replace your personal frustration with God's hope!

Speak It. Say it out loud – several times if you prefer. God's spoken Word has power. Plus, you'll be using several senses to experience God's Word. You're taking it in with your eyes, forming the words with your mouth, and hearing the words. It's like a double exclamation point!

Personalize It. What is God specifically saying to you in this season of your life? Insert your name, respond with a question, rephrase the promise – whatever it takes to absorb what God is saying to you and stand firmly on it as you take the next steps.

Live It. God doesn't intend for us to simply fill our heads with knowledge about his Word. He desires us to let it seep into every crevice of our lives. Let him guide you through challenges and encouragements of how you'll apply a verse into your daily life. Write a note about your plan – and then revisit this page to record your progress.

And God's peace, which is so great we cannot understand it, will keep your hearts and minds in Christ Jesus. Philippians 4:7

Speak It.

Personalize It.

Live It.

I told you these things so that you can have peace in me. In this world you will have trouble, but be brave! I have defeated the world. John 16:33

Speak It.

Personalize It.

Live It.

Come to me, all of you who are tired and have heavy loads, and I will give you rest. Accept my teachings and learn from me, because I am gentle and humble in spirit, and you will find rest for your lives. Matthew 11:28-29

Speak It.

Personalize It.

Live It.

My dear children, you belong to God and have defeated them; because God's Spirit, who is in you, is greater than the devil, who is in the world. 1 John 4:4

Speak It.

Personalize It.

Live It.

Faith means being sure of the things we hope for and knowing that something is real even if we do not see it. Hebrews 11:1

Speak It.

Personalize It.

Live It.

Christ gave you a special gift that is still in you, so you do not need any other teacher. His gift teaches you about everything, and it is true, not false. So continue to live in Christ, as his gift taught you. 1 John 2:27

Speak It.

Personalize It.

Live It.

Consider how the lilies grow; they don't work or make clothes for themselves. But I tell you that even Solomon with his riches was not dressed as beautifully as one of these flowers. Luke 12:27

Speak It.

Personalize It.

Live It.

Jesus said to all of them, "If people want to follow me, they must give up the things they want. They must be willing to give up their lives daily to follow me." Luke 9:23

Speak It.

Personalize It.

Live It.

Whoever is not willing to carry his cross and follow me cannot be my follower. Luke 14:27

Speak It.

Personalize It.

Live It.

Give all your worries to him, because he cares about you. 1 Peter 5:7

Speak It.

Personalize It.

Live It.

WEEK SEVEN

Make It Personal #3: *Hope*

We've been learning how to discern godly emotions from ungodly emotions. The true emotions of God versus the messy emotions of man. Healthy emotions versus unhealthy emotions. Sometimes we cling to what we know even when it's not healthy. Consider how your frustrations serve you. What benefits can you identify in your frustrations?

If you wrote nothing, I want to challenge you to try again. The only people who have no benefits of their frustrations must not have any frustrations. After all, why would you keep your frustrations if they're not serving some sort of benefit? Perhaps as you're writing down the benefits, you're thinking the benefits are silly. It's okay. Remember, identifying what seems misplaced or irrational in our lives is often the first step to realizing we need to replace it with something else. Not just weed it out, leaving a gaping hole – it's too easy to let the old grow back – but replacing the old with something new.

It's the same with our frustrations. We need to replace our frustrations with something new: hope. Frustrations are worries that nothing will change, dissatisfaction that something's not going well, discontentedness with our limited understanding, or disappointment in our relationships or situations. The reason it's important to identify what benefits frustrations are serving you is to recognize what you're clinging to. It's not the frustrations in and of themselves. That would negate the definition of frustrations. Frustrations are dissatisfying, and we want something to change… but they can also become comfortable – so comfortable, we choose them over change.

Today we're going to study hope, because hope is what God gives you to sustain you through situations of dissatisfaction, discontentedness, and disappointment. We're going to start a process today to help you release your death grip on frustrations and cling to hope instead. It's one of the easiest and most difficult things to do. Of course, it sounds like a "duh" choice. After all, who wouldn't choose hope over frustration? The theory of choosing hope sounds great but the practical application of releasing frustration and grasping hope so that it seeps into every corner of your life is challenging.

What do you learn from the following verses?

All those who compete in the games use self-control so they can win a crown. That crown is an earthly thing that lasts only a short time, but our crown will never be destroyed. So I do not run without a goal. I fight like a boxer who is hitting something—not just the air. 1 Corinthians 9:25-26

Our only goal is to please God whether we live here or there, because we must all stand before Christ to be judged. Each of us will receive what we should get—good or bad—for the things we did in the earthly body. 2 Corinthians 5:9-10

I do not mean that I am already as God wants me to be. I have not yet reached that goal, but I continue trying to reach it and to make it mine. Christ wants me to do that, which is the reason he made me his. Philippians 3:12

I keep trying to reach the goal and get the prize for which God called me through Christ to the life above. Philippians 3:14

Anyone who says, "I know God," but does not obey God's commands is a liar, and the truth is not in that person. But if someone obeys God's teaching, then in that person God's love has truly reached its goal. This is how we can be sure we are living in God: Whoever says that he lives in God must live as Jesus lived. 1 John 2:4-6

We have to know our goal. If you don't know where you're going, you'll end up somewhere… but likely not somewhere you would have chosen if you'd been deliberate. Goals point us toward the desired destination and help us along the journey. Goals help keep us motivated and measure progress. Goals also help us make decisions along the journey. If something will take us a step closer to the goal, we'll decide for it. If not, we'll decide against it. Or at least, we should.

The problem is we often don't set the *right* goal or we aren't specific in our goal, so we're meandering. *Seek first God's kingdom and what God wants. Then all your other needs will be met as well.* Matthew 6:33

We experience frustration when we have no goal, the wrong goal, or question our goal and progress. We experience frustration when we demand our own way. Selfish ambition might feel better in a temporary situation, but it will not end well. Selfishness will stir up more frustration. God has a pure and perfect purpose for you.

This is what God made us for, and he has given us the Spirit to be a guarantee for this new life. 2 Corinthians 5:5

If anyone sets an example of unselfishness, keeping his eyes on God's goal and will, it's Jesus. While being crucified, he prayed, *"Father, if you are willing, take away this cup of suffering. But do what you want, not what I want."* (Luke 22:42) When we commit to God's goal, when we seek God's righteousness, we minimize life's frustrations. We don't eliminate frustration, pain, questions, etc. When we yield to God's will, when we focus on giving of ourselves to God instead of getting from God and others, we'll get more than we can imagine. Spiritual dividends are the best investment fund.

When growing in our relationship with God is our life goal, we have hope through the messes. We have hope through the disappointments, dissatisfaction, and discontentedness. Those "D" words, and all frustrations, become situational. Hope is chronic.

Because of hope, you can set yourself aside. Because of hope, you can say, "I know God is taking care of me through this." Because of hope, you can say, "I don't have to stress and worry and be frustrated. I can focus on the main thing." The main thing…the main goal…your relationship with God. Because of hope, you won't be consumed with self-preservation, self-promotion, or self-enhancement. You might still struggle with these and more issues of self-focus, but hope whispers in your ear the truth God wants you to hear, claim, and stand firmly on. With the courage he gives you, you can stomp on the lies surrounding you. You can stamp out the embers of frustration before they catch a brisk wind and become an uncontrolled blaze.

It's not about you. Your sacrifice, yielding, and acknowledgement of God's sovereignty, dependability, and righteousness is the ultimate goal. God's glory will shine and prevail. Light up the world by emptying yourself of yourself so he can fill you up, and you will become so transparent, there will be no doubt that people see God in you.

You are the light that gives light to the world. A city that is built on a hill cannot be hidden. And people don't hide a light under a bowl. They put it on a lampstand so the light shines for all the people in the house. In the same way, you should be a light for other people. Live so that they will see the good things you do and will praise your Father in heaven. Matthew 5:14-16

There's a significant difference between the way we use the word hope in our everyday lives verses the hope of faith. Compare a commonly accepted definition of hope with several verses and look for differences that could create confusion.

Definition: Hope is the feeling that what is wanted can be had or that events will turn out for the best.

Praise be to the God and Father of our Lord Jesus Christ. In God's great mercy he has caused us to be born again into a living hope, because Jesus Christ rose from the dead. 1 Peter 1:3

And this hope will never disappoint us, because God has poured out his love to fill our hearts. He gave us his love through the Holy Spirit, whom God has given to us. Romans 5:5

Everything that was written in the past was written to teach us. The Scriptures give us patience and encouragement so that we can have hope. Romans 15:4

If our hope in Christ is for this life only, we should be pitied more than anyone else in the world. 1 Corinthians 15:19

We have troubles all around us, but we are not defeated. We do not know what to do, but we do not give up the hope of living. 2 Corinthians 4:8

The hope of our faith is certain.

He did not spare his own Son but gave him for us all. So with Jesus, God will surely give us all things. Romans 8:32

WEEK SEVEN

Make It Personal #4: *Emotional Check-Up*

It's time for a check-up! How are you growing through the *Pure Emotion* experience?

Frustration

How might frustration be distorting reality?

Is my frustration serving me – is it enhancing my life – or am I serving it – have I become enslaved to it?

Is frustration generally temporary or chronic for me?

How is my past experience with frustration affecting today?

How is frustration affecting my future?

Is frustration drawing me to or separating me from God?

Anxiety/Peace

How might anxiety be distorting reality?

Is my anxiety serving me – is it enhancing my life – or am I serving it – have I become enslaved to it?

Is anxiety generally temporary or chronic for me?

How is my past experience with anxiety affecting today?

How is anxiety affecting my future?

Is anxiety drawing me to or separating me from God?

Anger

How might anger be distorting reality?

Is my anger serving me – is it enhancing my life – or am I serving it – have I become enslaved to it?

Is anger generally temporary or chronic for me?

How is my past experience with anger affecting today?

How is anger affecting my future?

Is anger drawing me to or separating me from God?

Jealousy

How might jealousy be distorting reality?

Is my jealousy serving me – is it enhancing my life – or am I serving it – have I become enslaved to it?

Is jealousy generally temporary or chronic for me?

How is my past experience with jealousy affecting today?

How is jealousy affecting my future?

Is jealousy drawing me to or separating me from God?

Fear

How might fear be distorting reality?

Is my fear serving me – is it enhancing my life – or am I serving it – have I become enslaved to it?

Is fear generally temporary or chronic for me?

How is my past experience with fear affecting today?

How is fear affecting my future?

Is fear drawing me to or separating me from God?

WEEK SEVEN

Make It Personal #5: *God Space*

Let's start today by claiming the hope we have over and through our frustrations. Revisit your notes about your frustrations in the Starter Session. . Choose several to place in the spaces after "Frustration" below. Leave the "My hope is that God will help me…" sentences unfinished for now.

Frustration:
My hope is that God will…

Frustration:
My hope is that God will…

Frustration:
My hope is that God will…

Frustration:
My hope is that God will…

Frustration:
My hope is that God will…

Now it's time to claim your hope. Remember, hope is not a wish. It's not self-centered. Hope is God-centered. Seek and accept his will. As fully as he's revealing your next steps in each of your areas of frustration, complete the sentences above, beginning each with "My hope is that God will…"

God's hope will always unburden us, not burden us.

We must know God's truth, so we can discern what's not true.

We need to know who God is and what is godly in order to identify what is ungodly.

We need to sacrifice our selves to let God pour into and fill us.

The reality is, God will only fill your empty spaces. He won't crowd you out if you're determined to be filled with yourself.

You've been taking a hard look at yourself through *Pure Emotion*. You've been learning more about God so you can reflect him more completely. Each week, you've been evaluating yourself on how you're doing with the specific emotions we're studying. As we wrap up Week Seven, I want to give you some additional reflection time.

First, let's work with a visual. Consider your level of each "beaker" of emotion on your typical days. For instance, if you are generally very anxious, you might fill your anxiety beaker three-fourths full. Use a pencil to fill in the space where the liquid would go. If you're not a fearful person in general, you might have a very small amount filling your fear beaker.

I separated anxiety and peace even though we've mainly evaluated anxiety, and I've included the emotions we have yet to study. You can also draw additional beakers if there are other emotions you feel consume you and you want to intentionally release the unhealthy emotions to God so he can fill you with replacements of godly emotions.

Remember, you're filling your beakers with the emotions you're consumed with, so we're not talking about godly emotions. Even with peace and joy, even though they're godly emotions, consider to what level you try to achieve or acquire peace and joy with your own strength and by your own definitions. The goal is to identify how much of the beaker you're filling up with you and your own assumptions, responses and behavior.

Fear   Jealousy   Anger   Anxiety

Peace   Frustration   Guilt/Shame   Joy

Perhaps you can now imagine how much space you're leaving for God. This experience is intended to encourage you to yield to God, pouring yourself out and letting him pour into you. To encourage is to pour in or equip with courage. God will do the filling. You need to do the emptying.

Finally, review the check-ups you've been completing over the past several weeks. Take one emotion at a time and look through the check-up reports for each week. Use the space below to record ways you've been challenged and encouraged. Check in with God for a progress report. You might see some quick growth spurts as well as stunted growth. Assess where you are, be honest with yourself, and let God guide your next steps. There is always hope in your spiritual growth. Claim that hope – and grow!

Fear

Jealousy

Anger

Anxiety

Peace

Frustration

Week Eight: *Guilt and Shame*

Starter Session

Do not be shaped by this world; instead be changed within by a new way of thinking. Then you will be able to decide what God wants for you; you will know what is good and pleasing to him and what is perfect. Romans 12:2

I'm beginning this week's session with our key verse for *Pure Emotion*, because we're about to dig into some stuff that weighs heavily on us and can be difficult to sift through and discern. I've prayed this verse over you. Only a few moments ago, tears fell down my face, not because I know exactly where you are but because I know God does…and because I know the struggles that can tag along with guilt and shame. There are subtleties between godly guilt and shame and the guilt and shame you experience from within that have absolutely nothing to do with God. I also know the freedom from ungodly guilt and shame because I've experienced it. My tears for you aren't in mourning or sadness; they're in the joy of possible freedom. Freedom in God's grace.

But when a person changes and follows the Lord, that covering is taken away. The Lord is the Spirit, and where the Spirit of the Lord is, there is freedom. Our faces, then, are not covered. We all show the Lord's glory, and we are being changed to be like him. This change in us brings ever greater glory, which comes from the Lord, who is the Spirit. 2 Corinthians 3:16-18

There is freedom. Freedom in God to uncover our faces and not be ashamed but show God's glory. Freedom in vulnerability. Freedom to become like him. Freedom *in* him. I long for you to experience such freedom.

I don't want you to dwell in ungodly guilt and shame, so we're going to dig in right away, establishing God's truths. In the process, God will reveal when your guilt and shame is not of him. I pray that through the tenderness of those moments, you'll allow him to remove the covering of your face and your heart. Be vulnerable to him. Cry out to him. Be real with him. He created you and knows more about you than anyone else – even yourself. You can trust him. Not because I say you can trust him, but because God himself says you can trust him.

Jesus said, "Don't let your hearts be troubled. Trust in God, and trust in me." John 14:1

I encourage you to pray Romans 12:2. Speak it. Write it. Claim it.

At the end of today's Starter Session, I've included a large chart. I hope you'll refer to it throughout this week. When you find something that indicates true, godly guilt or shame, place it in the top boxes. If you find something that indicates ungodly, unhealthy, unproductive guilt or shame, include it in the bottom boxes. Here are some things that you might end up writing in the boxes:

- Scripture verses.
- Phrases in *Pure Emotion* that specifically speak to you.
- Memories.
- Experiences.
- Anything else God brings to mind or speaks to your heart that you need to grab onto and claim or loosen your grip and release.

To begin, let's take a look at a variety of verses and statements about guilt and shame. What's your response? How deeply do you live by each? Does each ring true or false to you, and is that because of a basis in absolute, unequivocal truth or learned and accepted ideas that you might be incorrectly assuming as truth?

"Guilt is the price we pay willingly for doing what we are going to do anyway." Isabelle Holland

I prayed, "My God, I am too ashamed and embarrassed to lift up my face to you, my God, because our sins are so many. They are higher than our heads. Our guilt even reaches up to the sky." Ezra 9:6

"Guilt is anger directed at ourselves." Peter McWilliams

Then I confessed my sins to you and didn't hide my guilt. I said, "I will confess my sins to the Lord, and you forgave my guilt." Psalm 32:5

"With shame, there is just painful feelings of depression, alienation, self-doubt, loneliness, isolation, paranoia, compulsive disorders, perfectionism, inferiority, inadequacy, failure, helplessness, hopelessness, narcissism." John Bradshaw

Then you can lift up your face without shame, and you can stand strong without fear. Job 11:15

"Guilt is perhaps the most painful companion of death." Coco Chanel

"Guilt is the very nerve of sorrow." Horace Bushnell

Pride leads only to shame; it is wise to be humble. Proverbs 11:2

"When we feel unbearable shame, the response often is violence, drug abuse, battering, harassment, incest. We feel ashamed of our bodies, which leads to eating disorders, anorexia, bulimia, compulsions, workaholism, in an effort to block out these feelings of worthlessness." John Bradshaw

Why did I have to come out of my mother's body? All I have known is trouble and sorrow, and my life will end in shame. Jeremiah 20:18

"You can bear anything-if it isn't your own fault." Katherine Fullerton Gerould

"If guilt means extending worry about what you have done, then it does not help." Jeffrey Hopkins

Look what the Lord has done for me! My people were ashamed of me, but now the Lord has taken away that shame. Luke 1:25

"Guilt is regret for what we've done. Regret is guilt for what we didn't do." Unknown

Let's claim what's true and weed out what isn't.

*First, how is godly and ungodly guilt different? What *is* guilt?

Guilt is the emotion that indicates you've done something wrong. Godly guilt = the real conviction that you're in disobedience to God's will.

*What are some examples of godly guilt in everyday life – either today or in your past? Be as specific as possible. Keep in mind this isn't a simple list of what you've done wrong; it involves the guilt or the conviction that you've done something wrong.

The Holy Spirit is our helper, guiding us through the discernment of what's right and wrong. God's Word instructs us, but we also need the Holy Spirit because

1. We don't know every word of the Bible. Let's not be lazy. We need to stay in God's Word consistently. Being familiar with God's Word is being familiar with God's character. Knowing who he is helps us more readily discern what he wants us to do or not do.
2. The situation or choice we're facing might not specifically be in the Bible, but I assure you the guidance we need is there. You might not find whether you're supposed to take Job A or Job B, move to an apartment or a house, or attend the college close to home or far away…but through instructions on finances, morality, relationships, and influences, you'll be able to choose well. Sometimes we wait for a clearer answer, and sometimes God wants us to grow through waiting. Just because a specific answer isn't in the Bible doesn't mean God's not speaking to you through his Word and Spirit.
3. God knew we'd need help! He gifted us with choice but also built a support system for us that is unfailing. We can be unyielding to the Holy Spirit's guidance but the Holy Spirit will never fail or guide us in an ungodly direction.

Godly guilt is true guilt. It involves some sort of offense or wrongdoing.

On the other hand, we can experience guilt when there hasn't actually been an offense or wrongdoing. This is false guilt, and it is not godly.

*What are some specific examples in your life when you've experienced guilt where there was no offense or wrongdoing?

False guilt can play a huge part in our lives. "If only…" "I wish I had…" "I should have…" might spark some burdensome guilt for you. You can probably even justify there was offense or wrongdoing because if you had done one thing differently, the situation would have changed. If you had just taken time to talk. If you hadn't been mad. If you'd done it yourself. The list is endless. Yes, your choices have consequences, but God is big and powerful, and you do not have the power you think you do if you believe you caused something to happen when there was actually no offense or wrongdoing involved. See it through God's eyes, not your own. He has a better view.

And then there is the false guilt we feel for the "little things." We forgot to call someone. We didn't go to the family reunion. We missed an important day at work because of a sick child. We missed staying home with a child because we had an important meeting at work. Our house wasn't clean when the neighbor stopped by. We spent time cleaning when the neighbor needed help. Pick a situation – any situation – and you can feel guilty about it.

I'm not saying there isn't validity in experiencing guilt in some of these circumstances, but you have to get to the bottom of the decisions that you make and how they compare to God's will. Is there an offense or wrongdoing God is convicting you of? Your guilt, in the context of his correction, is real and should motivate you to change, reconcile, or whatever "next step" he guides you through toward reconciliation and growth. But if there's no offense or wrongdoing except the ones you're creating, you might be experiencing false guilt, and it's time to label it for what it is and move on.

It's time to return from your guilt trip and unpack your bags.

What about shame? Shame is a deep sense of dishonor, disappointment, or condemnation. When shame comes from God, it always involves something we've done that is contrary to his will and separates us from God. It's deep, heavy and sorrowful.

Ungodly, or false, shame is usually self-driven. We imagined we've done something dishonoring, disappointing or condemning. In relation to God, we presume his reaction to us without asking him for his reaction. We're so disappointed in ourselves that we imagine we've dishonored him. Perhaps we've disappointed him, but we need to allow God to shame what we've done, not shame ourselves before we've lifted our faces to God to receive his reaction.

The biggest difference between godly and ungodly shame is while true shame focuses on something we've done, false shame focuses on who we are. Instead of our choice, action, or attitude being condemned, we think *we're* condemned. We can easily give up hope. We feel worthless, useless, and unloved. Those feelings don't come from God. Satan loves when you get tangled up in a mess of guilt and shame. When you're tangled in false guilt and shame, your eyes aren't on God. When you're not focused on God, you're not fulfilling the purpose he has for you. Guilt and shame easily multiply.

When have you felt guilty about being guilty?

Shame is closely related to sorrow. Sorrow is a deep sadness. While sadness might float on the surface, sorrow sinks below the surface, taking up temporary residence and impacting the flow of our lives. Sorrow can be godly or worldly. *What are the differences between godly and worldly sorrow?

Godly sorrow brings repentance that leads to salvation and leaves no regret, but worldly sorrow brings death. 2 Corinthians 7:10 (NIV)

The kind of sorrow God wants makes people change their hearts and lives. This leads to salvation, and you cannot be sorry for that. But the kind of sorrow the world has brings death. 2 Corinthians 7:10 (NCV)

Worldly sorrow is often temporary, and while it might involve regret, we move on fairly easily – and often choose the same or similar offenses or wrongdoings in the future – against God or others. Worldly sorrow is self-focused. Our sorrow is usually more about being caught and enduring consequences than responding to any true guilt and shame.

Godly sorrow is, obviously, connected to God. It involves the realization that we've offended God (even if the offense directly involves another person, anything contrary to God's will directly offends God)…and subsequent transparency and repentance with God. To say you can experience godly sorrow without asking for his forgiveness is contradictory. If what you're experiencing is truly godly, you will seek full restoration in your relationship with God.

You're likely seeing a pattern at this point. Godly guilt, shame or sorrow intimately involves God. It's true guilt or shame. False guilt or shame comes from self. I know it's not comfortable to hear that, because you think you don't want that false guilt and shame. You'd do just about anything to get rid of it. But the truth is, it's a twisted version of true guilt and shame, and you're going to have to sweat through the untwisting process, relying on God for strength and endurance.

We don't need to stay in a place of guilt and shame. God gives us grace. We can receive God's grace even when we don't deserve it. We still sweat it out, because we have to sacrifice ourselves in order to place ourselves in God's hands and receive his grace. We have to let go of our god of self-sufficiency to grab onto the God of *all* sufficiency. We might right a wrong out of our own pride in doing "the right thing," but God's grace mobilizes the recovery and restoration.

Shame invites us into grace.

Let's accept the invitation.

True Guilt	True Shame

False Guilt	False Shame

Week Eight

Make It Personal #1: *The Invitation of Grace*

Godly guilt and shame are always temporary, never chronic. Godly guilt and shame are productive, not destructive. Godly guilt and shame draw you closer to God, not distance you. When we regularly live with false guilt and shame, it affects our dignity and our hope. It's corrodes our joy. We fill in the following with all kinds of negative identities and judgments.

I am a _____.

How did Adam and Eve's shame impact their responses?

The woman saw that the tree was beautiful, that its fruit was good to eat, and that it would make her wise. So she took some of its fruit and ate it. She also gave some of the fruit to her husband who was with her, and he ate it.

Then, it was as if their eyes were opened. They realized they were naked, so they sewed fig leaves together and made something to cover themselves.

Then they heard the Lord God walking in the garden during the cool part of the day, and the man and his wife hid from the Lord God among the trees in the garden. But the Lord God called to the man and said, "Where are you?"

The man answered, "I heard you walking in the garden, and I was afraid because I was naked, so I hid." Genesis 3:6-10

Shame exposes us in our nakedness. The truth is God created us to be exposed. We're the ones who aren't okay with our exposure, because we feel vulnerable. When we're vulnerably exposed, we're ashamed because we can't live up to what we expect of ourselves or what we think others, including God, expect of us. We ask ourselves such questions as

- Could I have done better?
- Could I have made better choices?
- Would things be better if I had only done things differently?

And the answer is most frequently going to be yes! Let's hope we can grow in our choices; that's what growth is all about. Looking back can be excellent if it helps you move forward. But God has no intention of letting you get stuck in the past.

Adam and Eve didn't have the option of getting stuck in their pasts. God physically moved them out of the place of sin and into the next chapter of their lives. Of course, there were still ramifications of their sin. But ramifications aren't guilt and shame. We experience guilt and shame as a conviction that something needs to change and we need to rely on God for that change. As we accept God's forgiveness, we move on from the guilt and shame. We live with consequences, and have no choice in that. Our choice was what led to the consequences. But we have a choice to live or not live with the guilt and shame – to receive and embrace or not receive and embrace God's forgiveness. If we don't move on from it, we at least have to realize that the godly guilt and shame transforms into our own false guilt and shame, because God's guilt and shame is not lasting. He desires for you to grow.

Unlike Adam and Eve and others in the Old Testament, we live under the covenant of the New Testament: the promise of eternal salvation through Jesus. We live under grace.

What do you learn about Jesus and shame in Hebrews 12:2?

Let us look only to Jesus, the One who began our faith and who makes it perfect. He suffered death on the cross. But he accepted the shame as if it were nothing because of the joy that God put before him. And now he is sitting at the right side of God's throne.

Jesus shamed shame. When we have a relationship with Jesus, we experience God's grace. Grace is undeserved. It's God's way of saying…"regardless of where you've been and what you've done, and I know it all, I fully accept you as my child. I created you, and there is nothing that brings me more joy than to have you use the power of choice I gave you to humbly come to me and accept me as the one and only true and everlasting God."

God doesn't give us freedom *from* shame. He gives us freedom *in* our shame. That's grace. That's redemption. That's reconciliation with God.

Godly shame is redemptive. Ungodly shame is corrosive.

Which will you choose? Which do you choose on a daily, moment-by-moment basis?

Let God pour into you through the following verses.

Protect me and save me. I trust you, so do not let me be disgraced. Psalm 25:20

Then you will have plenty to eat and be full.

You will praise the name of the Lord your God, who has done miracles for you.

My people will never again be shamed.

Then you will know that I am among the people of Israel, that I am the Lord your God, and there is no other God. My people will never be shamed again. Joel 2:26-27

I love the word chosen in Psalm 25:20 to portray *shame*: disgraced. The word choice emphasizes what grace is and does…it dis-shames! God's people can be ashamed, but the blessing of God, his grace, means that we will never be put *to* shame. Praise God!

Our youngest daughter, Courtney, asked if we could forego traditional extended family Thanksgiving gathering and instead serve a meal to people in need. Something that happened while we were serving was a visual reminder of God's grace.

Tim and I worked the food line, filling trays, while Courtney was one of many who delivered food to tables where people were seated. I enjoyed watching her from across the room as she shared her bright beautiful smile with everyone she was serving. She'd lean down to look the person in the face and ask what he or she needed. One woman asked for tea. Courtney served her tea and asked if she needed anything else. "Tea." Courtney tried to explain that she'd already given her tea, but the woman obviously didn't understand, so Courtney picked up the cup and set it down again, delivering tea to her new friend. She checked on her later and asked if she needed anything. "Tea." This happened repeatedly. Courtney continued to "deliver" the tea.

Isn't that how we respond to God's grace? We ask for it, again and again, even though once we've humbly come to God and asked for his forgiveness, accepting Jesus as the Lord and Savior of our life, we have God's grace! Yet he repeatedly stoops to meet us where we are and meet our needs. Grace comes directly from God's love. I love how Donald Barnhouse expresses it: "Love that stoops is grace."

In what ways do you struggle with grace?

Romans 6:14 says *"Sin will not be your master, because you are not under law but under God's grace."* Under God's grace. It reminds me of standing under an umbrella.

An umbrella is protective. When I accept God's grace, it's not temporary. He covers me. I'm in a relationship with God that is ongoing and reliable – more than any other relationship I'll ever experienced.

Yes, I am sure that neither death, nor life, nor angels, nor ruling spirits, nothing now, nothing in the future, no powers, nothing above us, nothing below us, nor anything else in the whole world will ever be able to separate us from the love of God that is in Christ Jesus our Lord. Romans 8:38-39

What does this verse mean to you?

God's love, God's grace, is relentless. I don't know about you, but that makes me want to be relentless in my pursuit of him!

God sees everything about me. Everything.

When Jesus heard that they had thrown him out, Jesus found him and said, "Do you believe in the Son of Man?"

He asked, "Who is the Son of Man, sir, so that I can believe in him?"

Jesus said to him, "You have seen him. The Son of Man is the one talking with you."

He said, "Lord, I believe!" Then the man worshiped Jesus.

Jesus said, "I came into this world so that the world could be judged. I came so that the blind would see and so that those who see will become blind."

Some of the Pharisees who were nearby heard Jesus say this and asked, "Are you saying we are blind, too?"

Jesus said, "If you were blind, you would not be guilty of sin. But since you keep saying you see, your guilt remains." John 9:35-41

According the original Greek, the last verse could be written something like this: "If you were blind, you would have no sin. But since you keep saying you see, your sin remains."

Know where you stand with God. You might not have all the answers and understanding, but you can still have a relationship of trust.

Spiritually speaking, I don't want to be visually-impaired. How about you?

Earlier in today's study, we looked at Hebrews 12:2, where Jesus shamed shame. Let's look at it again in the context of its surrounding verses.

We are surrounded by a great cloud of people whose lives tell us what faith means. So let us run the race that is before us and never give up. We should remove from our lives anything that would get in the way and the sin that so easily holds us back. Let us look only to Jesus, the One who began our faith and who makes it perfect. He suffered death on the cross. But he accepted the shame as if it were nothing because of the joy that God put before him. And now he is sitting at the right side of God's throne. Think about Jesus' example. He held on while wicked people were doing evil things to him. So do not get tired and stop trying. Hebrews 2:1-3

What does this mean to you today?

Let's claim what it means. I've given you some spaces below. Each line begins with "..." and continues with "So..." Carefully study Hebrews 2:1-3. Pray over them. How is God encouraging and challenging you through them? Begin each line by rewording the part of the a verse God is highlighting for you. Then write what it means to you personally – in your daily life – behind the "so." I've shared one of mine with you to get you started!

*...Sin can easily hold me back from what God wants for me, **so**...I'm asking God to reveal hints of sin in my thoughts, attitudes, emotions, and actions so I can ask him to remove them and replace them with his purpose.*

...   **, so...**

...   **, so...**

...   **, so...**

...   **, so...**

...   **, so...**

WEEK EIGHT

Make It Personal #2: *Planting Seeds of Truth*

In the beginning there was the Word. The Word was with God, and the Word was God. He was with God in the beginning. All things were made by him, and nothing was made without him. John 1:1-3

We're taking a slightly different approach in today's Planting Seeds of Truth. I'm including only one set of verses. I want you to fully experience Psalm 40 as a prayer and praise for help. Choose one or more of the approaches we've been applying over the preceding weeks, and embrace the words of this psalm as you step one step closer to God!

Speak It. Say it out loud – several times if you prefer. God's spoken Word has power. Plus, you'll be using several senses to experience God's Word. You're taking it in with your eyes, forming the words with your mouth, and hearing the words. It's like a double exclamation point!

Personalize It. What is God specifically saying to you in this season of your life? Insert your name, respond with a question, rephrase the promise – whatever it takes to absorb what God's saying to you and stand firmly on it as you take the next steps.

Live It. God doesn't intend for us to simply fill our heads with knowledge about his Word. He desires us to let it seep into every crevice of our lives. Let him guide through challenges and encouragements of how you'll apply a verse into your daily life. Write a note about your plan – and then revisit this page to record your progress.

I waited patiently for the Lord.
He turned to me and heard my cry.
He lifted me out of the pit of destruction,
out of the sticky mud.
He stood me on a rock
and made my feet steady.
He put a new song in my mouth,
a song of praise to our God.
Many people will see this and worship him.
Then they will trust the Lord.

Happy is the person
who trusts the Lord,
who doesn't turn to those who are proud
or to those who worship false gods.
Lord my God, you have done many miracles.
Your plans for us are many.
If I tried to tell them all,
there would be too many to count.

You do not want sacrifices and offerings.
But you have made a hole in my ear
to show that my body and life are yours.
You do not ask for burnt offerings
and sacrifices to take away sins.
Then I said, "Look, I have come.
It is written about me in the book.
My God, I want to do what you want.
Your teachings are in my heart."

I will tell about your goodness in the great meeting of your people.
Lord, you know my lips are not silent.
I do not hide your goodness in my heart;
I speak about your loyalty and salvation.
I do not hide your love and truth
from the people in the great meeting.

Lord, do not hold back your mercy from me;
let your love and truth always protect me.
Troubles have surrounded me;
there are too many to count.
My sins have caught me
so that I cannot see a way to escape.
I have more sins than hairs on my head,
and I have lost my courage.
Please, Lord, save me.
Hurry, Lord, to help me.
People are trying to kill me.
Shame them and disgrace them.
People want to hurt me.
Let them run away in disgrace.
People are making fun of me.
Let them be shamed into silence.
But let those who follow you
be happy and glad.
They love you for saving them.
May they always say, "Praise the Lord!"

Lord, because I am poor and helpless,
please remember me.
You are my helper and savior.
My God, do not wait. Psalm 40

Make It Personal #3: *Humility*

Pride leads only to shame; it is wise to be humble. Proverbs 11:2

Isn't that the truth? In some verses, the word *dishonor* is used in place of *shame*. The truth is it's wise to be humble. List the situations in which you believe it's best to be humble.

I don't like it all the time, but humility is always the best position. I dedicated an entire week of *Pure Purpose* to humility, and as I talk with women about humility I find some interesting things.

1. Many women are uncomfortable talking about it.
2. Many women agree humility is important but aren't sure what that looks like in daily life.
3. A handful of women are proud of their humility. (If this doesn't strike you as odd, reread it.)
4. More than a handful of women believe that humility has something to do with self-condemnation.

Mark each of the above observations with a "+" if you could be included in the women I've observed and a "-" if you fall outside the group I've observed.

It might seem odd for me to plop a lesson in humility right in the middle of the study on guilt and shame, but I hope you'll soon discover the connection.

Humility establishes our position in relation to God. God doesn't want you to put yourself down…just as he doesn't want you to build yourself up. He wants you to see yourself the way he sees you.

So God created human beings in his image. In the image of God he created them. He created them male and female. Genesis 1:27

As God's creation, you reflect him. You will never be as great as God, and yet he desires to draw you closer and closer to him despite your imperfections. Each of us is unworthy because we're human…and God is God. Yet each of us was created by God to reflect and glorify him. He desires you.

Humility is not about putting yourself down. It's about a proper relationship with God. Look up to God. When we say "I can do this," we take God out of it and fail to acknowledge his existence. We become the focus. When we say "I can't," we take God out of it and fail to acknowledge his strength. We deflate ourselves or inflate ourselves, and both are wrong. We're not the source of the air. God is. When we only allow him to inflate us through his encouragement and deflate us through his discipline, we start all our sentences with God. We must acknowledge God.

When we inflate or deflate ourselves, we place ourselves as the source, the center. Only God should be the source of our air, inflating or deflating us.

What percentage of the time do you live as if you're the source of air, inflating and deflating yourself?

0% ━━ 100%

What percentage of the time do you live as God with the source of the air pressure of your life?

0% ━━ 100%

He knows just what we need when we need it.

God can do all things. Your worth is in him, and no one, including yourself, can make you worth any more or any less.[6]

Humility recognizes needs and weaknesses. When Tim and I got married, we determined we wouldn't say we'd never get a divorce. Not because we didn't think we were susceptible to divorce because we intended to be married for the rest of our lives. It's *because* we were susceptible that we made the commitment. If we put blinders on the possibility of anything catastrophic happening in our marriage, we wouldn't notice small changes and warning signs along the way. We'd feel blind-sided when we woke up one morning and realized we had nothing in common, didn't really like each other after all, and wanted nothing more than to run as far as possible from the other.

We wanted to recognize the possibility of growing apart, taking each other for granted, and hurting each other, because we're human. We knew, in all likelihood, those things would happen. You might be surprised to find out…those things *did* happen! We've been married over twenty years but it hasn't been a relaxing cruise the whole time! Marriage takes daily effort, and there are some days and situations that are just plain painful. I'm not talking about being the receiver of pain. I've inflicted plenty of wounds on our marriage!

Through the rough times, commitment – and God's grace – gets us through. I've often thought back to our early realization that we were susceptible and needed to be on guard. I'm certainly glad we were on guard, because I can't imagine the worse messes we would have been in.

Humility is the recognition that you have needs and weaknesses. You're susceptible. You don't have all the answers. And you might be weak in some areas you're not aware of being weak in. You can become so adamant that you won't do or be something that you don't watch the warning lights and end up exactly where you thought you wouldn't be.

Like Peter. What does his experience teach you about humility?

Jesus told his followers, "Tonight you will all stumble in your faith on account of me, because it is written in the Scriptures: 'I will kill the shepherd, and the sheep will scatter.' But after I rise from the dead, I will go ahead of you into Galilee."

Peter said, "Everyone else may stumble in their faith because of you, but I will not."

Jesus said, "I tell you the truth, tonight before the rooster crows you will say three times that you don't know me."

---

6   Lawrence, Susan. <u>Pure Purpose</u>. Bloomington IN: WestBow Press, 2010

But Peter said, "I will never say that I don't know you! I will even die with you!" And all the other followers said the same thing...

...Jesus answered, "Those are your words. But I tell you, in the future you will see the Son of Man sitting at the right hand of God, the Powerful One, and coming on clouds in the sky."

When the high priest heard this, he tore his clothes and said, "This man has said things that are against God! We don't need any more witnesses; you all heard him say these things against God. What do you think?"

The people answered, "He should die."

Then the people there spat in Jesus' face and beat him with their fists. Others slapped him. They said, "Prove to us that you are a prophet, you Christ! Tell us who hit you!"

At that time, as Peter was sitting in the courtyard, a servant girl came to him and said, "You also were with Jesus of Galilee."

But Peter said to all the people there that he was never with Jesus. He said, "I don't know what you are talking about."

When he left the courtyard and was at the gate, another girl saw him. She said to the people there, "This man was with Jesus of Nazareth."

Again, Peter said he was never with him, saying, "I swear I don't know this man Jesus!"

A short time later, some people standing there went to Peter and said, "Surely you are one of those who followed Jesus. The way you talk shows it."

Then Peter began to place a curse on himself and swear, "I don't know the man." At once, a rooster crowed. And Peter remembered what Jesus had told him: "Before the rooster crows, you will say three times that you don't know me." Then Peter went outside and cried painfully. Matthew 26:31-35, 64-75

In case you're not familiar with Peter, let me assure you he'd had many very faithful moments in his relationship with Jesus. If you were to observe his life, I doubt you'd identify him as a man of little faith. But he was susceptible, and he seemed ignorant in his susceptibility.

When we're humble, even when we can't identify our specific needs and weaknesses, we're in a position that recognizes we're vulnerable to poor choices, unhealthy responses, and sin.

Humility allows us to acknowledge guilt and shame. "I don't feel guilty. Why should I? It really wasn't my fault. She was just too sensitive." "Ashamed? Why would I feel ashamed? Who says what I did was wrong anyway?"

When we submit ourselves in humility, we accept guilt and shame because we know we're not the determiners of truth. We know who is. We let God define right and wrong, so even when we don't like it, we accept the guilt that comes from disobedience.

But humility does something else as well, and it's equally as important. Remember, humility isn't putting yourself down. It's putting yourself in a proper, appropriate relationship with God. He says who you are and who he intends you to be. You don't decide. But when you take on false guilt and shame, you're assuming you have the power to judge what guilt and shame is. You don't. That's God's job.

Being humble is not just acknowledging guilt and shame but discerning between godly and false guilt and shame. Because humility is being in a proper relationship with God, you can't personally decide what you measure against God's character and standards and what you don't. You accept your position with God, which includes all of God's character and standards. You don't define God. He defines you. And whether you think of yourself more highly or lowly than he intends, you're being proud.

God gets the glory. He wants you to yield it to him, but whether you're humble or not, he'll be glorified. If you want to be able to discern between godly and false guilt and shame (or any other emotions we're studying), humble yourself. It's one of the best steps you can take.

Humility positions us to accept grace. Whether you think you're too bad to be forgiven or too good to need forgiveness, you're once again putting yourself in the lofty and unworthy position of deciding whether or not you need grace. God gives. You receive. In order to receive, you must open your hands. When you deem yourself as someone who can't receive God's grace, you've clenched your fists. There are many people walking around with outstretched arms and clenched fists, desperately wanting to be poured into by God but withholding the last stretch of openness.

You have no secrets from God. He's not extending grace to you out of ignorance. He knows you – and he's still extending grace. You're not defined by the past, by what you have done – good or bad. Nor are you defined by what others may have done to you.

In your humility, you are who God says you are. Run to him in humility and accept the grace he's already holding outstretched to you.

Guilt and shame have a lot more to do with humility than you might think at first glance.

Even the foolishness of God is wiser than human wisdom, and the weakness of God is stronger than human strength.

Brothers and sisters, look at what you were when God called you. Not many of you were wise in the way the world judges wisdom. Not many of you had great influence. Not many of you came from important families. But God chose the foolish things of the world to shame the wise, and he chose the weak things of the world to shame the strong. He chose what the world thinks is unimportant and what the world looks down on and thinks is nothing in order to destroy what the world thinks is important. God did this so that no one can brag in his presence. Because of God you are in Christ Jesus, who has become for us wisdom from God. In Christ we are put right with God, and have been made holy, and have been set free from sin. 1 Corinthians 1:25-30

WEEK EIGHT

Make It Personal #4: *Emotional Check-Up*

It's time for a check-up! How are you growing through the *Pure Emotion* experience? You just went through a more intense check-up last week, so you might not need to answer every question this week. Of course, answer the guilt/shame questions so you'll have a reference point for future check-ups. For the other emotions, you might want to look through the questions and respond to the ones you're most struggling with or the ones in which you're experiencing the most significant challenges and growth.

Guilt/Shame

How might guilt/shame be distorting reality?

Is my guilt/shame serving me – is it enhancing my life – or am I serving it – have I become enslaved to it?

Is guilt/shame generally temporary or chronic for me?

How is my past experience with guilt/shame affecting today?

How is guilt/shame affecting my future?

Is guilt/shame drawing me to or separating me from God?

Frustration

How might frustration be distorting reality?

Is my frustration serving me – is it enhancing my life – or am I serving it – have I become enslaved to it?

Is frustration generally temporary or chronic for me?

How is my past experience with frustration affecting today?

How is frustration affecting my future?

Is frustration drawing me to or separating me from God?

Anxiety/Peace

How might anxiety be distorting reality?

Is my anxiety serving me – is it enhancing my life – or am I serving it – have I become enslaved to it?

Is anxiety generally temporary or chronic for me?

How is my past experience with anxiety affecting today?

How is anxiety affecting my future?

Is anxiety drawing me to or separating me from God?

Anger

How might anger be distorting reality?

Is my anger serving me – is it enhancing my life – or am I serving it – have I become enslaved to it?

Is anger generally temporary or chronic for me?

How is my past experience with anger affecting today?

How is anger affecting my future?

Is anger drawing me to or separating me from God?

Jealousy

How might jealousy be distorting reality?

Is my jealousy serving me – is it enhancing my life – or am I serving it – have I become enslaved to it?

Is jealousy generally temporary or chronic for me?

How is my past experience with jealousy affecting today?

How is jealousy affecting my future?

Is jealousy drawing me to or separating me from God?

How might fear be distorting reality?

Is my fear serving me – is it enhancing my life – or am I serving it – have I become enslaved to it?

Is fear generally temporary or chronic for me?

How is my past experience with fear affecting today?

How is fear affecting my future?

Is fear drawing me to or separating me from God?

Fear

Make It Personal #5: *Freedom in Obedience*

Are you claiming God's grace, my friend? I knew when starting this week that it was going to be a rough one, and I'm so proud of you for sticking with it. I know God, and I trust him to pour into you every step of the path. I know it's agonizing at times. I also know it's thrilling and joyous much of the time. Live in his freedom!

We're going to claim that freedom today. We're going to be authentic with God and ourselves, revealing vestiges of guilt and shame and fully embracing his grace. I realize it's a process, but we need to practice consistently, and that's what today is all about.

We're preparing the way for next week's study on joy. I just want to breathe it in deeply in anticipation.

I'm providing you with a variety of verses and giving you the opportunity to reflect on each one.

1. Begin by admitting and writing any areas of guilt and shame. You don't need to go into details. Include basic key words if you prefer. But if God's prompting you to write it all out, grab some paper and extra pencils!

2. Ask God to help you discern between godly guilt and shame and false guilt and shame. Draw a line through anything false, and as you do, give it to God.

3. Listen to how God is prompting you to respond in obedience to the verse. What's your next step? How does he want you to bring the verse alive and make it relevant in your life? Even if you haven't listed anything in the guilt and shame area, you might be challenged to set goals and reflect in the obedience section.

As always, you don't need to fill in every space. This isn't about checking the lesson off your to do list. This is about your spiritual growth. Seek, listen, and obey. God will guide and provide.

Love the Lord your God with all your heart, all your soul, all your mind, and all your strength. The second command is this: Love your neighbor as you love yourself. There are no commands more important than these. Mark 12:30-31

Guilt and Shame   **Obedience**

If you love me, you will obey my commands. John 14:15

Guilt and Shame   **Obedience**

Do not let all kinds of strange teachings lead you into the wrong way. Your hearts should be strengthened by God's grace, not by obeying rules about foods, which do not help those who obey them. Hebrews 13:9

Guilt and Shame   **Obedience**

So go and make followers of all people in the world. Baptize them in the name of the Father and the Son and the Holy Spirit. Matthew 28:19

Guilt and Shame   **Obedience**

Finally, all of you should be in agreement, understanding each other, loving each other as family, being kind and humble. Do not do wrong to repay a wrong, and do not insult to repay an insult. But repay with a blessing, because you yourselves were called to do this so that you might receive a blessing. 1 Peter 3:8-9

Guilt and Shame   **Obedience**

When you talk, do not say harmful things, but say what people need—words that will help others become stronger. Then what you say will do good to those who listen to you. Ephesians 4:29

Guilt and Shame   **Obedience**

But Jesus answered, "Stop complaining to each other." John 6:43

Guilt and Shame   **Obedience**

Then Jesus said to them, "Be careful and guard against all kinds of greed. Life is not measured by how much one owns." Luke 12:15

Guilt and Shame   **Obedience**

Do not owe people anything, except always owe love to each other, because the person who loves others has obeyed all the law. Romans 13:8

Guilt and Shame   **Obedience**

Then Jesus called the crowd to him, along with his followers. He said, "If people want to follow me, they must give up the things they want. They must be willing even to give up their lives to follow me." Mark 8:34

Guilt and Shame   **Obedience**

Week Nine: *Joy*

Starter Session

You've been working through some tough stuff in recent weeks, yet I pray the encouragement you're getting through the truth of God's Word is energizing you along your spiritual journey. The truth is whether your guilt and shame (and regret of any kind) are real or false, dwelling on past mistakes or shortcomings can rob your life of the abundant joy that can be yours. When your life is full of joy, even though others will have to choose to embrace joy or not, it will definitely be apparent among your family and friends.

According to the survey, women experienced joy as positive. No one said they struggled with joy (which surprised me a little, because I think there are plenty of women who struggle with finding joy in difficult situations), and joy received the second most responses when asked what emotion women wouldn't want to live without. (Love received the highest number of responses.)

*What gets in the way of your joy?

I've put together a few things you might believe rob you of joy. To think of it from another perspective, imagine you're experiencing joy and a voice interrupts, so your experience of joy is minimized, or joy seems swept away altogether. Check all the sources of interruptions you experience. You can classify them with letters based on the frequency of interruptions.

C=Consistently   O=Occasionally   R=Rarely   N=Never

❏ Faith _____
❏ My past _____
❏ Negative self-talk _____
❏ Doubt _____
❏ Uncertainty _____
❏ Pressure from others _____
❏ Habits _____
❏ Addictions _____
❏ Other _____
❏ Other _____

It's important to be aware of joy-stealers in your life, but it's even more important that you realize you can claim joy and hang onto it, locking it into your life so that no one and no situation

191

can steal it. The problem is we equate joy with feeling good, very similar to being happy. Joy isn't static. It can become a constant in our lives, but our experience of it changes through those situations. It's not that we have less or more joy. We can be full of joy through any circumstance, but there are times we'll struggle more to find, realize and embrace it. There are times we'll realize we've been taking joy for granted.

Unlike other emotions we've been studying, joy is godly. Period. We don't need to look at the ungodly side of joy, but we do need to discern joy from happiness. Happiness is the human twist on joy. We've taken godly anger and twisted it into human anger and justified the twists. We've taken godly fear, jealousy and other emotions and done the same. God has promised us joy, and we've twisted it into a promise for happiness. So the first thing we need to do is separate the two.

*How do you believe joy and happiness differ?

Throughout this week, you'll see a variety of words associated with joy: rejoice, enjoy, joyful, joyous. Keep in mind these are all related words. But happiness is different.

I remember the smiley face phase when there were smiley face tshirts, bumper stickers, and school supplies. Many of them read "Happiness is…" and the statement was finished with a wide variety of words and phrases.

Happiness is being married.
Happiness is being single.
Happiness is a warm puppy.
Happiness is fishing.
Happiness is being a grandma.
Happiness is shopping.
Happiness is a choice.
Happiness is impossible.

Create your own. *If your car came with a mandatory "Happiness is…" bumper sticker, how would you finish it?

Happiness is circumstantial.
Happiness makes a person smile, but sadness can break a person's spirit. Proverbs 15:13
When good people triumph, there is great happiness, but when the wicked get control, everybody hides. Proverbs 28:12
The vines have become dry, and the fig trees are dried up. The pomegranate trees, the date palm trees, the apple trees— all the trees in the field have died. And the happiness of the people has died, too. Joel 1:12

Happiness is certainly enjoyable, but it's also fleeting. If circumstances are favorable, you're happy. If not, you're unhappy. Your happiness is dependent on what's happening around you — and your perception of what's happening around you.

I imagine we all know people who seem "happy" even when what's going on around them doesn't seem happiness-worthy…and people who seem miserable even when they're surrounded by fantastic circumstances. What we're actually seeing isn't so much happiness or unhappiness but joy or lack of it.

Joy is a firm confidence that all is well regardless of the circumstances. Philippians 3:1 says *"Be full of joy in the Lord."* God is the source of joy, and God is the object of joy. We're joyful because God is who he says he is, and that means we can trust him, fully relying on his guidance and provision through any circumstance. Our joy isn't circumstantial, because our faith isn't circumstantial. We're joyful because of God but also *with* God. As we live close to God, we experience life with the glimpse of his perspective. Because God has the big picture, we can trust there is always hope, and if nothing else, we can find joy in hope.

Knowing God, being in a dynamic relationship with him, transcends any and all temporal circumstance. Knowing God is inextricably connected with obeying God, and obeying God gives us peace and assurance even in uncertainties.

Like right now. As I'm writing today's session, I'm in a circumstance of uncertainty. "A season of transition" is what I like to call it. I like change and even a bit of uncertainty…but within a bit of structure, and the last 24 hours have had very little structure and certainty. I got some great news yesterday, followed by disappointing news an hour ago and uplifting news thirty minutes ago. I think God wants me to have good material to write about. I briefly considered my next steps. Should I turn off my phone and sign off my computer, virtually sticking my head in the sand so no one can contact me? Not likely. I'm just glad my joy isn't dependent on my circumstance. Oh, I'd be okay some of the time, but I'm not willing to surrender to the situational unhappiness of life. Not just because I'm a positive person but because it's not what God intends, and above my own misery, happiness, or anything else that centers on me and my situations, I want to be in the center of where God wants me to be and respond how he wants me to respond.

Joy is God's gift to every believer. Arguing that you're just not a joyful person or someone else just has that gift of joy isn't going to get you very far. You might wish that was the case, but it's not true. The Holy Spirit gifts us, but joy isn't a *gift* of the Holy Spirit; joy is the *fruit* of the Holy Spirit.

But the Spirit produces the fruit of love, joy, peace, patience, kindness, goodness, faithfulness, gentleness, self-control. Galatians 5:22-23

*What do you learn about joy from the following verses?

Then Nehemiah the governor, Ezra the priest and teacher, and the Levites who were teaching said to all the people, "This is a holy day to the Lord your God. Don't be sad or cry." All the people had been crying as they listened to the words of the Teachings.

Nehemiah said, "Go and enjoy good food and sweet drinks. Send some to people who have none, because today is a holy day to the Lord. Don't be sad, because the joy of the Lord will make you strong."

The Levites helped calm the people, saying, "Be quiet, because this is a holy day. Don't be sad." Then all the people went away to eat and drink, to send some of their food to others, and to celebrate with great joy. They finally understood what they had been taught. Nehemiah 8:9-12

I love that the people "finally understood what they had been taught." We have joy because we've learned. Sometimes we don't fully understand the details, but we understand God. We know who he is and accept he has the big picture and all the details in his view. We embrace his love for us and rest in his grace. And find joy. (As you'll study tomorrow, joy and grace share deep roots.)

God wants us to be full of joy, regardless of our circumstances. He doesn't say he wants us to be partially full. He's not satisfied with almost full. He wants us to be joy-full!

It's a difficult concept to comprehend, especially when we allow ourselves to think of joy as happiness, circumstantial, or when we think of joy being diminished by sadness, trials, or struggles. But remember that joy is fruit of the Spirit. The Holy Spirit nourishes us, pouring into us everything that we need to live out the life God intends…to fulfill his purpose for us…to fully experience the process of life. As the Holy Spirit nourishes us, and as we're obedient, relying on him for all guidance and discernment, we grow. Fruit buds and grows and flourishes. You're not going to automatically produce fruit, which means your life isn't going to automatically be filled with joy. You'll have to yield to God, yield to the Holy Spirit working through you.

I'll be the first to admit yielding isn't easy, but we've definitely seen how important it is throughout *Pure Emotion*. God requires it consistently. It's inextricably linked with faith. Remember the week you drew a line on each beaker to indicate how much you were filling yourself up with a particular emotion. How much room are you giving the Holy Spirit? I know it's a challenge to determine, but take a guess and place a line indicating how much of your life is driven by and filled up with yourself – your thoughts, dreams, task lists, etc.

The remaining space is filled by the Holy Spirit. But God wants you to be completely filled. Filled with the Holy Spirit. Filled with joy.

For the remainder of today's session, explore a variety of verses that refer to the fullness of joy. Let God speak to you through them. *How is he encouraging you? *How is he challenging you? *What is he prompting you to do? Let him work in you through these verses.

You will teach me how to live a holy life. Being with you will fill me with joy; at your right hand I will find pleasure forever. Psalm 16:11

The Lord your God is with you; the mighty One will save you. He will rejoice over you. You will rest in his love; he will sing and be joyful about you. Zephaniah 3:17

This is what the Lord All-Powerful says: "The special days when you fast in the fourth, fifth, seventh, and tenth months will become good, joyful, happy feasts in Judah. But you must love truth and peace." Zechariah 8:19

People will hate you, shut you out, insult you, and say you are evil because you follow the Son of Man. But when they do, you will be blessed. Be full of joy at that time, because you have a great reward in heaven. Their ancestors did the same things to the prophets. Luke 6:22-23

As Jesus rode toward Jerusalem, others spread their coats on the road before him. As he was coming close to Jerusalem, on the way down the Mount of Olives, the whole crowd of followers began joyfully shouting praise to God for all the miracles they had seen. They said, "God bless the king who comes in the name of the Lord!" Psalm 118:26

There is peace in heaven and glory to God! Luke 19:36-38

I have told you these things so that you can have the same joy I have and so that your joy will be the fullest possible joy. John 15:11

They called the apostles in, beat them, and told them not to speak in the name of Jesus again. Then they let them go free. The apostles left the meeting full of joy because they were given the honor of suffering disgrace for Jesus. Every day in the Temple and in people's homes they continued teaching the people and telling the Good News-that Jesus is the Christ. Acts 5:40-42

So Paul and Barnabas shook the dust off their feet and went to Iconium. But the followers were filled with joy and the Holy Spirit. Acts 13:51-52

Be joyful because you have hope. Be patient when trouble comes, and pray at all times. Romans 12:12

Be full of joy in the Lord always. I will say again, be full of joy. Philippians 4:4

My brothers and sisters, when you have many kinds of troubles, you should be full of joy, because you know that these troubles test your faith, and this will give you patience. James 1:2-3

You have not seen Christ, but still you love him. You cannot see him now, but you believe in him. So you are filled with a joy that cannot be explained, a joy full of glory. 1 Peter 1:8

Your hope is in God, not the messiness of this world. *God is strong and can help you not to fall. He can bring you before his glory without any wrong in you and can give you great joy.* (Jude 1:24) God can give you great joy. Let's not settle for "enough joy" or "adequate joy." Let's go for great!

Make It Personal #1: *Joy in Grace*

Crying may last for a night, but joy comes in the morning. Psalm 30:5

I know you've cried through a night. I don't know if your night was actual nighttime. I don't know if your night was twelve hours, twelve days, twelve weeks, or longer. But I know your night was dark. Josh Wilson captures the experience well in *Before the Morning.*

> *Do you wonder why you have to feel the things that hurt you?*
> *If there's a God who loves you, where is He now?*
> *Maybe there are things you can't see, and all those things are happening to bring a better ending.*
> *Someday, somehow, you'll see, you'll see.*
> *Would you dare, would you dare, to believe that you still have a reason to sing,*
> *'cause the pain you've been feeling can't compare to the joy that's coming.*
> *So hold on, you got to wait for the light. Press on, just fight the good fight. Because*
> *the pain you've been feeling – It's just the dark before the morning.*

I encourage you to YouTube the video and soak up the rest of the lyrics and music.

The truth is, as we studied yesterday, joy can be a constant in our lives. Because the Holy Spirit resides in us, and because the fruit of the Spirit is joy, we have constant access to joy. It's just that sadness and crying can pile on top of the joy through the night so that we don't acknowledge the joy. Remember, joy isn't circumstantial. It's different than happiness. Joy is godly. Happiness, while it *can be* godly, isn't always. It can be driven by our own desires, preferences and experiences.

Joy is deeply rooted in faith. As faith deepens, we experience joy more deeply. The two are intricately tied. Remember in last week's study, we looked at grace as it is foundational in our faith. Let's dig a little deeper, where we'll find shared roots between joy and grace.

Chara is the Greek word for joy. It means just what you think it means: joy, delight, gladness, etc. And it means *a result of* God's grace. We have joy because of God's grace. We have joy because we experience God's grace. Joy *is* an experience of God's grace.

The Greek word for grace is *charis*. Where *chara* (joy) is a feeling experienced in one's heart, *charis* (grace) is the divine influence upon the heart. God gives us grace, and we experience joy. Here's what I think is really cool about how tightly the two of these words are related. While we experience joy because of God's grace, the word for joy is the root word for grace. In other words, take one away, and the other can't be defined.

Let's consider this with another illustration. Perhaps you've heard that there's no rhyming word for orange. Well, not exactly. There's no *English* word that rhymes with orange, but there's a hill in Wales – Blorenge – that is a perfect rhyme to orange. If you were asked to create two lines of perfectly rhymed poetry with orange on the end of one and only line, and you were forbidden to use the word Blorenge, you couldn't do it. Pull one out of the equation, and you don't have a complete rhyme.

Pull joy or grace out of the equation, and you can't fully experience the other. That's how intricately tied they are. They're inseparable.

What does the inseparability of God's grace and joy mean to you?

(Just one note about the word *charis*, or grace. When you see the word grace in Scripture, it's not always referring specifically to God's grace, or unmerited favor, to people, although all references to grace are somehow related to God's grace. The word grace can also reflect the goodwill or benevolence people extend to each other as a reflection of God's grace. Or it can be a gracious appreciation or thankfulness, as it reflects and glorifies God. Just something to keep in mind as you're studying.)

Let's continue to explore the depth of joy. What relationships do you find among the following verses?

You will teach me how to live a holy life. Being with you will fill me with joy; at your right hand I will find pleasure forever. Psalm 16:11

Then an angel of the Lord stood before them. The glory of the Lord was shining around them, and they became very frightened. The angel said to them, "Do not be afraid. I am bringing you good news that will be a great joy to all the people. Today your Savior was born in the town of David. He is Christ, the Lord." Luke 2:9-11

But from now on, the Son of Man will sit at the right hand of the powerful God. Luke 22:69

Since you were raised from the dead with Christ, aim at what is in heaven, where Christ is sitting at the right hand of God. Colossians 3:1

Joy. Holy Spirit. Grace. Jesus. Heaven. God. I love the complexity of God's creation, will and plan. And I only grasp a very small bit of understanding!

So what does this mean when you're in the middle of a mess?

Let's start with the bigger picture. What role does faith take in your life when things are going smoothly by your own standards?

What role does faith take in your life when things are rough by your standards?

Let's dig into what God's Word says.

Since we have been made right with God by our faith, we have peace with God. This happened through our Lord Jesus Christ, who through our faith has brought us into that blessing of God's grace that we now enjoy. And we are happy because of the hope we have of sharing God's glory. We also have joy with our troubles, because we know that these troubles produce patience. And patience produces character, and character produces hope. And this hope will never disappoint us, because God has poured out his love to fill our hearts. He gave us his love through the Holy Spirit, whom God has given to us.

When we were unable to help ourselves, at the right time, Christ died for us, although we were living against God. Very few people will die to save the life of someone else. Although perhaps for a good person someone might possibly die. But God shows his great love for us in this way: Christ died for us while we were still sinners. Romans 5:1-8

These verses are packed with so much of what we've been studying. I don't know about you, but sometimes my head can swim with all the details of the verses I'm reading. Let's list what we learn about each of the following. Of course, it's okay to mention relationships among two or more of the following when you're searching each one. Remember, we're letting God reveal the relationships and connections. They aren't mutually exclusive!

Peace

Jesus

Grace

Happy

Hope

Glory

God

Joy

Troubles

Patience

Character

Love

Fill/full

Holy Spirit

Life/live

Death/die

We/I

Consider what you wrote in response to the questions about how your faith lives out when your life is rough and when it's smooth. How do these verses speak to you about the highs and lows of life?

The Highs…

The Lows…

One more thing before we close our study for the day. I want you to have every opportunity to declare these verses for your life and stand firmly on them in the days to come. I've provided the same verses slightly reworded with some blanks. The first blank is for your name. In all the remaining blanks, write "my" as you claim the truth surrounding it. You can complete this within the book, or you can rewrite it on a piece of paper to keep close to you throughout your regular routine, so you can remind yourself of the truths of these verses. Personally, I like to use sticky index cards. They're a great size, and they don't easily fall out of my appointment book or Bible.

Blessings, my friend!

Since _____ has been made right with God by _____ faith, I have peace with God. This happened through _____ Lord Jesus Christ, who through _____ faith has brought me into that blessing of God's grace that I now enjoy. And I am happy because of the hope I have of sharing God's glory. I also have joy with _____ troubles, because I know that these troubles produce patience. And patience produces character, and character produces hope. And this hope will never disappoint me, because God has poured out his love to fill _____ heart. He gave me his love through the Holy Spirit, whom God has given to me.

When I was unable to help ourselves, at the right time, Christ died for me, although I was living against God. Very few people will die to save the life of someone else. Although perhaps for a good person someone might possibly die. But God shows his great love for me in this way: Christ died for me while I was still a sinner. Romans 5:1-8

Make It Personal #2: *Planting Seeds of Truth*

Remember the final lesson on last week's study on guilt and shame, when you reflected on verses, identified guilt and shame connected with those verses or topics and allowed God to convict you toward obedience? It's time to check your progress! There's little sense in making goals without checking the progress toward those goals. Before you get started with today's verses, use the space below to reflect on your progress and perhaps set more refined goals.

Now it's time to get started with our verses for today. I've kept them limited since you've spent time reflecting on your obedience toward goals and challenges as well!

Speak It. Say it out loud – several times if you prefer. God's spoken Word has power. Plus, you'll be using several senses to experience God's Word. You're taking it in with your eyes, forming the words with your mouth, and hearing the words. It's like a double exclamation point!

Personalize It. What is God specifically saying to you in this season of your life? Insert your name, respond with a question, rephrase the promise – whatever it takes to absorb what God's saying to you and stand firmly on it as you take the next steps.

Live It. God doesn't intend for us to simply fill our heads with knowledge about his Word. He desires us to let it seep into every crevice of our lives. Let him guide you through challenges and encouragements of how you'll apply a verse into your daily life. Write a note about your plan – and then revisit this page to record your progress.

And you will joyfully give thanks to the Father who has made you able to have a share in all that he has prepared for his people in the kingdom of light. Colossians 1:12

Speak It.

Personalize It.

Live It.

Always be joyful. 1 Thessalonians 5:16

Speak It.

Personalize It.

Live It.

If people please God, God will give them wisdom, knowledge, and joy. But sinners will get only the work of gathering and storing wealth that they will have to give to the ones who please God. So all their work is useless, like chasing the wind. Ecclesiastes 2:26

Speak It.

Personalize It.

Live It.

Give me back the joy of your salvation. Keep me strong by giving me a willing spirit. Psalm 51:12

Speak It.

Personalize It.

Live It.

WEEK NINE

Make It Personal #3: *Joy of Parables*

Joy is powerful, and it's rich in variety. If it's part of God's kingdom, we can rejoice in it. We perhaps struggle the most with finding joy in pain and trials, but there are so many more aspects of joy...

Joy in faith. I pray that the God who gives hope will fill you with much joy and peace while you trust in him. Then your hope will overflow by the power of the Holy Spirit. Romans 15:13

Joy of obedience. Remain in me, and I will remain in you. A branch cannot produce fruit alone but must remain in the vine. In the same way, you cannot produce fruit alone but must remain in me. I am the vine, and you are the branches. If any remain in me and I remain in them, they produce much fruit. But without me they can do nothing. If any do not remain in me, they are like a branch that is thrown away and then dies. People pick up dead branches, throw them into the fire, and burn them. If you remain in me and follow my teachings, you can ask anything you want, and it will be given to you. You should produce much fruit and show that you are my followers, which brings glory to my Father. I loved you as the Father loved me. Now remain in my love. I have obeyed my Father's commands, and I remain in his love. In the same way, if you obey my commands, you will remain in my love. I have told you these things so that you can have the same joy I have and so that your joy will be the fullest possible joy. John 15:4-11

Joy of God's Word. Happy are those who don't listen to the wicked, who don't go where sinners go, who don't do what evil people do. They love the Lord's teachings, and they think about those teachings day and night. They are strong, like a tree planted by a river. The tree produces fruit in season, and its leaves don't die. Everything they do will succeed. Psalm 1:1-3

Joy in forgiveness. Create in me a pure heart, God, and make my spirit right again. Do not send me away from you or take your Holy Spirit away from me. Give me back the joy of your salvation. Keep me strong by giving me a willing spirit. Then I will teach your ways to those who do wrong, and sinners will turn back to you. Psalm 51:10-13

The more details of God's joy we know, claim, and celebrate, the more readily we will be able to find joy in the tribulations.

Jesus regularly included joy in his teachings. He often taught in parables, which make up about one-third of Jesus' teachings in the Bible. These parables are memorable stories conveying everyday life. Within the simplicity of parables are deep messages central to Jesus' teachings.

Let's dig into three parables today. Because you'll have significant reading for each parable, I encourage you to interact with the verses as you read. Underline, circle, star, and take notes in the margins. My two favorite quick study marks to make are exclamation points when I have an "aha" moment I want to easily refer to later and question marks when I know I need to revisit the point and explore.

I've listed a couple questions at the begin of each set of verses so you'll be able to consider them as you're reading, but I encourage you not to simply "read for the answers." Let the verses soak into you, reflect, and then express yourself!

The Parable of Planting Seed
What does Jesus teach about joy?

How can/will you apply Jesus' teaching into your daily life?

How does Jesus explains his teaching style?

That same day Jesus went out of the house and sat by the lake. Large crowds gathered around him, so he got into a boat and sat down, while the people stood on the shore. Then Jesus used stories to teach them many things. He said: "A farmer went out to plant his seed. While he was planting, some seed fell by the road, and the birds came and ate it all up. Some seed fell on rocky ground, where there wasn't much dirt. That seed grew very fast, because the ground was not deep. But when the sun rose, the plants dried up, because they did not have deep roots. Some other seed fell among thorny weeds, which grew and choked the good plants. Some other seed fell on good ground where it grew and produced a crop. Some plants made a hundred times more, some made sixty times more, and some made thirty times more. Let those with ears use them and listen."

The followers came to Jesus and asked, "Why do you use stories to teach the people?"

Jesus answered, "You have been chosen to know the secrets about the kingdom of heaven, but others cannot know these secrets. Those who have understanding will be given more, and they will have all they need. But those who do not have understanding, even what they have will be taken away from them. This is why I use stories to teach the people: They see, but they don't really see. They hear, but they don't really hear or understand. So they show that the things Isaiah said about them are true:

'You will listen and listen, but you will not understand.
You will look and look, but you will not learn.
For the minds of these people have become stubborn.
They do not hear with their ears, and they have closed their eyes.
Otherwise they might really understand
what they see with their eyes
and hear with their ears.
They might really understand in their minds
and come back to me and be healed.' Isaiah 6:9–10

But you are blessed, because you see with your eyes and hear with your ears. I tell you the truth, many prophets and good people wanted to see the things that you now see, but they did not see them. And they wanted to hear the things that you now hear, but they did not hear them."

"So listen to the meaning of that story about the farmer. What is the seed that fell by the road? That seed is like the person who hears the message about the kingdom but does not understand it. The Evil One comes and takes away what was planted in that person's heart. And what is the seed that fell

*on rocky ground? That seed is like the person who hears the teaching and quickly accepts it with joy. But he does not let the teaching go deep into his life, so he keeps it only a short time. When trouble or persecution comes because of the teaching he accepted, he quickly gives up. And what is the seed that fell among the thorny weeds? That seed is like the person who hears the teaching but lets worries about this life and the temptation of wealth stop that teaching from growing. So the teaching does not produce fruit in that person's life. But what is the seed that fell on the good ground? That seed is like the person who hears the teaching and understands it. That person grows and produces fruit, sometimes a hundred times more, sometimes sixty times more, and sometimes thirty times more." * Matthew 3:1-23

The Parable of Three Servants
What does Jesus teach about joy?

How can/will you apply Jesus' teaching into your daily life?

"The kingdom of heaven is like a man who was going to another place for a visit. Before he left, he called for his servants and told them to take care of his things while he was gone. He gave one servant five bags of gold, another servant two bags of gold, and a third servant one bag of gold, to each one as much as he could handle. Then he left. The servant who got five bags went quickly to invest the money and earned five more bags. In the same way, the servant who had two bags invested them and earned two more. But the servant who got one bag went out and dug a hole in the ground and hid the master's money.

"After a long time the master came home and asked the servants what they did with his money. The servant who was given five bags of gold brought five more bags to the master and said, 'Master, you trusted me to care for five bags of gold, so I used your five bags to earn five more.' The master answered, 'You did well. You are a good and loyal servant. Because you were loyal with small things, I will let you care for much greater things. Come and share my joy with me.'

"Then the servant who had been given two bags of gold came to the master and said, 'Master, you gave me two bags of gold to care for, so I used your two bags to earn two more.' The master answered, 'You did well. You are a good and loyal servant. Because you were loyal with small things, I will let you care for much greater things. Come and share my joy with me.'" Matthew 25:14-23

The Parable of a Lost Sheep
What does Jesus teach about joy?

How can/will you apply Jesus' teaching into your daily life?

The tax collectors and sinners all came to listen to Jesus. But the Pharisees and the teachers of the law began to complain: "Look, this man welcomes sinners and even eats with them."

Then Jesus told them this story: "Suppose one of you has a hundred sheep but loses one of them. Then he will leave the other ninety-nine sheep in the open field and go out and look for the lost sheep until he finds it. And when he finds it, he happily puts it on his shoulders[6] and goes home. He calls to his friends and neighbors and says, 'Be happy with me because I found my lost sheep.' In the same way, I tell you there is more joy in heaven over one sinner who changes his heart and life, than over ninety-nine good people who don't need to change." Luke 15:1-7

You've now been studying joy for several days as well as studying emotions, discerning your own responses with godly emotions, for several weeks. What is God teaching you? How is he challenging you? What would you say about your spiritual growth?

You have this faith and love because of your hope, and what you hope for is kept safe for you in heaven. You learned about this hope when you heard the message about the truth, the Good News that was told to you. Everywhere in the world that Good News is bringing blessings and is growing. This has happened with you, too, since you heard the Good News and understood the truth about the grace of God. Colossians 1:5-6

WEEK NINE

Make It Personal #4: *Emotional Check-Up*

It's your final week for a check-up. Next week, I'll give you a new tool to use beyond *Pure Emotion*. I've slightly reworded the questions for this week's topic, joy. I urge you to take no short cuts this week. Pour yourself into your study time so you'll get much out of it. Spiritual growth is worth the effort!

How might I be distorting reality with my concept or experience of joy?

How is joy enhancing my life? Do I long for it, live by it, or both?

Is joy generally temporary or chronic for me?

Joy

How is my past experience with joy affecting today?

How is joy affecting my future?

Are my perceptions and experiences of joy drawing me to or separating me from God?

Guilt/Shame

How might guilt/shame be distorting reality?

Is my guilt/shame serving me – is it enhancing my life – or am I serving it – have I become enslaved to it?

Is guilt/shame generally temporary or chronic for me?

How is my past experience with guilt/shame affecting today?

How is guilt/shame affecting my future?

Is guilt/shame drawing me to or separating me from God?

Frustration

How might frustration be distorting reality?

Is my frustration serving me – is it enhancing my life – or am I serving it – have I become enslaved to it?

Is frustration generally temporary or chronic for me?

How is my past experience with frustration affecting today?

How is frustration affecting my future?

Is frustration drawing me to or separating me from God?

Anxiety/Peace

How might anxiety be distorting reality?

Is my anxiety serving me – is it enhancing my life – or am I serving it – have I become enslaved to it?

Is anxiety generally temporary or chronic for me?

How is my past experience with anxiety affecting today?

How is anxiety affecting my future?

Is anxiety drawing me to or separating me from God?

Anger

How might anger be distorting reality?

Is my anger serving me – is it enhancing my life – or am I serving it – have I become enslaved to it?

Is anger generally temporary or chronic for me?

How is my past experience with anger affecting today?

How is anger affecting my future?

Is anger drawing me to or separating me from God?

Jealousy

How might jealousy be distorting reality?

Is my jealousy serving me – is it enhancing my life – or am I serving it – have I become enslaved to it?

Is jealousy generally temporary or chronic for me?

How is my past experience with jealousy affecting today?

How is jealousy affecting my future?

Is jealousy drawing me to or separating me from God?

Fear

How might fear be distorting reality?

Is my fear serving me – is it enhancing my life – or am I serving it – have I become enslaved to it?

Is fear generally temporary or chronic for me?

How is my past experience with fear affecting today?

How is fear affecting my future?

Is fear drawing me to or separating me from God?

Make It Personal #5: *Life's Not Fair*

You've probably heard "Life's not fair." many times. Perhaps your parents told you "Life's not fair" when you had an early disappointment. Or you've told your own children "Life's not fair" as they've whined about not getting what they wanted. The truth is…life isn't fair if we take fairness literally. Life's not impartial. Life doesn't always fit into the rules. What are the rules anyway? Who decides? With a changing perception of who and what is right and wrong and who gets to decide what's right and wrong anyway, how can we actually even tell whether life's fair because what's fair to you might not be fair to me!

And so goes the cycle of the fairness of life. Let's face it. We live in a tolerant society – sort of. We seem to be able to tolerate anything except what infringes on our "rights," which end up being defined by our wants, convenience, and preferences.

The truth is Truth. Capital T. We can pretend there's no absolute truth. We can behave as if there's no absolute truth. We can teach there's no absolute truth. But that doesn't make it so. The truth is, whether you like it or not, there is a God. He created the earth. He created you. He gives you a choice to be in a relationship with him or not. Seeking him or not. Living with him in eternity or not.

Life's not suddenly easy when you start living based on God's will. Life isn't completely understandable when you start living based on his standards. But it certainly has more meaning. Life has significance, not just because of the promise of life for eternity but because it makes life's highs a bit more high and life's lows a bit more low.

So if God is a loving God, why isn't life fair? Let's think this through a bit. Finish the following sentence with as many words and phrases as you can think of in a couple minutes. I urge you not to give the Sunday School answer. Surely, at some point in your life, you thought something wasn't fair. Maybe now you have a different perspective, but it can be beneficial to revisit some earlier thoughts for a few reasons. (1) You can rejoice in growth. (2) You can relate to others who are experiencing something similar right now. (3) A memory might trigger a similar thought you've had recently that you hadn't consider as significant.

Life's not fair when….

One more step. Look through your list and determine which God would declare as unfair. Life isn't fair, but God is.
He loves what is right and fair; the Lord's love fills the earth. Psalm 33:5

In God's world, what's fair is right and just...by God's standards. We can inflict a lot of unnecessary pain on ourselves when we determine what's fair, right and just by our own standards. We can even feel life isn't fair when something happens we know is against God's will but there doesn't seem to be any ramification from it. Have you ever thought that someone deserved something that they didn't get? This works both ways: deserving something worse than they get or deserving something better than they get.

I can tell you one person: me. And I'm certain you, too. And likely every single person who has ever lived. We think we and others don't get what they deserve when what they get doesn't meet our expectations. We put ourselves in the judgment seat. Whether we decide something isn't fair because we're using our own standards or because we're not seeing God's standards being upheld, the end result is the same. In both cases, we're trying to take control. When I know something has been done contrary to God's will and I don't see the result I expect, I can easily step up to the judge's seat and declare "Life's not fair!" What I'm doing in that process is basically declaring, "God doesn't know what he's doing because he hasn't done what I expect him to do."

God doesn't have to meet my expectations. I assure you God is consistent. He doesn't change. He's dependable. He is never contrary to his Word. I can fully declare God's Word. I can know God's character – at least with my limited understanding, but there's something I don't and can't share with God: his perspective. You see, God sees what I can't. He sees every detail of the past and every detail of the future, and he knows how it all fits. I can get fidgety and uncomfortable because I think something is unfair, but the truth is...God is just, and he won't do anything that contradicts his justice. He balances justice, fairness, love, and grace in a way I can never fully understand.

But I can experience grace even though I didn't – and don't – deserve it. There have been times he could have struck me dead because of things I've done and said. But he gives me choice: to trust and step closer to him or to try it on my own – even though I'm never on my own – and take a step away. There are so many times he has patiently and generously taught me...and then taught me again years later when I stopped applying what I'd already learned. There are times he's held my feet to the fire, and I've known without a doubt to choose one thing would be obedience and to choose the other would be disobedience.

The thing is...whether or not life is fair is irrelevant. God doesn't want us to get stuck in this life. He wants to correct our eyesight so we see into eternity. This life on earth is important, because it's where we live out our faith. We seek, learn and grow. God doesn't want us to waste one minute of it. That's not to say we're supposed to be perfect. After all, we often learn most through those trials. We experience the most intense joy after a dark night.

God doesn't want us to waste life, not because it's about us, but because, ultimately, it's about him and our relationship with him.

How are you finding joy in life with God?

In order to find and savor joy, you need to set aside your focus on justice. If God prompts you to take up his cause, like we studied in the chapter on anger, by all means take up the cause, but be certain to know when you're taking up God's cause because it's his will and when you take up your own or even God's cause because you think it's a great idea. It's all about obedience.

God is generous with joy. Remember, he wants to *fill* you with joy. Can you be filled with joy if you're consumed with justice and fairness? Let's revisit the fruit of the Spirit to see how much the Spirit nurtures justice and fairness in us.

But the Spirit produces the fruit of love, joy, peace, patience, kindness, goodness, faithfulness, gentleness, self-control. Galatians 5:22-23

While fairness isn't mentioned specifically, which of the fruit of the Spirit might *involve* fairness?

Love and peace jump out to me immediately, although I'm sure we could search and find more ties. We know God's love is corrective, so fairness is involved. We know to establish and maintain peace, we have to confront at times. Peacemaking involves fairness. Fairness isn't listed as fruit of the Spirit, but it's part of the fruit-producing process. Consider farming. We use equipment in the process of farming that's not the actual end product. We need tools to cultivate the growth process, and the tools have significant impact on the crop. But the tools aren't the crop in and of themselves.

Let's think about joy again. What tools go into the cultivation of joy in your life?

I've noticed something in my own life. When I get discouraged, when I feel I've been wronged or unappreciated, when I start to focus on myself more than others, the best thing I can do is to serve…generously. When I pour onto others, I seem to get rid of myself, and God fills me up beyond my expectations. And just a hint…it's most fun to serve in secret – or at least quietly – when possible. The more generously I give of myself, the less I'm concerned with fairness.

There's a Jewish parable about a farmer with two sons. As soon as the sons were old enough to walk, the farmer took them to the fields and taught them everything he knew about growing crops and raising animals. When he got too old to work, the boys took over the chores and when the father died, they decided to keep working together. Each brother contributed what he could and would then equally divide what they had produced. The older brother never married. The younger brother married and had eight children. Years later, when they were having a great harvest, the older brother thought, "My brother has ten mouths to feed. I only have one. He needs more of his harvest than I do, but I know he's much too fair to renegotiate. I know what I'll do. During the night, I'll take some of what I have in my barn and slip it into his barn to help him feed his children."

At the same time, the younger brother was thinking, "God has given me this wonderful family, but my brother hasn't been so fortunate. He needs more of this harvest for his old age than I do, but I know him. He's much too fair. He'll never renegotiate. I know what I'll do. In the dead of the night, I'll take some of what I've put in my barn and slip it into his barn." So one night when the moon was full, those two brothers came face to face, each on a mission of generosity.

Although there wasn't a cloud in the sky, a gentle rain began to fall. It was God weeping for joy because two of his children had realized generosity is the deepest characteristic of holiness, and because we are made in God's image, generosity is the secret to our joy as well.

That's what grace is all about.

How will you extend grace today?

How will you receive grace today?

I pray that the God who gives hope will fill you with much joy and peace while you trust in him. Then your hope will overflow by the power of the Holy Spirit. Romans 15:13

Week Ten: *Emotionally Pure*

Starter Session

During our first week of study, we explored the tie between emotions and vulnerability, and I shared how vulnerability is similar to being on an island. Not the relaxing resort beach where refreshing drinks and snacks are readily available, but a deserted beach. The sun beats down, and I'm exposed to the elements. There's little escape from attack, because I'm visible to everyone who is in the area. Exposure feels unsafe and unsettling. We often experience emotions as unsafe and unsettling, too.

I can feel just as exposed in the depths of the island jungle, where the vines and bushes are overgrown and hide the path. It's a different kind of exposure. I'm not as exposed to attacks and weather, but I'm exposed to the unknown and uncertainty. I can easily get lost, and I feel vulnerable to whatever is lurking in the overgrowth. We often experience emotions as tangled messes that make us vulnerable.

Exposure or vulnerability feels unsafe, and as we search for truth about godly emotions, we find emotions are often braided with vulnerability and safety. Just as we've declared truth about godly emotions, we need to discern truth about vulnerability and safety, too, so as we unbraid the assumptions, we're exposing the truth.

The truth is…God isn't safe.

He's bold and just, which doesn't always equate with safety. It doesn't mean we're not safe when in his care, but how we define safety and how God defines safety are two different things. We tend to define safety as the absence of something: risk, danger, discomfort, harm. God defines safety as the presence of something: eternal security. But we're not living in eternity yet. We're still on earth, which is messy. While we're here, we're vulnerable and unsafe…except for the security of eternal salvation because of a relationship with Jesus. But when we're referring to the experience of our emotions leaving us exposed and feeling unsafe, we need to realize…we can still be secure in our relationship with God even when we feel exposed and unsafe.

In fact, when we're vulnerable and exposed, God works in us. Through our vulnerability, we can rely on him more completely and be more sensitive to his guidance. When you're covered by a hard shell, it's difficult to mold you. Can God do it? Sure, he can do anything!

*What do you learn about God and vulnerability in the following verses?

But Lord, you are our father. We are like clay, and you are the potter; your hands made us all. Isaiah 64:8

How terrible it will be for those who try to hide things from the Lord and who do their work in darkness. They think no one will see them or know what they do. You are confused. You think the clay is equal to the potter. You think that an object can tell the one who made it, "You didn't make me." This is like a pot telling its maker, "You don't know anything." Isaiah 29:15-16

He uncovers the deep things of darkness and brings dark shadows into the light. Job 12:22

Consider a time you felt vulnerable, perhaps even throughout this study. *What words come to mind?

*What do the promises of the above (and other) verses assure you about those experiences of vulnerability?

Our faces, then, are not covered. We all show the Lord's glory, and we are being changed to be like him. This change in us brings ever greater glory, which comes from the Lord, who is the Spirit. 2 Corinthians 3:18
- The change in us comes from God.
- The change glorifies God.
- We change to be more like God.
- The change comes when we're uncovered, unveiled, vulnerable.
- When we're uncovered, we show God's glory.

If you believe these statements to be true, speak them aloud. Highlight them. Punctuate them with exclamation marks or smiley faces. Declare them!

Let's revisit the analogy of being on an island.

Think about the dark, inner, tangled messes. There are parts of my life, including my emotions, that have definitely been dark, tangled messes. The truth is I'm somewhat comfortable with the mess. My eyes adjust, and I know the obstacles – or at least I think I do. It might be easier to walk on cleared trails, but there's comfort in the known, so I spend extra time and energy working around the overgrowth and tangled vines.

What quickly comes to mind as being a comfort to you even if you know it's a mess in your life? You don't need to share this right away, and I'm not going to ask you to give up your beloved security blankets right now, but I'm challenging you to look at what you're tightly clinging to.

Where do you run when life is tough?

When do you crawl into bed and pull the covers over your head? Or flop onto the couch and let time slip away as you lose yourself in a series of television shows?

Or perhaps you have the opposite reaction, and you run, run, run when the tangled mess surfaces. You might exercise excessively, bury yourself in work, or find any and every reason to put one more thing in your already crowded schedule.

Sometimes it's difficult to identify our tangled messes…because they're tangled messes. It's challenging to pull one vine away from another and find out what's truthful and justified and what's debilitating and rationalized.

Here's the great thing – you don't have to clear it all by yourself!

God helps you clear it. He *wants* to clear it. He has the machete in his hand and he'll sometimes hand it to you because doing the clearing work is important for the process. You need to sweat it out sometimes to see the effort behind the mess in your life. It's painful and gratifying all at once. But if you don't take hold of that machete handle and start swinging, you'll remain in the dark, tangled mess.

So…what about your island?

Consider where various emotions and experiences would fit on your island and map it out. What emotions are in the tangled mess and what emotions are untangled but leave you feeling unprotected as you stroll the beach? If a different analogy fits better for you, draw another graphic and explore!

As you clear the way with God's help, you'll see a path you've never seen before. You'll go in a direction you've never gone before. You'll stumble less. Light peers through the trees. You'll see colors and shadows and critters you've never seen. You've been too busy finding your way through the mess. But you – and I – must be vulnerable, exposed, willing to be molded in order to explore the changes. Where you are might not change but what you're experiencing does.

*What comes to mind when you consider the statement "Where I am might not change but what I'm experiencing changes."?

There are many things in life we just can't change. It doesn't mean we should give up, but we need to start with what we *can* change. We often experience an interesting phenomenon when we're doing a Bible study like this or we're listening to a series of messages or reading a book. We think, "I wish so-and-so would listen to/read this."

I'm not saying we shouldn't "want" for other people…but keep your motivation in check. Trust God's timing. What seems to you to be perfect content and perfect timing for a friend or family member might not sink in at all right now, but God will weave something similar into the person's life a couple months or years down the road and it will have a more significant impact.

Recall a big moment in your life – perhaps a significant situation or exchange with someone that had a lasting impact on your spiritual growth. You might have perceived it as positive or negative at the time. *Now consider the impact of changing the timing of that same experience. What would have been different if you'd experienced it several years earlier or several years later?

Of course, we don't know for sure what would have happened if the timing would have been different, and we don't want to get into a "what if" mentality. One of my favorite coaches often said, "Would've, Could've, Should've means you didn't." The best thing we would, could, and should do is be in the center of God's will. When we are, God's timing and provision will always be "just right." We won't experience everything as positive because we live in a messy world, but we'll be right where we're supposed to be when we're supposed to be there. It's not easy to be in the center of God's will, because we have to constantly discern and be obedient. When we are, we not only grow closer to God, but we yield others to him as well. Instead of trying to pull and push others into where we think God wants them, because we're seeking to be in the center of God's will, we'll trust him to guide us into and out of relationships, when to speak and when to be quiet, when to lead and when to follow. We'll talk more about the delicate balance between yielding control and taking responsibility later this week.

Life requires balance. Life involves emotions, and emotions require balance. Balance not between what's right and wrong. When we're discerning emotional responses, we're not on a child's seesaw. Perhaps you've tried to stand on the middle of the long board, finding a balance as you shift weight from side to side until the board evens out. Both ends of the board are in the air, because you aren't favoring one side or the other.

But we don't want to be neutral when it comes to emotions. We need to choose godly emotions over our humanly-driven emotions. We're created in God's image, and we want to give up our own distorted emotions to yield to his, becoming transparent so people see him in us. We're not on a seesaw. We're on a balance beam.

Enter through the narrow gate. The gate is wide and the road is wide that leads to hell, and many people enter through that gate. But the gate is small and the road is narrow that leads to true life. Only a few people find that road. Matthew 7:13-14

I was in gymnastics for many years when I was young. Perhaps you're familiar with the balance beam and have seen girls walk, flip, and leap on it. It's not as easy as they make it seem. If you've watched much women's gymnastics, you've seen some falls off the balance beam as well. One of the most critical elements to staying on the balance beam is focus.

When trying to balance on the playground seesaw, the focus fluctuates between both ends. As you feel a pull to one side, you compensate your weight to the opposite side. The pull of one determines the responsive push to the other. Not the case on the balance beam. The focus is on the beam itself. You must keep your eyes on the beam – but not where you're currently standing on the beam. The focus is on the end of the beam. The focus is where you're going. If you narrow your perspective too much, you can become disoriented. You'll waver or overcompensate. Perhaps you remember experiencing something similar as a new driver (or being a passenger in the car with a new driver). The car seems to bounce back and forth between the lines because the driver focuses on where she is right now. Too close to the middle line? Swerve to the right. Then too close to the outer line? Swerve left. Continue until everyone in the car has motion sickness.

When the driver lifts her eyes to gaze ahead on the road, it's easier to move smoothly toward the distant reference point. The shortest line between two points is a straight line. When your focus point is close to where you are, you might make a straight line to that point but then have to quickly find another focus point…over and over.

When your focus stretches to a farther point, the line – your path – straightens.

Your path won't be easy. God tells us the way is straight and narrow, not easy. Let's not get the two confused. Walking on the balance beam is straight and narrow, but it's not easy. Add a leap, turn, and flip, and the difficulty level increases. The difficulty in your life increases through trials, relationships, and pain.

We fall, and it's easier to stay down than climb back up.

We shake and feel paralyzed in an attempt to steady ourselves.

We take our eyes off the goal and see all the distractions around us. We sway in the sea of uncertainties.

If you take a look at the balance beam, you'll notice basics, such as it's 10 centimeters wide and 125 centimeters high (a little over 4 feet). It's not easy to stay on the straight and narrow balance beam, but here are a few things I learned as I became familiar with it.

- 10 centimeters doesn't seem very wide, but it's plenty wide for my foot.
- Just because the beam itself is straight and narrow doesn't mean my foot has to fit exactly. In fact, the best way to move on the beam is to slightly turn my foot out so I can use my toes to feel and wrap the edge. Plus, my best posture for balance is to have slightly turned out feet.
- The beam isn't perfectly flat. It's created with a slight dip…not enough to keep me from falling but enough to give me a little extra guidance as I move my feet.
- The beam is covered with a suede-like material, providing a little extra grip and cushion.
- The beam is deeper than it is wide. The sides are slightly outwardly bowed to help my hands grip the sides when necessary.
- New skills are learned on lower beams. Or pads are built up on either side of the beam. As the person gets comfortable with the skill, the pads are gradually lowered. Discipline and security go hand in hand.

*How might some of these same concepts and facts apply within your spiritual journey?

Emotions require balance. Not seesaw balance, but balance beam balance. Emotions are part of our spiritual journey. The way is straight and narrow.

This is the final week of *Pure Emotion*, but it's not the final week of your pure emotions. This is a journey. It reminds me of a journey we see in Scripture.

The Bible begins with Genesis, which includes Adam and Even in the garden and the mess of sin that started when Satan visited and convinced them to question God's intentions and will.

*Consider the negative, ungodly emotions included within those first several chapters of Genesis.

Fast forward to the end the Bible. Revelation. The culmination of God's will. Heaven (and hell).

*Consider the culmination of God's will and eternity in heaven. What godly emotions do you think of as being a part of God's ultimate plan?

Genesis to Revelation is a journey. It's messy throughout the journey – beginning to end. I challenge you to find one place in Scripture where you can camp under and claim "This is it. I have arrived and I'm not looking back or forward." God doesn't want us to "not arrive" because he's withholding himself from us. He doesn't want you to punish yourself for not measuring up or not being where you *could* be. He doesn't want you to be content with where you are. He wants you to stick with him on the journey, acknowledging the truth of who he is, where you are, who he created you to be, and where you're going…with him.

Keep on.

We know that everything God made has been waiting until now in pain, like a woman ready to give birth. Not only the world, but we also have been waiting with pain inside us. We have the Spirit as the first part of God's promise. So we are waiting for God to finish making us his own children, which means our bodies will be made free. We were saved, and we have this hope. If we see what we are waiting for, that is not really hope. People do not hope for something they already have. But we are hoping for something we do not have yet, and we are waiting for it patiently. Romans 8:22-25

WEEK TEN

Make It Personal #1: *Emotional Monuments*

When asked what thrills them most about emotions, women responded…
* Emotions serve as indicators in my life. (54%)
* Any emotion enhances my experiences. (29%)
* Subdued emotions help me maintain control. (12%)
* Intense emotions add to life. (5%)

How did you answer this question the first week of *Pure Emotion*? Would your answer be different today?

Regardless of your personal response to this question, let's focus on one thing in today's study: Your emotions are moments, not monuments.

What does this statement mean to you?

God's very clear that we're to have no idols – including emotions. When your emotions become your measuring stick or your frame of reference, you're in danger of building emotional monuments. Monuments are for remembering, not for camping under.

After all the people had finished crossing the Jordan, the Lord said to Joshua, "Choose twelve men from among the people, one from each tribe. Tell them to get twelve rocks from the middle of the river, from where the priests stood. Carry the rocks and put them down where you stay tonight."

So Joshua chose one man from each tribe. Then he called the twelve men together and said to them, "Go out into the river where the Ark of the Lord your God is. Each of you bring back one rock, one for each tribe of Israel, and carry it on your shoulder. They will be a sign among you. In the future your children will ask you, 'What do these rocks mean?' Tell them the water stopped flowing in the Jordan when the Ark of the Agreement with the Lord crossed the river. These rocks will always remind the Israelites of this."

So the Israelites obeyed Joshua and carried twelve rocks from the middle of the Jordan River, one rock for each of the twelve tribes of Israel, just as the Lord had commanded Joshua. They carried the rocks with them and put them down where they made their camp. Joshua also put twelve rocks in the middle of the Jordan River where the priests had stood while carrying the Ark of the Agreement. These rocks are still there today.

The priests carrying the Ark continued standing in the middle of the river until everything was done that the Lord had commanded Joshua to tell the people, just as Moses had told Joshua. The people hurried across the river. After they finished crossing the river, the priests carried the Ark of the Lord to the other side as the people watched. The men from the tribes of Reuben, Gad, and East Manasseh obeyed what Moses had told them. They were dressed for war, and they crossed the river ahead of the other people. About forty thousand soldiers prepared for war passed before the Lord as they marched across the river, going toward the plains of Jericho. Joshua 4:1-13

What do you learn from these verses?

    Let's tenderly take the next journey together. I'm going to challenge you to think of a painful time in your life. It might be a season of pain or perhaps a particular experience. Get as close as you can to the specifics. Consider the rock that stands tall to mark that time in your life.

    Mine was many years ago. It was painful. I dealt with it the best I could (which looking back, seems like not dealing with it at all), and I moved on. A few years later, I could feel it poking at me again. I felt like I was right back at the rock even though time had passed. I felt as if I hadn't grown or healed with the passing time. So I worked it out again, a little differently, hopefully a little more deeply…and I moved on. Again.

    A few years passed and it started sticking out again. I trudged back to the rock. Repeated coping and healing. Fast forward. Trudge back. Repeat. Fast forward. Trudge back. Repeat. It was an exhausting process. I didn't think about it much in the "in between" times, but each time I trudged back, the effort and pain caught up with me. Each time I thought I was ready to move on. Each time I was caught off guard with the pull back to the rock.

    And then, several years ago, I'd had enough. I felt the sharp poking, and I knew what was coming. The exhaustion set in, and I wasn't happy about it. I was downright angry and said, "God. Why do you keep pulling me back to that place? I thought we'd dealt with this!" I clearly heard his answer in the depth of my soul: "Susan. I'm not taking you back there. You're trudging back there on your own."

What?! Why would I put myself through the agony? Yet I wanted to learn and grow, and I was tired of the weariness, so I listened. And God taught.

Consider the trauma like a burn. I've never experienced a severe burn, but I understand it's excruciating. When someone suffers a severe burn, the focus isn't on reconstruction. It's on easing the trauma and stopping the burn. No reconstruction can immediately take place. The swelling has to subside. Tissue has to heal. And then reconstruction can take place…after some time.

From what I understand, the reconstruction can be more painful than the original burn. I'm sure there are some similarities. Just as I felt the pull back to the original pain and trudged back to it, a burn victim might feel that initial trauma. Similar pain, but different. The healing that's taking place couldn't have taken place at the time of the trauma. But it feels similar enough – and might even feel more painful – and it brings up all kinds of excruciating pain.

After the reconstruction, time must pass in order for the swelling to subside and tissue to heal…in preparation for yet another reconstructive procedure, at which time the process cycles yet again. Feels like the same pain as the trauma. Perhaps worse. But it's another stage of healing.

And the process repeats itself. Perhaps a little different each time but part of the same journey.

I thought God was pulling me back to the original trauma. But he was healing me a little more along the way. He knew I needed rest in between. He knew it was best for the healing process – and still is. My journey of healing isn't over, but now it looks like this…

A series of standing stones. You see, each time God worked on me, there's a monument to commemorate it. I move on from the stone. If I were to camp under it, I wouldn't need the monument to remind me of the journey. Instead, the stone reminds me of the relationship I have with God. He works on me, and I set a stone of remembrance. And another and another. I keep journeying. Instead of trudging back to an earlier place along the journey, I can stand right where I am, turn my head…

…and see a line of standing stones as a testament of the dependability of God. I can see and declare, "God was there for me. And there and there and there. He brought me here. And he is here with me, too. I can depend on him for everything at every place along the journey." Praise God!

Your emotions are moments, not monuments.

We can be pulled back to monuments we've erected when we're experiencing emotional responses. Current pain reminds us of past pain, and we return to the monument. Current frustration reminds us of a pattern of frustration, and we return to the monument. Current fear reminds us of past fears, and we run to hide behind the monument.

But today's emotion isn't yesterday's emotion. Similar? Yes. But if you're growing in your relationship with God…if you're asking him to reveal his godly emotions to you and reveal the discrepancies between himself and you…if you're drawing closer to the center of his will, your emotions of today only have hints of yesterday's emotions – an aftertaste. And today's emotions are a mere appetizer of tomorrow's emotions. God has a feast planned for you!

Rejoice, and celebrate. How have you grown throughout your *Pure Emotion* journey?

What are you looking forward to as you anticipate the tomorrows of your journey?

Emotions enhance our experiences and give us clues as to where we are in our relationship with God. Are you relying on yourself and your emotions or are you trusting God and letting him use emotions to speak to, guide, and challenge you?

Whether you feel in or out of control with your emotions, I assure you you're not in control. Being in control isn't the goal of faith. You were created in God's image, and your goal is deepening your relationship with him so you reflect and glorify him. Yielding is more important than control.

God is who he says he is, and he is where he says he is.

You can trust him. Encounter him today.

WEEK TEN

Make It Personal #2: *Emotional Check-Up*

We're digging into our Emotional Check-Up early this week with a slightly different approach. As you've reflected on your responses to each emotion week after week, I'm certain you're being challenged and beginning to see growth. Be patient. Changing your perspective and replacing the habits of emotional responses with God's truth and will about those emotions will take time. You're not going to get it "right" all the time. Give yourself some breathing space. Celebrate the small steps along the way.

And that's what we're going to do today! I've provided space for each emotion we've studied. The space is yours to use in whatever way God is leading you. Perhaps these prompts will jumpstart your thoughts...

- What have I learned about this emotion that stands out the most to me?
- How have I experienced a replacement of an unproductive, unhealthy habit or emotional response with a more godly emotional response?
- What are my goals in responding with this emotion and what small steps have I taken so far?
- What's a specific situation I can celebrate as I've begun to grow in this area?

Be honest! The reality is you began *Pure Emotion* struggling with some emotions more than others. You're going to grow at different rates with different emotional responses. It's going to be more difficult to replace longstanding unhealthy habits in some situations, and you'll easily jump in with both feet in others. Avoid comparing yourself to others – or comparing how you've grown in one emotion but not as much in another.

We've been searching God for truth throughout our study. Don't stop now! Continue to seek God's truth as you reflect on each emotion...and that includes God's truth in how he's seeing your growth and potential. Make appointments with God in the coming weeks and months. Write notes in your appointment book two weeks, 6 weeks, and 3 months from now to revisit this page and reflection questions from other Emotional Check-Up pages through *Pure Emotion*. Keep growing.

God is on this journey with you, and he's deeply invested in your life!

Fear

Jealousy

Anger

Anxiety

Peace

Frustration

Guilt

Shame

Joy

Week Ten

Make It Personal #3: *Perseverance*

Brothers and sisters, be patient until the Lord comes again. A farmer patiently waits for his valuable crop to grow from the earth and for it to receive the autumn and spring rains. You, too, must be patient. Do not give up hope, because the Lord is coming soon. Brothers and sisters, do not complain against each other or you will be judged guilty. And the Judge is ready to come! Brothers and sisters, follow the example of the prophets who spoke for the Lord. They suffered many hard things, but they were patient. We say they are happy because they did not give up. You have heard about Job's patience, and you know the Lord's purpose for him in the end. You know the Lord is full of mercy and is kind. James 5:7-11

Patience. We all want more of it, but we joke about not praying for it…perhaps because we're a bit hesitant of what we'll have to endure to grow in patience.

I've been on an emotional roller-coaster while writing *Pure Emotion*. I hadn't made some connections until my friend Tracie left a message on my phone on a particularly trying day:

"Isn't it just like God to give you the blessing of a roller coaster of emotions as you're writing about emotions? He's good about always providing that way!"

She was right. I might not enjoy the roller coaster, but I can certainly appreciate it. I shared the phone message with Tim. He paused before saying, "Please don't tell me you're planning to write a study on patience. I don't think I'm ready for it."

He was kidding of course. Sort of.

Think back to the fruit of the Spirit.

But the Spirit produces the fruit of love, joy, peace, patience, kindness, goodness, faithfulness, gentleness, self-control. There is no law that says these things are wrong. Galatians 5:22-23

Patience is fruit. It grows in us out of the Spirit.

Patience isn't just a quality or skill we have. It's a process of growth. Let's explore the specifics of James 5:7-10.

The word *patient* is scattered throughout the first few verses, and it means what you'd likely guess: forbearing, long-suffering, to wait patiently, to endure. In the last verse, you see the phrase "did not give up." In the NASB, this is expressed as "endurance." In the NIV, "persevere" is used. There's a tight connection between patience and perseverance. In fact, the two words used in these passages, *makrothumia* for patience and *hupomeno* for perseverance, are synonyms. The Greek word for patience is typically used in the context of people, and the word for perseverance is used in the context of circumstances.[7]

Emotions involve both people and circumstances, but let's remember…no one controls your emotions. Something someone does might impact your emotional response. To be honest, something someone does *will* impact your emotional response, but you will nearly always be able to get to a circumstance that underlies your response. Even when your response involves people, there's a circumstance involved. We need to be patient *with* people, but we must persevere *through* circumstances.

---

7   Zodhiates, Spiros. <u>Hebrew-Greek Key Word Study Bible</u>. Chattanooga TN: AMG, 2009

We often entwine the two so tightly that the confusion we create becomes a frustration in and of itself. We can't separate a person from a circumstance. We can't separate a circumstance from a person. Or at least we *think* we can't. But when I respond to Tim out of frustration because he stops listening to me in the middle of a conversation, it's not really patience with Tim that I'm struggling with; it's the circumstance of not being heard. When I misapply the source of my frustration, my response most definitely doesn't reflect God. When I keep it in context and realize it's the circumstance I'm most frustrated with, I'm (more) able to step back and approach the situation with perseverance. (For the sake of authenticity, let me tell you that I failed this little test this morning, which is why it's fresh in my mind. I'm learning!)

The more we authentically look at our emotions and take responsibility for them, the less we'll blame others or rationalize how others impact us. We'll see our emotions in the context of specific – and patterns of – circumstances…and as God reveals the truth about our emotions to us, we can persevere through the circumstances.

What does the world tell you about perseverance?

Hupomeno comes from two words, *hupo* (under) and *meno* (to remain). The world might tell us to persevere in our own power, but God tells us otherwise. In order to persevere, or have patience through circumstances, we must remain under him. This doesn't mean we sit inactively. Life with God isn't inactive. God's perseverance means we endure in following him. We're steadfast in our obedience. Perseverance isn't about taking control; it's about yielding control. What a readjustment for many of us raised in a world focused on independence and individualism.

Just as we've been realigning our definitions of godly emotions, we have to realign our definitions and applications of many other concepts. We make assumptions of the words and phrases we encounter in the Bible. Dig in deep, my friend. God wants you to question and explore! He's not intimidated by your questions. He's strong enough to handle them, and he welcomes the discourse. Of course, he requires respect, but we can respectfully question someone. In fact, it's the people we most respect that we need to question, because they're most likely to be authentic with us, challenging our assumptions and guiding us toward growth and truth.

Explore the following verses about perseverance and consider how they challenge and encourage you, particularly in the context of your emotions.
Love does not delight in evil but rejoices with the truth. It always protects, always trusts, always hopes, always perseveres. 1 Corinthians 13:6-7 (NIV)

So do not throw away your confidence; it will be richly rewarded. You need to persevere so that when you have done the will of God, you will receive what he has promised. Hebrews 10:35-36 (NIV)

Blessed is the one who perseveres under trial because, having stood the test, that person will receive the crown of life that the Lord has promised to those who love him. When tempted, no one should say, "God is tempting me." For God cannot be tempted by evil, nor does he tempt anyone; but each person is tempted when they are dragged away by their own evil desire and enticed. Then, after desire has conceived, it gives birth to sin; and sin, when it is full-grown, gives birth to death. James 1:12-15 (NIV)

How has this journey of *Pure Emotion* involved perseverance?

Make It Personal #4: *Planting Seeds of Truth*

We've been planting and watering seeds of truth throughout *Pure Emotion*. We've dug into many verses, exposing our assumptions and being challenged to grab onto God's truth, allowing it to change our daily lives.

Today, you'll revisit the Planting Seeds of Truth studies from previous weeks, searching for the key verse that God is highlighting for each emotion we've studied. Perhaps you'll notice an excess of notes about a particular verse, or you'll recall how God brought a specific verse to your mind in the middle of a trying situation.

Choose one verse for each week or emotion. As always, avoid becoming legalistic about filling in these blanks. Of course, I don't want you to be lazy. More important, God doesn't want you to be lazy. He wants you to stretch and grow, so be sure to search out the words he's specifically highlighting for you to grasp and claim. It's okay to write two verses or to leave a space blank if you're not challenged or encouraged by a specific verse.

And it's okay to look beyond your Planting Seeds of Truth pages. Perhaps you remember a verse embedded into our other study days and want to search for it. Or perhaps you've been studying on your own and a verse has particularly spoken to you regarding your emotional maturity. Be flexible. God will pour into you!

Fear

Jealousy

Anger

Anxiety

Peace

Frustration

Guilt

Shame

Joy

To help you remember and apply these truths in your daily life, I encourage you to rewrite each verse on a sticky index card. Keep all the cards together, or place them in a variety of locations so you'll see them throughout the coming days to serve as consistent reminders and encouragement.

Week Ten

Make It Personal #5: *God's Goodness*

This is it – our final day of study together. What a journey we've had! I trust God has poured encouragement and challenges over you in the weeks leading up to today. Trust him with your whole heart, soul, and mind. He loves you and wants the very best for you…and *he's* the very best for you!

Surely your goodness and love will be with me all my life, and I will live in the house of the Lord forever. Psalm 23:6

God's goodness is appealing, pleasant, useful, abundant, and benevolent. When have you experienced God's goodness?

God is love. 1 John 4:8

God invests his love in you. We've studied throughout *Pure Emotion* that God's emotions are always constructive and never destructive. God's love is the same. He will pour into you, not withdraw from you. Of course, he wants to and will prune you of all that is unnecessary in you and is hindering your growth, but the pruning process is ultimately constructive.

Tim recently said to me, "I love you and I want you to experience that love in everything I do. When I do something that makes you think I don't love you, it devastates me."

I don't want to take a detour about how intensely my husband loves me (but he does). I know his love for me is vastly limited in comparison to God's love for me. But what Tim said to me not only spoke to me as a wife, but God spoke through him and encouraged me as God's child. God loves me and wants me to experience his love in everything he does.

And the second part of Tim's statement? Well, God can't do anything that doesn't reflect his love! When I perceive something as unloving, it's either (1) actually unloving and therefore not of God, or (2) not unloving at all, because God is love – and only love.

God loves you and wants you to experience his love in everything he does.

Keep in mind love is not always the sappy, touch-feely experience we often think of. What realities of love challenge you? What realities of love encourage you?

Love is patient and kind. Love is not jealous, it does not brag, and it is not proud. Love is not rude, is not selfish, and does not get upset with others. Love does not count up wrongs that have been done. Love takes no pleasure in evil but rejoices over the truth. Love patiently accepts all things. It always trusts, always hopes, and always endures. Love never ends. 1 Corinthians 13:4-8

We have access to God's love. We receive God's love. God's love flows out of us onto those around us...when we're willing vessels. Our relationship with God is a balance. We must be obedient in relationship, and we must also be passionately engaged in relationship. Which do you struggle with the most and how?

Both have something in common. If we can simply grasp the commonality, we embrace both obedience and passionate engagement. The commonality? Surrender.

When we surrender, we submit in obedience, because it's God's will.

When we surrender, we passionately engage with God, because it's God's will.

When we surrender, we yield. We seek, accept and live by God's will.

When we surrender, our will, desires, and passions overlap more and more with God's will, desires, and passions.

As we surrender, our fear becomes godly fear.

As we surrender, our jealousy becomes godly jealousy.

As we surrender, our anger becomes godly anger.

As we surrender, our anxiety becomes godly anxiety.

As we surrender, our peace becomes godly peace.

As we surrender, our frustration becomes godly frustration.

As we surrender, our guilt and shame becomes godly guilt and shame.

As we surrender, our joy is godly joy.

God longs for you to surrender to him. He created you with a craving that only he can fulfill. He created you in his image – including his emotions – to reflect and glorify him. And he gave you a choice. Will you surrender? Will you yield?

My prayer for you is this...

Do not be shaped by this world; instead be changed within by a new way of thinking. Then you will be able to decide what God wants for you; you will know what is good and pleasing to him and what is perfect. Romans 12:2